Language Endangerment

Cognitive Linguistic Studies
in Cultural Contexts (CLSCC)

ISSN 1879-8047

This book series aims at publishing high-quality research on the relationship between language, culture, and cognition from the theoretical perspective of Cognitive Linguistics. It especially welcomes studies that treat language as an integral part of culture and cognition, that enhance the understanding of culture and cognition through systematic analysis of language – qualitative and/or quantitative, synchronic and/or diachronic – and that demonstrate how language as a subsystem of culture transformatively interacts with cognition and how cognition at a cultural level is manifested in language.

For an overview of all books published in this series, please see
http://benjamins.com/catalog/clscc

Volume 7

Language Endangerment
Disappearing metaphors and shifting conceptualizations
Edited by Elisabeth Piirainen and Ari Sherris

Language Endangerment

Disappearing metaphors
and shifting conceptualizations

Edited by

Elisabeth Piirainen
Ari Sherris

John Benjamins Publishing Company

Amsterdam / Philadelphia

The paper used in this publication meets the minimum requirements of the American National Standard for Information Sciences – Permanence of Paper for Printed Library Materials, ANSI z39.48-1984.

DOI 10.1075/clscc.7

Cataloging-in-Publication Data available from Library of Congress:
LCCN 2015023211 (PRINT) / 2015029733 (E-BOOK)

ISBN 978 90 272 0410 3 (HB)
ISBN 978 90 272 6809 9 (E-BOOK)

John Benjamins Publishing Co. · https://benjamins.com

Table of contents

CHAPTER 1

Introduction

Elisabeth Piirainen and Ari Sherris
Steinfurt, Germany / Texas A&M University-Kingsville, USA

Languages with decreasing numbers of speakers, or decreasing domains in which a constant or expanding number of speakers employ their languages, have become a major focus of research. This often means developing the traditional architectures of phonetics, phonology, morphology, and syntax through sketches, dictionaries and reference grammars. In contrast, this volume focuses on non-literal language, including conceptual metaphors and metonymies, idioms and other figurative units, which are not always in the forefront of published efforts. At the progressive edge of this research are endeavors to document, interpret, and disseminate knowledge of a dying language, often for maintenance and revitalization efforts. This research is often multidisciplinary in nature for it is initiated by scholars from linguistics, education, public policy, and sociology, as well as by scholars from hybrid epistemological spaces such as applied linguistics and sociolinguistics (Spolsky, 2011). The popular press (Edwards, 2011; Roberts, 2010; Tobin, 2011), scholarly journals (e.g., http://www.elpublishing.org/), conferences (e.g., the Stabilization of Indigenous Languages Symposium), and Internet websites (e.g., http://ethnologue.com) reference or specialize in language endangerment with burgeoning interest. Introductory texts on languages of the world place language endangerment front and center, as well as advocacy for language revitalization, targeting broad cross-sections of university students in an effort to inform and increase public discussion (e.g., Tetel Andresen & Carter, 2015).

More importantly, efforts to arrest the trajectory of extinction are underway on every continent with tacit support from UNESCO, language ecologists, and an expanding civic engagement as the topic moves forward in public conversations, and to a limited extent in political discourse. Once again, however, figurative language is underserved by these interests and has been virtually excluded from language endangerment research until recently. Nevertheless, in many places turnaround actionable plans, micro- and macro-political agendas, and activism maintain and revitalize languages through language policy initiatives

DOI 10.1075/clscc.7.001int
© 2015 John Benjamins Publishing Company

and bilingual and immersion schooling via acquisition planning (Combs & Penfield, 2012). In contexts where intergenerational transmission has shifted to a dominant language, renewed efforts at adult education under the banner of heritage language with themes that might initiate, increase, or encourage intergenerational transmission begin to appear instead of, or in addition to, acquisition planning. Indeed, the representation of endangerment and revitalization should not be underestimated if it is to become part of public discourse and an actionable issue for the institutions of civil society.

In the last 500 years, approximately 50% of the known languages have become extinct (Romaine, 2013). Today, estimates of the number of living languages hover close to 7000 (Austin & Sallabank, 2011; Lewis, Simons, & Fennig, 2015; Romaine, 2010; Sallabank, 2012). Predictions of their sustainability are bleak. Most measurements of language vitality, no matter the metric, indicate that approximately 90% will vanish within 100 or so years (Krauss, 1992; Harrison, 2007; Nettle & Romaine, 2000; UNESCO, 2001 cited in Romaine, 2013). When a language vanishes knowledge of flora and fauna, culture, and language are lost. Inexorable forces, both natural and manmade, take a heavy toll.

The majority of the world's languages is spoken by the world's indigenous peoples who on every continent are themselves endangered ethnic communities. Indeed, their languages and cultures, for the most part, have been marginalized as they as peoples, have been minoritized by the policies of nation-states (Romaine, 2009). Direct and indirect social, political, and cultural forces of hegemony, equations of bigotry, neoliberal commodifications of culture, repression, displacement, and linguicide have played out and continue to play out in restrained and unrestrained ways that are visible and hidden (Phillipson & Skutnabb-Kangas, 2013; Sherris, Pete, & Haynes, 2014).

Romaine (2013) puts the broader issues this way, "Communities can thrive and transmit their languages only when their members have a decent environment to live in and a sustainable economic system" (p. 774). However, as long as neoliberalism is popular (Harvey, 2014) and patrimonial capitalism threatens democratic mechanism for social justice worldwide (Piketty, 2014), it is dubious whether a sustainable economic system will take root in many of the indigenous communities worldwide. This is as true of the examples in this book from uberneoliberal contexts such as Europe, North America, and New Zealand, as it is from sub-Saharan Africa, and island nation-states such as Papua New Guinea and the Philippine Archipelago, which are also represented (Wurm, 2007). When an indigenous community cannot thrive, their metaphors cannot either.

At the same time, cosmopolitan perspectives (Canagarajah, S., 2013; Todd, 2009), as well as complex systems perspectives (Larsen-Freeman & Cameron, 2008), often take pains to articulate the facts on the ground as no less cultural artifacts to be treasured: all, it is argued, sociolinguistic patterns which are urban, rural, and cyber-spatial and that have been characterized as examples of superdiversity (Blommaert & Rampton, 2011). Linguistic repertoires are cited as pluralist discourse arrangements that would include an expanding core of receptive phonological skills across varieties of lingua-franca, regionally dominant languages and languages from countervailing forces, albeit often smaller and endangered. The global flows of people, goods, services, knowledge, and information increasingly no longer just the preoccupations of elite, shrink the circle of nation-state power, so the cosmopolitans argue, partially relocating to supranational levels (Wright, 2012). However these forces are as neoliberal as those of nation-states, their ideational progenitors. Many argue, therein lies the danger for indigenous communities, peoples, and their languages and cultures. This is no less true of metaphors and figurative units of endangered languages, yet they are often forgotten in the race to construct orthographies, dictionaries, and sketch grammars.

Metaphors in flux

The disappearance of endangered metaphor and idiom is the focus of this volume. It comprises part of a broader process of minority language loss that includes the displacement of knowledge, ways of knowing, and habits of mind (Harrison, 2007). The non-literal language, "everyday poetry of mind" in Gibbs' (1994) words, of which metaphor and idiom are subsets, as it were, is put into abeyance by contact in so many new ways today that futures become an uncertainty for many ways of speaking and interacting throughout the world. The superdiverse world we increasingly inhabit, where remote areas are often reached through wireless Internet means on handheld smart devices is an advancing real-politic (Blommaert & Rampton, 2011). In some place a smart device such as a wireless phone is one-to-a-village, which extends the pathways languages are in contact, however incrementally at first, rarely discussed in the literature of endangerment. Knowledge of how this affects conceptual metaphor is a new frontier.

At the same time, and perhaps of a cosmopolitan turn, these same handheld smart devices become ways of re-investing in the heritage language, or the disappearing forms of a dialect or variety, by activists with websites and educationists creating interactive dictionaries and language learning modules. Therefore, to only work with a concept of language endangerment that follows a strict metric, would not capture the shifts and loss as poignantly and fail somehow to project the breadth of change today.

Indeed, this book explores Waray, and how some of its "everyday poetry" is shifting despite, or because of, its high status as a language used for wider communication. Since 1991 Waray is the statutory language of provincial identity in Samar, Leyte Islands. Yet another chapter in this book explores Tatar, whose status is unclear. It is, along with Russian, the co-official language of the Republic of Tatarstan and – despite a large number of speakers – strongly under pressure from Russian. With the end of the Soviet Union, Tatar can be counted among the many endangered languages of oppressed minorities in the former Soviet Union. Fluent speakers are aging, and transmission of the language to the younger generations is not guaranteed. In Ghana, Safaliba, discussed in this volume, is one of approximately 68 languages that go unrecognized by schools, government agencies, healthcare units and non-government agencies, although efforts are being made to generate the conditions for literacy, for which knowledge of metaphor, metonymy and idiom are significant to highlight. In these three examples alone, this book extends the watch, as it were, and challenges activists in the field of revitalization to address metaphor as they would the lexical and grammatical architectures of endangered languages.

Finally the volume sees value in extending the discussion of metaphor and idiom loss by looking through the lens of dialect shift too. In this case, Jutlandic, a slowly disappearing dialect of Danish, is the focus of an additional chapter. Research focuses on the documentation of idioms and metaphors with the help of modern methods of field research and lexicography before they are relinquished by their speakers.

What's new in this Volume

The present volume is partly based on its predecessor, "Endangered Metaphors" (Idström & Piirainen, 2012; cf. reviews by Díaz-Vera, 2012, Stone, 2012, and Martí Solano, 2013). However, this volume can be read on its own, for it covers different topics and problems. In what follows, we will briefly compare "Endangered Metaphors" (EM for short) and the present book "Language Endangerment" (LE for short).

Indeed, both volumes evidence a wide geographic and methodological range. What distinguishes the present book from EM, however, is the fact that the emphasis is no longer exclusively on the documentation of figurative language that will be lost in the near future. Instead, the new volume begins to examine new domains where endangered languages may be exhibiting revitalized vitality as in online social networking and educational practice.

Furthermore, both volumes provide novel empirical data of languages from six of the seven continents, for there is nothing on the indigenous languages of Antarctica, as well as a large variety of language families and world cultures.

Oceania / Australia is represented by languages of Papua New Guinea (PNG) and New Zealand. EM is concerned with the PNG languages Siroi and Kewa and LE with six *PNG vernacular* languages in comparison with Tok Pisin as well as *Māori* (New Zealand). EM analyzes several languages of the Americas, including three varieties of Athapascan (Canada, Alaska), Nahuatl (Mexico) and Ashéninka Perené (Peru). EL analyzes *Flathead Salish*, a critically endangered American Indian language (Montana, USA). While EM explores only one language of Africa (*Chumburung* spoken in Ghana), EL contributes to *Safaliba* as well as *Bété* (Ivory Coast). Asia is represented with one article in each volume: EM compares two minority Tibeto-Burman languages spoken in India (*Dimasa* and *Rabha*) while LE has a detailed article on Waray (Philippines). In contrast to the five languages of Europe studied in EM, ranging from *Inari Saami* in North Finland and *Roma lects* in Finland to *Basque, Scottish-Gaelic* and a *Low German dialect*), LE explores only two European varieties: Tatar (Russia) and Jutlandic (a dialect of Denmark).

No less varied than the languages and their continental coverage, the linguistic objects of study are varied too. Most of them fall into two large groups, namely metaphors (e.g., conceptual metaphors or metaphoric models, metonymies, one-word metaphors and other kinds of metaphorically used linguistic entities) on the one hand, and conventional figurative units (e.g., idioms, proverbs or figurative compounds) on the other. The difference is that idioms are elements of the mental lexicon while metaphor covers both novel metaphorical expressions and lexicalized ones. Besides, a small group of articles also deals with coded or tabooed *language* and *veiling circumlocutions* (e.g. the articles on Kewa, the two Tibeto-Burman languages and Low German in EM, and on Māori in LE). An exception is *symbolically* used numbers (Chumburung, EM). What all these non-literal linguistic units have in common is their semantic ambiguity: in most cases they can be processed on two conceptual levels: on the level of their figurative meaning and on the level of their literal meaning. As has often been pointed out, large complexes of cultural knowledge encoded in these specific cognitive systems will be lost when traditional idioms or the entire metaphorical system of a language undergo fundamental changes, knowledge for example, of how language communities categorize their world, or which source concepts they use to verbalize abstract concepts such as emotions.

Different linguistic data require different theoretical frameworks. Hence, two main directions of figurative language research – each of which developed their own meta-linguistic apparatus – run through both volumes: the Conceptual Metaphor Theory (CMT) in the sense of Lakoff & Johnson (1980 and later developments) on the one hand, and European phraseology research (cf. Burger et al., 2007; Dobrovol'skij & Piirainen, 2005; Piirainen, 2008, 2012), on the other. Most articles of the two volumes refer to CMT, either directly because they use it as basis of their research or indirectly, dealing with it critically. Terms developed by CMT such as *source domain, target domain, metaphoric model, conceptual mapping* proved to be helpful across different frameworks. European phraseology research in turn emphasizes the different levels of description. Figurative units can be described either on the *superordinate level* of the conceptual metaphor or on the *basic level of the rich image*. As it turns out, it is more likely on the latter level that cultural implications can readily be detected (cf. the articles on Bété, Tatar and Jutlandic in LE). However, still other theoretical frameworks are discussed in the volumes. The contribution to Waray (LE) deals with CMT and three further metaphor theories, while the article on Nahuatl (EM) uses "Conceptual Blending Theory" and an adequate exploration of Inari Saami idioms (EM) requires the "Relevance Theory".

The linguistic findings of present volume are consistent with those of EM. As in the previous volume, new frontiers for study are opened in each chapter as well as an expanding agreement that the so-called "universality" of conceptual metaphors does not exist. Many of the new papers find implicit or explicit disfavor the Anglocentrism or essentialism of the Lakoffian "metaphor theory". Even bodily based metaphors are not universal, but rather constrained by cultural conceptions, as a number of our contributions show (cf. e.g. articles on Basque, Ashéninka Perené, Low German and others in EM and most articles of LE, and similar findings by Dobrovol'skij & Piirainen, 2005, pp. 121–144; Piirainen, 2008, pp. 217–219). There are also new results for idiom research. As has been expected, idioms reflect the natural surroundings and respective traditional material culture. What is new is the realization that idioms and proverbs of languages without literature tradition also are based on "intertextuality". Of course these are not literary texts as in the Western standard languages, but myths, folk stories, legends, narrations of all kind that are passed on orally from one generation to another (see Upper Tanana Athabascan and Inari Saami in EM and especially Bété in LE). The number of these findings could be continued.

Evidence of language endangerment is also confirmed. We encounter the two kinds of "vanishing voices" across all contributions of both volumes: metaphors and idioms that will be lost when a language becomes extinct and metaphors and idioms that are endangered themselves, due to radical changes in the linguistic situation, i.e. by replacing or borrowing from figurative units of the given majority language. As the articles of EM those of the present volume point to the same direction: figurative units of a language are vulnerable. "They start to vanish at the very beginning of a language becoming endangered" (Idström & Piirainen, 2012, p. 18). In the next section we briefly highlight each chapter of this volume.

About this book

Chapter 2 (J. King) analyses shifting conceptualizations of Māori metaphors of DEATH in contemporary accounts with an emphasis on data from web-based social networking platforms such as Facebook and Twitter. The chapter highlights historical manifestations of *poroporoaki* tradition (farewell rituals to send the dead on to the next world), its flexibility with respect to Christian themes and the strengths of its formulaic nature in preserving more traditional metaphoric stances. Conceptual metaphors like DEATH IS A JOURNEY are known in Māori but, contrary to English, not used euphemistically in the sense of "avoidance language". Other Māori DEATH metaphors have no counterpart in the standard European languages which so far constituted most of our knowledge of conceptual metaphors (e.g. THE DEAD ARE FALLEN TREES; THE DEAD ARE STARS). The Revitalization efforts that got underway in the mid-1980s as well as an encapsulated account of earlier historical aspects of Māori language and culture are backdrops.

Chapter 3 (P. King) contrasts metaphors using TASTE as source domains in six Papua New Guinea vernacular languages (Dawawa, Gadsup, Gwahatike, Guhu Samane, Kamano Kafe, and Tairuma) and then compares them to languages of wider communication (Tok Pisin and English). The degree of conventionality of the expressions is also taken into account. It appears that the source domain TASTE is more culturally conditioned than other sensory domains and its metaphorical extension to target domains differ from language to language, especially in terms of items considered in English as sour, spicy and bitter (lemons, chili and quinine). Moreover, salty and sweet substances share classifications in all Papua New Guinea languages, unlike English. SPEECH is the most common target domain of TASTE metaphors. TASTE metaphors are not only a novelty of metaphor research in itself but contrasting them in small and nationwide languages also produces clear results.

Chapter 4 (Palagar) examines metaphors of Waray, spoken in the Philippine Archipelago, referred to as a "curtailed language". Based on rich linguistic data the article develops a taxonomy of metaphors across various *source domains* or *vehicles* (cosmological, geographic and spatial, zoological, botanical, somatic, social, and general tangible and intangible elements) and more abstract *target domains* or *tenors* (emotion, time, space, among other things). The author presents evidence of a novel principle in metaphor processing, the "Principle of Domain Non-Transmissibility", with some exceptions, and explores these topics with detail. The chapter is characterized by in-depth discussions of four metaphor theories, which are applied consistently to the juxtaposition of the vehicles and tenors of Waray metaphors.

Chapter 5 (Schaefer) examines metaphors from the Safaliba language, among the smallest Ghanaian languages that is the principal way of communicating for approximately 7000 Ghanaians across multiple domains. The comparison of Safaliba metaphors with those of four of other Oti-Volta languages from contiguous Ghanaian discourse communities reveals intriguing variations. For metaphor research the most important result is the fact that many of the conceptual metaphors referred to as "universal" do not exist in the languages of Northern Ghana. As the author concludes, the more languages are examined, especially minority varieties distant from European languages, the more questionable becomes "universality" in the realm of metaphor.

Chapter 6 (Sherris, Pete, & Haynes) analyzes primary Flathead Salish metaphors. Flathead Salish is spoken by less than 50 American Indian speakers in Montana, USA. In order to link the analysis to efforts at acquisition planning and broader revitalization efforts, a task-based language teaching approach is developed so that the work is useful in heritage language schooling. Flathead metaphors are compared to English metaphors for this purpose too. From a theoretical perspective this comparison contributes to our knowledge of *conceptual metaphors*: It turned out that – starting from the *source domains* – conceptual mappings are by no means "universal" as was claimed earlier. About half of the Flathead Salish metaphors have no corresponding source domain in English. These findings are used to improve the methodological approaches to revitalization, language planning and educational programs.

Chapter 7 (Zouogbo) examines idioms and proverbs of Bété, one of the endangered languages spoken in the Ivory Coast. On the one hand, Bété figurative units are deeply rooted in the culture of Bete people, in their ideas of cosmogony and in oral narrative traditions (various expressions summarize the gist and moral of a well-known narrative). On the other hand, the use of figurative language has special social functions. Transmitting a message by means of an idiom or a proverb indicates not only language competence but also knowledge of the traditional culture and therefore means authority. The chapter shows that the function of idioms and proverbs in an oral society differ significantly from those known in societies with literary traditions. In addition, conclusions are made on the relationship of figurative units, imagery and cognition.

Chapter 8 (Arboe) explores the recession of figurative units (mainly idioms) in the Jutlandic dialects in Denmark. The opposite semantic fields under consideration (RICHNESS VS. POORNESS; CLEVERNESS VS. STUPIDITY; SLOWNESS VS. RAPIDITY; WASTEFULNESS VS. THRIFT; LUCK VS. MISFORTUNE; HIGH SPIRITS VS. DISCONTENT; SELFISHNESS VS. COOPERATION and LIFE VS. DEATH) reveal the same tendency to abandon dialectal idioms and replace them by units of the standard language. Main reason is the fact that the speakers want to achieve a greater range of communication and therefore give up idioms becoming obsolete to standard Danish speakers. This chapter is a good example to illustrate how the figurative lexicon of many dialects (once) spoken in Europe vanished or changed fundamentally since the last century. The study also produces results for dialect lexicography.

Chapter 9 (Gizatova) analyzes Tatar idiom loss in the Republic of Tatarstan, Russia. Tatar is one of the many languages being strongly under pressure from Russian. Speakers of the genuine Tatar language are aging; Russian is the predominant language of education and almost all official domains. After examining authentic Tatar idioms related to traditional historical and intertextual knowledge the author explains that Tatar figurative language is changing rapidly and its transmission to the younger generations is not guaranteed. The development of Tatar toward a mixed variety, especially in the field of figurative expressions, may be seen representative of a large number of languages of oppressed minorities in the Eurasian continuum.

Future directions for endangered metaphor studies

This volume and the earlier volume testify to the unabated power of metaphor, metonymy, and idiom in the many ways they frame knowledge and reify culture across a plethora of human conditions, circumstances, contexts, and domains. When languages diminish, humankind loses these unique symbols of everyday creativity. Mappings from abstractions to concrete, more fundamental human experiences, sometimes sensory-motor creature-stirrings, metaphor and idiom reverberate with a depth of meaning that links language to mind and human cognition. Broken links, lost maps, silenced languages, stain and darken human history, scaring cultures, and erasing records of collective memory, imprints of who we are and what we do. The fragility, temporality, and mortality of metaphor are merciless and unmitigated, as each author has shown us with a fidelity to place and time. Any future agenda should craft an increased rate of metaphor research, stronger collaborations with indigenous interlocutors, and a pact with heritage language learners, activists, and enthusiasts through a more powerful set of tools for research, dissemination, and advocacy. Consequently, we recommend research and development along three parameters: metaphor metrics, intensified research of online domains, and open-access metaphor, metonymy and idiom archiving.

Just as several metrics for categorizing levels of language vitality or endangerment have been created (Brenzinger et al., 2003; Fishman, 1991; Krauss, 2007; Lewis, 2008; Lewis & Simon, 2010), future field linguists might begin to construct or adapt a metaphor-specific metric of vitality. This might include surveys, interviews, and focus groups of speakers. The audio recorded data might then be transcribed and analyzed for frequencies of primary and complex metaphor mappings according to age, topic, or domain. An elicitation protocol in Figure 1 requires speakers to finish the sentence in the left column. It would be conducted in the target language. The column on the right simply presents what has been termed representative primary metaphors (Lakoff & Johnson, 1999, pp. 50–54).

Elicitation protocol for primary metaphors	English examples of primary metaphors
Affection is …	Affection is …warmth
Important is …	Important is …big
Happy is …	Happy is …up
Intimacy is …	Intimacy is …closeness
Bad is …	Bad is …stinky
Difficulties are …	Difficulties are …burdens
More is …	More is …up
Categories are …	Categories are …containers
Similarity is …	Similarity is …closeness
Linear scales are …	Linear scales are …paths
Organization is …	Organization is …physical structure
Help is …	Help is …support
Time is …	Time is …motion
States (of mind) are …	States (of mind) are …locations
Change is …	Change is …motion
Actions are …	Actions are …self-propelled motions
Purposes are …	Purposes are …desired objects or destinations
Causes are …	Causes are …physical forces
Relationships are …	Relationships are …enclosures
Control is …	Control is …up
Knowing is …	Knowing is …seeing
Understanding is …	Understanding is …grasping
Seeing is …	Seeing is …touching

Figure 1.

The above protocol is incomplete, of course, and should be extended topically during the interviewing or focus group session itself. Through review of record-ings and notes on the recordings to expand the personal data collection between each recording session, converging and diverging cultural evidence of use might be collected. There is also a need to use stimulus prompts (Bowern, 2008) and a stimulated recall (Lyle, 2003) format to bring language use to the attention of its users in directions that deepen the ways they share their understandings with outsiders, including ethnographers, linguists, language teachers, and community revitalization activists.

Our second recommendation for future research is perhaps obvious. It is currently most promising for indigenous peoples expanding their electronic borderlands. Indeed, as a result of the burgeoning domains of online discourse, field linguists of metaphor, metonymy and idiom might consider emails, social networking sites, and blogs for data collection environments as one paper in this collection has. This is promising, where possible, of course, because it brings in the new literacies or new discourses (e.g., "translingual" data collected by Canagaragah, 2013) that are expanding languages, as well as bring languages in contact in important ways, while protecting them in other ways (Jones & Ogilvie, 2013). Needless to say, there is a sad lack of research on either the transformative or conservative influences of communication use on metaphor in these open-access online environments.

Finally a strong caveat is our third recommendation. Metaphor field work in endangered languages and endangered dialects might begin to be archived so that future researchers, community activists, teachers, and educators, might take advantage of the sources for maintenance and revitalization efforts. Archives ensure the data has a life in perpetuity (e.g., ELAR: Endangered Languages Archive at the University of London). Moreover, with additional funding, archived materials can later become websites. Many online bilingual and learner dictionaries are exemplary of how research data that has been archived might enhance maintenance and revitalization. The data from metaphor, metonymy, and idiom could become an additional layer of information to existing online dictionaries. Alternatively, visual and interactive word maps of source and target metaphors could be a next step. The technology, including concordance software, exists to support any of these endeavors; indeed, a new threshold is there for any of us to step across.

Our deepest appreciation goes to the communities who bring vitality to the metaphors and idioms in our work and to the work of the scholars who contributed to this volume. Special heartfelt thanks go to Anna Idström who conceived of this book and who was instrumental in moving the idea forward in its early days.

References

Austin, P., & Sallabank, J. (2011). Introduction. In P. Austin & J. Sallabank (Eds.), *The Cambridge handbook of endangered languages* (pp. 1–24). Cambridge, UK: Cambridge University Press. DOI: 10.1017/CBO9780511975981.001

Blommaert, J., & Rampton, B. (2011). Language and superdiversity. *Diversities*, 13(2), 1–22. Retrieved from: http://unesdoc.unesco.org/images/0021/002147/214772e.pdf#214780

Bowern, C. (2008). *Linguistic field work: A practical guide.* NY: Palgrave.

Brenzinger, M., Yamamoto, A., Aikawa, N., Koundiouba, D., Minasyan, A., Dwyer, A., Grinevald, C., Krauss, M., Miyaoka, O., Sakiyama, O., Smeets, R., & Zepeda, O. (2003). *Language vitality and endangerment. Language vitality and endangerment.* Paris: UNESCO. Retrieved from http://www.unesco.org/culture/ich/doc/src/00120-EN.pdf

Burger, H., Dobrovol'skij, D., Kühn, P., & Norrick, N. R. (Eds.) (2007). *Phraseology. An international handbook of contemporary research.* Berlin & New York: de Gruyter.

Canagarajah, S. (2013). *Translingual practice: Global Englishes and cosmopolitan relations.* London: Routledge.

Combs, M. C., & Penfield, S. D. (2012). Language activism and language policy. In B. Spolsky (Ed.), *The Cambridge handbook of language policy* (pp. 461–474). Cambridge, UK: Cambridge University Press. DOI: 10.1017/CBO9780511979026.028

Díaz-Vera, J. E. (2012). Review of Idström, A.; Piirainen, E. (Eds.), Endangered Metaphors. Amsterdam/Philadelphia: John Benjamins. *Metaphor and the Social World,* 2(2), 263–269. DOI: 10.1075/msw.2.2.06dia

Dobrovol'skij, D. O., & Piirainen, E. (2005). *Figurative language: Cross-cultural and cross-linguistic perspectives.* Amsterdam [etc.]: Elsevier.

Edwards, V. (2011, June 27). Compensation for lost languages. *The Australian.* Retrieved from http://www.theaustralian.com.au/higher-education/compensation-for-lost-languages/story-e6frgcjx-1226082975633.

Fishman, J. (1991). *Reversing language shift: Theory and practice of assistance to threatened languages.* Clevedon, UK: Multilingual Matters.

Gibbs, R. W. (1994). *The poetics of mind. Figurative thought, language, and understanding.* Cambridge: University Press.

Harrison, D. (2007). *When languages die: The extinction of the world's languages and the erosion of human knowledge.* Oxford, UK: Oxford University Press.

Harvey, D. (2014). *Seventeen contradictions and an end of capitalism.* Oxford, UK: Oxford University Press.

Idström, A., & Piirainen, E. (2012). Introduction. In A. Idström & E. Piirainen (Eds.), *Endangered Metaphors* (pp. 15–19). Amsterdam: John Benjamins. DOI: 10.1075/clscc.2.02ids

Idström, A., & Piirainen, E. (Eds.). (2012). *Endangered metaphors.* Amsterdam: John Benjamins [Series: Cognitive Linguistic Studies in Cultural Contexts 2]. DOI: 10.1075/clscc.2

Jones, M. C., & Ogilvie, S. (Eds.). (2013). *Keeping languages alive: Documentation, Pedagogy, and Revitalization.* Cambridge, UK: Cambridge University Press. DOI: 10.1017/CBO9781139245890

Krauss, M. (1992). The world's languages in crisis. *Language,* 68(1), 1–42. DOI: 10.1353/lan.1992.0075

Krauss, M. (2007). Classification and terminology for degrees of language endangerment. In M. Brenzinger (Ed.), *Trends in linguistics, studies and monographs: Language diversity endangered* (pp. 1–8). Berlin: Walter de Gruyter.

Lakoff, G., & Johnson, M. (1980). *Metaphors we live by.* Chicago: University of Chicago Press.

Lakoff, G., & Johnson, M. (1999). *Philosophy in the Flesh. The embodied mind and its challenge to Western thought.* New York: Basic Books.

Larsen-Freeman, D., & Cameron, L. (2008). *Complex systems and applied linguistics.* Oxford, UK: Oxford University Press.

Lewis, P. (2008). Evaluating endangerment: Proposed metadata and implementation. In K. King, N. Schilling-Estes, L. Fogle, J. Lou, & B. Soukup (Eds.), *Sustaining linguistic diversity: Endangered and minority languages and language varieties* (pp. 35–49). Washington, DC: Georgetown University Press.

Lewis, P., & Simons, G. (2010). Assessing Endangerment: Expanding Fishman's GIDS. *Revue Roumaine de Linguistique*, 2, 103–120.

Lewis, M. P., Simons, G. F., & Fennig, C. D. (Eds.). (2015). *Ethnologue: Languages of the world* (18th ed.). Dallas, Texas: SIL International. Online version: http://www.ethnologue.com.

Lyle, J. (2003). Stimulated recall: A report on its use in naturalistic research. *British Educational Research Journal*, 29(6), 861–878. DOI: 10.1080/0141192032000137349

Martí Solano, R. (2013). Review of Idström, A.; Piirainen, E. (Eds.), Endangered Metaphors, Amsterdam/Philadelphia: John Benjamins. *Yearbook of Phraseology*, 4, 79–83.

Nettle, D., & Romaine, S. (2000). *Vanishing voices: The extinction of the world's languages.* Oxford, UK: Oxford University Press.

Phillipson, R., & Skutnabb-Kangas, T. (2013). Linguistic imperialism and endangered languages. In T. K. Bhatia & W. C. Ritchie (Eds.), *The handbook of bilingualism and multilingualism* (2nd ed.), (pp. 495–516). Malden, MA: Wiley-Blackwell.

Piirainen, E. (2008). Figurative phraseology and culture. In S. Granger & F. Meunier (Eds.), *Phraseology: An interdisciplinary perspective. Louvain-la-Neuve, 13–15 October 2005* (pp. 207–228). Amsterdam: John Benjamins. DOI: 10.1075/z.139.20pii

Piirainen, E. (2012). *Widespread Idioms in Europe and beyond: Toward a Lexicon of common figurative units.* New York [etc.]: Peter Lang [International Folkloristics, 5].

Piketty, T. (2014). *Capital in the 21st century.* Cambridge, MA: Belknap/Harvard University Press.

Roberts, S. (2010, April 28). Listening to (and saving) the world's languages. *The New York Times.* Retrieved from http://nytimes.com

Romaine, S. (2009). Language, culture, and identity issues across nations. In J. Banks (Ed.), *Routledge international companion to multicultural education* (pp. 373–384). London: Routledge.

Romaine, S. (2010). Contact and language death. In R. Hickey (Ed.), *The handbook of language contact* (pp. 320–339). West Sussex, UK: Wiley-Blackwell. DOI: 10.1002/9781444318159.ch16

Romaine, S. (2013). Linguistic and ecological diversity. In R. Bayley, R. Cameron, & C. Lucas (Eds.), *The Oxford handbook of sociolinguistics* (pp. 773–791). Oxford: Oxford University Press.

Sallabank, J. (2012). Diversity and language policy for endangered languages. In B. Spolsky (Ed.), *The Cambridge handbook of language policy* (pp. 100–123). Cambridge, UK: Cambridge University Press. DOI: 10.1017/CBO9780511979026.008

Sherris, A., Pete, T., & Haynes, E. (2014). Task-based language teaching practices that support Salish language revitalization. In M. C. Jones & S. Ogilvie (Eds.), *Keeping languages alive: Documentation, pedagogy, and revitalization* (pp. 155–166). Cambridge, UK: Cambridge University Press.

Spolsky, B. (2011). Language and society. In P. Austin & J. Sallabank (Eds.), *The Cambridge handbook of endangered languages* (pp. 141–156). Cambridge, UK: Cambridge University Press. DOI: 10.1017/CBO9780511975981.008

Stone, M. (2012). Review of: Idström, A.; Piirainen, E. (Eds.), Endangered Metaphors, Amsterdam/Philadelphia: John Benjamins. *The Linguist List* 23.5.5181, 11/12/2012.

Tetel Andresen, J., & Carter, P. M. (2015). *Languages in the World: How history, culture, and politics shape language*. Malden, MA: Wiley-Blackwell.

Tobin, L. (2011, February 21). Half of living languages face extinction. *The Guardian*. Retrieved from http://theguardian.com

Todd, S. (2009). *Toward an imperfect education: Facing humanity, rethinking cosmopolitanism*. Boulder, Co: Paradigm Publishers.

Wright, S. (2012). Language policy, the nation, and nationalism. In B. Spolsky (Ed.), *The Cambridge handbook of language policy* (pp. 59–78). Cambridge, UK: Cambridge University Press. DOI: 10.1017/CBO9780511979026.006

Wurm, Stephen A. (2007). Threatened languages in the Western Pacific area from Taiwan to, and including, Papua New Guinea. In M. Brenzinger (Ed.), *Language diversity endangered* (pp. 374–390). Berlin: Mouton de Gruyter.

CHAPTER 2

Metaphors we die by
Change and vitality in Māori

Jeanette King
Canterbury University, New Zealand

Accounts of metaphors of death from various languages and cultures typically report the use of euphemisms used to talk about death. In contrast euphemisms are not the main focus of metaphors of death in Māori. Indeed, the dead are a palpable presence to those living and are routinely acknowledged in important Māori greeting rituals through the formulaic episode *poroporoaki* (farewells to the dead), the main focus of which are to send the dead on to the next world. Accordingly, *poroporoaki* typically feature formulae based on the DEATH IS A JOURNEY conceptual metaphor. With the introduction of Christianity in the 19th century, *poroporoaki* now also include formulae derived from the biblically based DEATH IS SLEEP conceptual metaphor. Since the commencement of widespread language revitalization initiatives in the 1980s *poroporoaki* have been adapted for inclusion at the beginning of television and radio programs, and, more recently, are used in Facebook and Twitter messages. A corpus of broadcast Māori forms the basis of this analysis of metaphors used in modern day *poroporoaki*. Besides the conceptual metaphors already mentioned, the corpus also contains examples of honorific metaphors which liken the dead to stars, or to trees which have fallen. In changing and adapting to new situations *poroporoaki* exemplify the important role of metaphoric formulae in maintaining the vitality of important cultural elements as languages adapt to changing technologies.

Keywords: Māori, formulae, metaphor, death, endangered language

1. Introduction

Many of the studies of metaphors of death in different languages and cultures focus on the rich variety of euphemistic circumlocutions to report that someone is dead or dying (Allan & Burridge, 1991; Bultinck, 1998; Fernández, 2006;

DOI 10.1075/clscc.7.01kin

Franklin, 2012; Pound, 1936; and Piirainen, 2012).[1] Euphemisms are described as "alternatives to dispreferred expressions … [which] may be taboo, fearsome, distasteful, or for some other reason have too many negative connotations" (Allan & Burridge, 1991, p. 14). Thus euphemisms regarding death show the difficulty many cultures have in accepting death, in that these idioms attempt to take away the power of death (Fernández, 2006, pp. 103–104). These euphemisms are often numerous, but, because they do not exist within a formulaic variety, they are often a part of the phrasal lexicon which is quickly eroded in situations of shift away from an endangered language (Piirainen, 2012; King & Syddall, 2011).

Māori culture has a very different approach to death. Firstly, while some euphemisms exist, they are few, and tend to be honorific rather than a straight avoidance of using more direct wording. In reporting a death that has just occurred, modern day speakers make much use of a proverb which compares the deceased to a mighty tree which has fallen (see Section 3.3). However, more generally, there are very few options to saying that someone is no longer alive, the most common wording being:

(1) *kua mate ia*
     'he/she is dead'

Since euphemisms are the focus of metaphors of death in other cultures we might be mistaken in believing that the pragmatic Māori do not use metaphors or images as far as death is concerned. In fact, death rituals play an integral part in Māori ceremony and there are a number of death related metaphors conventionally employed in such situations. The importance of death rituals is manifest in the presence of a formulaic episodic in Māori commonly referred to as *poroporoaki* (farewells to the dead). This paper investigates the major metaphors and images used to refer to the dead in Māori in the more recent adaptation of *poroporoaki* to the broadcast medium and the online forum of Twitter.

It is important at this point to note that while the discussion of metaphors here will include reference to conceptual metaphors as defined by Lakoff and Johnson (1980), strict definitions will not be adhered to, in line with Mühlhäusler (2012, p. 3) who notes that precise agreement on definitions is not required in order to engage in meaningful discussion. To be able to understand the use of metaphors which appear in *poroporoaki* the following two subsections give an overview of the Māori language and rituals of encounter respectively.

---

1.   The title of this chapter plays on the title of the seminal book on conceptual metaphor by Lakoff and Johnson (*Metaphors we live by*), published in 1980. The title 'Metaphors we die by' has also been used by many other authors in discussions of metaphors of death (in its widest sense), including Romaine (1996), Bultinck (1998), Horowitz (2002) and Nerlich & Jaspal (2012).

1.1   The Māori language

With the arrival of Polynesian voyagers by canoe in about 1300 (Wilmshurst et al., 2008), New Zealand became the last major land mass on our planet to be inhabited by humans. Over the following centuries the Polynesian language that the Māori brought with them to New Zealand evolved into the language we know today, the closest linguistic relatives of which are Rarotongan and Tahitian (Harlow, 2007). After initial encounters with European voyagers Abel Tasman in 1642 and James Cook in 1769–1774, European settlement of New Zealand began with sealers, whalers and missionaries from the early 19th century. European settlers started arriving in larger numbers from 1840 onwards. Linguistically, colonization led the Māori populace to shift away from speaking Māori from the early 20th century onwards (Benton, 1991) until the 1980s when large scale revitalization of Māori began with the instigation of the popular and successful *kōhanga reo* (language nests). In summary, most Māori were largely monolingual in Māori until the late 1800s, increasingly bilingual through to the 1950s, and increasingly monolingual in English until the last 30 years (Benton, 1991).

Besides well recognized immersion education initiatives, a key part of the revitalization of Māori has been its increasing use in radio and television broadcasting. Māori language radio stations began in 1988 with an urban based station, expanding so that today there are 21 publicly funded stations throughout the country each broadcasting at least eight hours a day in Māori (Te Puni Kōkiri, 2008). Most of these stations are tribally based and focused.

With regard to Māori language television broadcasting, there have been regular news broadcasts and documentary style programs on government funded channels since 1983 (Te Puni Kōkiri, 2011). A nationwide Māori television station began broadcasting programs in Māori and English in 2004 and a sister Māori language only channel since 2008. The extension of the Māori language into these new environments has meant the development of new stylistic registers. See, for example, Kuiper, King & Culshaw (2014) for an explanation on the development of rugby commentary in Māori as well as the adaption of familiar forms to the new media. See also Nikora et al. (2013) for a discussion on the role of print media in the reporting of the funeral of the Māori Queen in 2006.

Despite revitalization initiatives, the Māori language is regarded as "unsafe" according to UNESCO's language vitality assessment (UNESCO, 2003) and can accordingly be described as an endangered language. Concerns about the vitality of the language have led to the production of, for example, a dictionary of Māori idioms published by the Māori Language Commission (Te Taura Whiri i te Reo Māori, 1999) which had the express purpose of increasing the use of idioms in the speech of younger speakers. There are also documented changes in the sound system of Māori in response to the influence of New Zealand English (Harlow et al., 2009).

In order to understand the imagery used to refer to death in the Māori language it is necessary to understand a little of the social background of the Māori experience and the importance and features of Māori rituals of encounter.

1.2   Rituals of encounter

The epitome of Māori cultural expression is to be found in the rituals of encounter on the *marae*, the open space in front of the ceremonial meeting house. This is where welcome ceremonies (*pōwhiri*) and funeral ceremonies (*tangihanga*) are enacted, ceremonies of encounter which have a long-standing and important role in Māori society (Higgins & Moorfield, 2004b). Because these ceremonies are public these rituals of encounter between host and visitor groups have survived the movement of Māori into cities where urban *marae* have been established (Walker, 1975). In addition, *pōwhiri* also occur at schools and government offices, as almost any space can be made to perform the function of a *marae*, particularly for welcome ceremonies. Indeed, visiting celebrities and dignitaries are routinely accorded a ritual Māori welcome on arrival in New Zealand.

Typically the *pōwhiri* begins with high pitched calls of welcome *(karanga)* from senior women in the host group, signaling to the visitors to proceed forward into the designated *marae* space. These calls are responded to by senior women in the visiting party. After the visitors and hosts are seated in separate groups (usually outside, in front and to either side of the meeting house) the speeches *(whaikōrero)* begin, these being given by senior males from both groups, each followed by an appropriate song *(waiata)*. More details about the forms of welcome ceremony can be found in Salmond (1975), Higgins and Moorfield (2004a), and Mead (2003). The use of the Māori language is obligatory in these proceedings (Salmond, 1974, p. 199; Kāretu, 1993). When the series of speeches has concluded the hosts and guests form lines and greet each other individually with *hongi* ('pressing of noses') and shaking of hands. The final part of the ritual is the sharing of food.

A specialized ritual of encounter is the *tangihanga* ('funeral'). Commentators from the early 19th century noted that:

> the *tangihanga* was a crucial ceremony in Maori life, that there was nothing like it in scale, or anything which places the same obligations upon the members of the society. If there is a key to the Maori world view then this is where it must be sought.   (Oppenheim 1973, p. 13)

The purpose of the *tangihanga* was to ritually send the deceased to the next world. Accordingly, the elements of this specialized ritual of encounter focus on addressing the deceased through farewells contained in both *karanga* and *whaikōrero* (for further details see Best, 1905; Salmond, 1975; Kāretu, 1975; and Rewi, 2010). The *poroporoaki* at *tangihanga* are distinguished by focusing completely on the deceased, and include extensive tributes. Consequently, it is traditional in Māori *poroporoaki* for the speaker to address the dead, rather than talk about them (Best, 1905, p. 170). It is important to note that this practice contrasts with European tradition, where although the deceased may very occasionally be directly addressed (see, for example, Allan & Burridge, 1991, pp. 163–164), this is more likely to be in a written rather than oral context.

Perhaps one reason why these funeral rituals are regarded as the epitome of Māori rituals of encounter (Dansey, 1975, p. 134) is that *poroporoaki* addressing a particular deceased person are adapted to a more generalized and formalized format in *pōwhiri* where both *karanga* and *whaikōrero* contain *poroporoaki* in which the dead in general are typically addressed and farewelled (Ngata, 2005). As outlined by Salmond (1975, pp. 169–170) these more general *poroporoaki* comprise three elements:

evocation –	the dead are called upon
valediction –	the dead are farewelled
segue –	statement signaling that the speaker is moving from addressing the dead to addressing the living.

While none of these elements is obligatory, in practice the valediction is usually present. In addition, although these three elements are in a free order sequence most examples follow the order given. Tributes to the dead can also be included, and can appear as part of any of the three elements. *Poroporoaki* are referred to here as a type of 'formulaic episode' to acknowledge that they are an episode which can be incorporated within a variety of speech acts and that they are typically comprised of a number of formulaic phrases. As for the types of metaphors we would expect to find in *poroporoaki* it is first necessary to understand Māori beliefs pertaining to death.

In Māori culture, after death the *wairua* (spirit, soul) of dead people travel to the northernmost point of New Zealand, Te Reinga, where they variously jump down into *te pō* (the underworld), travel across the ocean to Hawaiki, the homeland of the Māori (Best, 1905), or ascend to the sky (Mead, 2003, p. 147). From the conceptual metaphor framework we would understand this as the DEATH IS A JOURNEY conceptual metaphor. However, in line with Mühlhäusler's argument about the cultural relativity involved in deciding what is metaphoric and what is literal (2012, p. 1), it is important to point out that the travelling of the soul after the physical death of the body is not regarded traditionally by Māori as being metaphoric; it was an actual journey. Accordingly, one of the principle purposes of speeches to the dead at *tangihanga* is to encourage the deceased's soul to leave the body and start on the journey. That is, *poroporoaki* were efficacious. Consequently, the study of metaphor where DEATH IS A JOURNEY explains an abstract process using a concrete image comes from a very different belief system than that of the Māori (Orbell, 1978, p. 7).

Considering the important role Christianity has played in Māori culture (Head, 2005), it would not be surprising to find that Christian metaphors have become part of *poroporoaki*. This was confirmed in a previous study by King and Syddall (2011) who found that the euphemistic DEATH IS SLEEP/REST metaphors had entered *poroporoaki* with both the form and cultural context being calqued. In this more detailed study we would expect to find representations of both of these metaphors, and also perhaps further euphemisms, since euphemisms are such a strong feature of English expressions of death.

2. Research materials

In order to understand how speakers of Māori have adapted *poroporoaki* into a new situation, the main study here centers on the use of *poroporoaki* in introductory greetings *(mihi)* in radio and television broadcasts. These *mihi* are taken from the Māori Broadcast Corpus (MBC) which contains approximately one million words of running text, comprising mostly Māori language material broadcast on radio and television in 1995 (Boyce, 2006). As this analysis focuses on a modern adaptation of *poroporoaki* into the introductions to radio and television programs, excluded from this analysis are other material in the MBC corpus which also contains *poroporoaki,* namely, *whaikōrero* and *karanga* recorded at *pōwhiri* and *tangihanga.*

The material analyzed here comprises 63 *mihi* spoken by nine different speakers, all of whom are male. These *mihi* will be referred to as "the corpus". Of the *mihi* analyzed, 24 were from various radio programs, and 39 were from television programs. Significantly, the magazine type television documentary programs all started with a *mihi*. Typically, the presenter is seated in a studio and talks directly to the audience. Ostensibly, his principle task is to introduce the topic of the program. It is important to note that some of the *mihi* were undoubtedly scripted, in that several presenters presented very similar *mihi* on each occasion in the corpus. However, due to the number of speakers and the variety of programming (several speakers presented in both radio and television formats) the corpus contains a variety of styles and presentations. Metaphors used in the *poroporoaki* in these *mihi* were categorized and the results are presented in the following sections.[2]

The online Māori Niupepa Collection (Keegan et al., 2001) has also been used to compare written use of some of the metaphors, formulae and phrases under study. The Māori Niupepa Collection contains Māori language material from 34 newspapers published by various government, religious and Māori sources from the second half of the 19th century through to the first 30 years of the 20th century. While the Māori Niupepa Collection is a written, rather than an oral, corpus it gives some indication about the presence of metaphors and euphemisms which may have entered *poroporoaki* since European colonization.

More recent representations of *poroporoaki* from the Twitter feed relating to the death of popular New Zealand politician Parekura Horomia in April 2013 are also referred to in order to evaluate present day usage of the metaphors under discussion. For this analysis tweets were collected between 28 April to 3 May 2013. A total of 101 of these tweets used three of the conceptual metaphors under study here: DEATH IS A JOURNEY (29 instances), DEATH IS SLEEP (87 instances) and PEOPLE ARE TREES (14 instances). This includes, respectively eight, 42 and three occasions where English variants of the Māori metaphors were employed. The rationale for including tweets is that Twitter and other social networking sites are being increasingly used, especially by younger Māori, to maintain relationships and kinship ties (O'Carroll, 2013) so it is of interest to see how the metaphors under study are represented in this medium. However, it needs to be borne in mind that many of the tweets included here were not produced by Māori, or by speakers of Māori. Note also that most of the tweets contained both Māori and English phrases and that very few tweets were entirely in Māori. It appears that in these media the use of Māori and English phrases is being used emblematically by both Māori and Pākehā (New Zealanders of European descent) to pay tribute to the deceased. Accordingly, these tweets are a good example of translingual practice (Canagarajah, 2013) where Māori and English are being used together as a semiotic resource to provide an effective way of communicating meaning and identity.

---

2. The *mihi* element which has introduced the *Waka Huia* television documentary series since its inception in 1985 seems to have been discontinued about 2007. Since then the programme has adopted a more typical documentary style beginning.

3.   Results

As expected, the valediction component of the *poroporoaki* in the corpus contained the most metaphors with several formulae representing the DEATH IS A JOURNEY and DEATH IS SLEEP conceptual metaphors. In this respect the results seem to be similar for studies of other languages such as the Kenyan EkeGusii language (Nyakoe & Matu, 2012). However, there are major differences in that the Māori use of the DEATH IS A JOURNEY conceptual metaphor is not, as previously discussed, euphemistic, contrary to descriptions from English (see, for example, Pound, 1936 and Allan & Burridge, 1991). The results for these two conceptual metaphors are presented in Sections 3.1 and 3.2. Other conceptual metaphors with euphemistic qualities, PEOPLE ARE TREES and THE DEAD ARE STARS also appeared in tribute formulae and these are presented in Sections 3.3 and 3.4 respectively.

In by far the majority of *poroporoaki* (52) the presenter follows convention and addresses the dead. However, in nine *poroporoaki* the presenter does not address the dead, but rather only talks about them. These results are carried by one speaker who consistently talks about the dead on seven occasions, this being highly correlated with his use of the DEATH IS SLEEP metaphor.

These findings show that the convention of addressing the dead directly is still highly associated with *poroporoaki,* but suggests that this convention is less likely to be followed when the DEATH IS SLEEP metaphor is used. As noted by King and Syddall (2011), this is indicative of not only the calquing of the form of the metaphor but also its cultural context.

3.1   DEATH IS A JOURNEY

Examples from *poroporoaki* in the 19th and 20th century (Best, 1905; Salmond, 1975) suggest that the DEATH IS A JOURNEY metaphor was the sole metaphor used in valedictions in *poroporoaki*. Unsurprisingly, this metaphor is also strongly represented in the MBC where 47 of the 63 *mihi* have at least one valedictory phrase which sends the dead on their journey. The most frequent forms of this metaphor used the verb *haere* ("to go"), either stated once, twice, or three times. In total, metaphoric valedictions based on the verb *haere* occurred 68 times in the corpus.

Three of the most common realizations of this valediction are formulae generated from the template in Example (2).

(2)   *haere (haere) (haere)(atu rā)*
      'farewell (farewell) (farewell) (thither)'

As can be seen in Example (2), the basic word *haere* can be repeated a number of times. Triple repeats are a common rhetorical device in Māori oratory (Salmond, 1975, p. 164). The grammatical structure of the phrases generated in (2) are commands. That is, they are addressed to the dead and instruct or invite them to leave and go on their way. All of the occurrences of *haere* as valedictions in the corpus were direct address. In other words, valedictions using *haere* maintain the traditional form of directly addressing the dead.

Another verb associated with journeys, *hoki* ("to return"), is also used metaphorically 17 times in the corpus, and all but four of these were used in phrases of direct address. The verb *hoki* functioned similarly to *haere*, with Example (3) showing the most common formula with ten occurrences.

(3) *hoki atu koutou*
     'return there all of you'

Indeed, in the 47 *mihi* that contain variations of the DEATH IS A JOURNEY metaphor there are a total of 85 instances of variations of formulae with *haere* or *hoki*. In other words, on average, each of these *mihi* contain approximately two metaphorical formulae using *haere* and/or *hoki*.

About a third of the phrases which use the verbs *haere* and *hoki* are extended with phrases describing the location to which the deceased is being farewelled to. In total, there were 21 destination phrases, the most frequent being the instruction for the deceased to join the spirits of the ancestors, most commonly through variations of the phrase *ki te kāpunipuni o te wairua* ("to the gathering place of the souls"). Interestingly, this particular formulation seems to be somewhat modern with only one example appearing in the written Māori Niupepa Collection.

The second most frequent destination cited in this corpus is the underworld, most often articulated with variants of the phrase *ki (tua o) Paerau* "to (the further side of) Paerau". This destination has early attestations, being mentioned in Best (1905) and also appearing in the Māori Niupepa Collection. There was one example of a phrase where the deceased is sent to a constellation of stars *ki te Pūtahitanga-o-Rehua* ("to Canis Major"). There were no examples of this phrase in the Māori Niupepa Collection.

There was one example where the dead were sent to both to the homeland of Hawaiki and the meeting place of the spirits: *ki Hawaiki-nui, ki Hawaiki-roa, ki Hawaiki-pāmamao, ki Te Hono-i-wairua* ("to great Hawaiki, to distant Hawaiki, to far away Hawaiki, to the meeting place of the spirits"). Both these destinations are also well attested from traditional sources (Best, 1905, p. 172).

The DEATH IS A JOURNEY conceptual metaphor was also associated with the use of the phrase *ki tua o te ārai* ("beyond the veil") which, on the face of it appears to be euphemistic. In the corpus there are only five examples, but it is a relatively well-known phrase which is commonly heard in *poroporoaki* (Tauroa & Tauroa, 1986, p. 53). The phrase "beyond the veil" has biblical origins and is a reference to the curtain inside the temple separating the tabernacle (which contained the Ark of the Covenant) from less sacrosanct parts of the temple. The tabernacle was considered holy and was only entered by the high priest on one day of the year (the day of atonement). The reference therefore is to a very holy place in which one is in communion with God. The Bible was gradually translated into Māori from the 1820s onwards so several generations of Māori would have been exposed to this image. Despite its ubiquity in Māori this phrase is rarely known or used in modern English contexts. Bultinck refers to "behind the veil" (1998, p. 37) but neither Pound's exhaustive list of euphemisms for death (1936) or Fernández's analysis of Victorian obituaries (2006) refer to it.

A search for the phrase *tua o te ārai* in the Māori Niupepa Collection revealed only six examples, all appearing in religious newspapers no earlier than the 1890s. All but one of these examples were used in Christian or European contexts. This suggests that this image entered the Māori language in the late 19th century. Considering the Christian origins for this phrase it is not surprising that four of the five examples of this phrase in the corpus are produced by Anglican Ministers.

This phrase was introduced with a wide range of verbs of motion, for example *tae* ("to reach, arrive"), *huri* ("to turn") and *peka* ("to branch off"). The underlying metaphor is thus a variant of DEATH IS A JOURNEY. Three of the five examples in this corpus were used to refer indirectly to the dead, rather than addressing them. In other words, this phrase, calqued from English, also retains the English contextualization of being used to refer to the dead rather than to address them.

While the conceptual metaphor DEATH IS A JOURNEY is found in other cultures, it is often associated with a euphemistic way of describing death (Fernández, 2006; Aubed, 2011), and is particularly associated with Christian thought (Nyakoe & Matu, 2012). In English, for example, there are some expressions which refer to death as a journey to another world, for example, "he went to heaven", or "Hades" (Bultinck, 1998, p. 36). There are also some expressions which refer to meeting up with the souls of other dead people, for example, "he joined the angels" and "be gathered to one's fathers" (Bultinck, 1998, p. 37). However, in general, the range of Māori valedictory exhortations for the deceased to depart and leave appears to lack euphemistic intent, in that they are not examples of 'avoidance language' (Allan & Burridge, 1991, p. 3). Instead, the phrases discussed here form part of a series of appropriate phrases to be used to farewell the dead.

Despite the DEATH IS A JOURNEY conceptual metaphor being the most productive metaphor in the corpus, this is not the case with in the Twitter analysis where it was second most frequent, with variations on the valediction using *haere* being most frequent (13) with another eight using the verb *hoki* to send the dead politician on his way. Destinations were included on eight occasions with ancestors being the most frequently cited. Interestingly, of the eight non-Māori versions of this metaphor used in direct address, one was Latin *vale*, with the others being "go well" and "farewell".

3.2   DEATH IS SLEEP

The conceptual metaphors DEATH IS SLEEP and the related metaphor DEATH IS REST derive from a long-standing English euphemism where "sleep ... [is] regarded as a temporary death" (Allan & Burridge, 1991, p. 162). These metaphors are particularly pervasive in Christian rhetoric and have been incorporated into *poroporoaki*. As detailed in King and Syddall (2011), the Māori verb *moe* ("to sleep"), which has many cognates across Polynesia and reconstructs to the Proto-Polynesian **mohe* (Greenhill & Clark, 2011) seems to have been extended in meaning since European settlement of New Zealand to also mean "to die".

In the corpus there were a total of 44 examples of formulae evoking the conceptual metaphor DEATH IS SLEEP. Three different verbs were employed: *moe* ("to sleep"), *okioki* ("to rest") and *takoto* ("to lie down") with 16, 17 and 6 examples respectively. King and Syddall (2011) argue that the extension of the meaning of *moe* to metaphorically encompass death is a post-Christian one. By extension this argument also covers the related verbs *okioki* and *takoto*. We will examine the use of each of these three verbs in this conceptual metaphor in turn.

Moe is used in two formulae in the *poroporoaki*. There are nine examples of the phrase *moe mai* ("sleep"), which is a command addressed to the deceased. Similar to the *haere atu* ("farewell") formulae, *moe mai* is often repeated to give effect. The other seven examples are of the noun phrase *moenga roa* ("long sleep") which is used with the verbs *takoto* and *okioki* to form, on six of the seven occasions, descriptive, rather than direct address phrases giving the equivalent meaning of the English phrase "sleeps the long sleep" (Pound, 1936, p. 197). As the use of *moe* appears to be a calque from the Bible (King & Syddall, 2011, pp. 59–60) it is not surprising that four of the 16 examples of *moe* were produced by two speakers who were Anglican priests. For reasons which are unclear the other 12 examples were produced by two speakers from the Tūhoe tribe.

Moving on to the use of the verb *okioki* ("to rest"). The use of this verb was divided almost equally between descriptive and direct address uses (eight and nine, respectively). When used in direct address to the deceased it was in the formula *okioki atu (rā)* ("resting there"). Although the verb *takoto* ("to lie down") is not in itself metaphoric in that a deceased person is literally lying in a supine position, on six occasions the conceptual metaphor DEATH IS SLEEP/REST was evoked with this verb being used in the metaphoric formula *takoto i te moenga roa* ("resting in the long sleep").

With regard to the Twitter analysis, the conceptual metaphor DEATH IS SLEEP/REST was the most frequent, comprising about 72% of the 130 metaphoric phrases found in the tweets. This contrasts with the corpus where the DEATH IS A JOURNEY conceptual metaphor is most frequent. In addition, while in the corpus there was a fairly equal distribution between two of the three main verbs used to invoke this metaphor, in the tweets, all but 2 of the examples in Māori used the verb *moe* ("to sleep"). The majority of occurrences (41) were accounted for by the formula *moe mai (rā).* All uses were direct address. This phrase also appeared on one occasion as a hashtag, and in fact to date there have been a total of six tweets over the whole lifespan of Twitter using that hashtag to reference a death. This compares to the hashtag *haerera* ("farewell") which in contrast has only been used twice to reference a death. This suggests that the conceptual metaphor DEATH IS SLEEP/REST has a higher salience in the wider community than the DEATH IS A JOURNEY metaphor. The conceptual metaphor DEATH IS SLEEP/REST was also strongly represented in the English phrases in the tweets, with the most common form being centered on the use of the word "rest", the most frequent forms being "RIP" or "Rest in Peace".

3.3   PEOPLE ARE TREES

One word commonly used in the corpus to refer to those that have died is *hinga* ("to fall from an upright position"). Variants of this word occur 18 times, more particularly in the radio broadcasts. Example (4) shows the most frequent formulation.

(4)   *te hunga e hingahinga mai nā*
     'those who continue to die'

All occurrences in the corpus refer to the dead indirectly, rather than directly and phrases with *hinga* are used by five of the nine speakers.

With regard to the meaning of *hinga*, it is important to note that since the time of European settlement this word may have acquired a metaphorical meaning in addition to its literal one. In this case *hinga* "to fall" has also come to mean "to be defeated" and "to be killed". The word *hinga* has many cognates amongst the

Fijian-Polynesian languages, reconstructing to the Proto-Polynesian form *siga* (Greenhill & Clark, 2011). None of these cognates are recorded as having metaphorical meanings. In addition, metaphoric meanings for *hinga* did not enter the authoritative William's Dictionary until the greatly enlarged 5th edition in 1917 (Williams & Williams, 1917). On the other hand, there are some metaphoric uses of *hinga* in an early collection of written texts in Māori first published in 1854 (Grey, 1971). While it seems possible that these metaphorical meanings are a post-European phenomenon, it is impossible to be definitive about this since lack of data is not definitive evidence.

While the use of *hinga* here can readily be understood as metaphoric there are further levels of meaning, largely opaque to those without a knowledge of Māori, where formulae using *hinga* are used to honor the deceased. This is because the use of this word contains several cultural referents which need to be understood in order to appreciate its full meaning. An understanding of these referents reveal that the underlying conceptual metaphor involved in the use of *hinga* is THE DEAD ARE FALLEN TREES.

Firstly, the use of *hinga* references a popular proverbial saying, given as Example (5), which is nowadays used as the default way to announce publically that someone has died.

(5)   *Kua hinga te tōtara i te wao nui a Tāne*[3]
      "A tōtara tree in Tāne's great forest has fallen"
      'Someone important has died'

To anyone without cultural knowledge, the literal translation of this saying contains few clues as to its meaning. As per Wray's "Needs only analysis" (2002) a phrase such as this is parsed as one unit, with the meaning here being that someone important, either to the speaker or writer, or, more commonly, in the wider community, has died. While well known today, this proverbial saying seems to be of relatively recent origin. However, it has strong antecedents in Māori culture.

Firstly, as with other cultures, there are numerous Māori proverbs about human behavior which reference elements of the natural world, in particular trees and birds (Mead & Grove, 2001; Royal, 2012). With respect to trees, the wood of the *tōtara* was highly prized for its many uses, being "straight grained, easily worked, and […] durable" (Orbell, 1985, p. 58) and it was therefore regarded as a "chiefly tree" (Best, 1977, p. 106). Accordingly, the dead were often compared to trees, and, in particular, the *tōtara* (Orbell, 1985, p. 172). In the authoritative

---

3.   Other formulations of this proverb often vary in the use of particles with the verbal particle *kua* being replaced by *ka* and the particle *i* for *o* (see Mead & Grove, 2001).

modern book of Māori proverbs (Mead & Grove, 2001) the *totara* tree is mentioned in more proverbs than any other tree with all 22 of these proverbs referring to the strength or preciousness of the tree and its wood. Indeed, a common tribute to a deceased person in the 19th century was to address them as a *tōtara haemata* ("strong-growing totara"). The combination of *tōtara* in a longer phrase including *hinga* occurs approximately five times in the Māori Niupepa Collection, with all instances appearing in the first quarter of the 20th century, and none having this wording. In fact the earliest written example of this particular formulation seems to be in a book of proverbs published in 1951 (Kohere, p. 20).

In addition, the word *hinga* references the idea of "the fallen", those who have died in war. Particularly since World War I this word has gained a strong foothold with the publication of Laurence Binyon's poem "For The Fallen" (Binyon, 1915, pp. 28–29), the 4th verse of which, known as the Ode of Remembrance, is recited at annual war memorial ceremonies in New Zealand and elsewhere. Many Māori fought and died in both World Wars and their involvement has played an important role in the consolidation and validation of Māori identity (Oppenheim, 1973, p. 22). The warrior allusion here is a powerful one, as in traditional Māori culture to die in battle was a noble death (Best, 2001, p. 71). Thus the use of *hinga* ennobles the deceased. In fact, the use of *hinga* to mean "death" is common in collections of *waiata tangi* (laments for the dead).[4] Tāne, mentioned in this proverb, links both these traditional ideas together. An important figure in traditional Māori consciousness, his name is the personification of the word for "male", he is both the god of the forest, as well as being associated with strength and warrior type qualities of humankind (Orbell, 1995, pp. 179–181).

In summary, short phrases using variations of the verb *hinga* are used in the corpus to pay tribute to those who have died recently. Often the reduplicated form of the verb (*hingahinga*) is used to emphasize the large numbers of deceased. The phrases refer to the deceased, rather than addressing them directly, and the use of *hinga* indexes ideas of valor as well as referencing the more well-known phrase used to announce the death of an important individual. It is thus a succinct way to pay tribute. The underlying conceptual metaphor PEOPLE ARE TREES has strong roots in Māori metaphoric tradition, and this has been adapted and refined to reference Māori and European traditions of the valor of death on the battlefield.

---

4. See the *Ngā Mōteatea* collection published as Ngata 1972 (originally published by the Polynesian Society in 1928) and Ngata & Te Hurinui, 1961 & 1980.

3.4   THE DEAD ARE STARS

In the corpus there is another phrase which also valorizes the dead by referring to them as stars. Used by four of the nine speakers, the most common form of this phrase is shown in Example (6).

(6)   *rātou kua whetūrangitia*
        'those who have become stars'

The association of people with stars is a traditional one (Orbell, 1995, pp. 164–165). It is well-known that the Polynesians had extensive knowledge of the night sky and were highly skilled at using stars and constellations to travel across the Pacific (Howe, 2006). Because of the apparent movement of the stars from east to west, the stars were particularly associated with the homeland of Hawaiki (Orbell, 1995, p. 165), and thus an appropriate image to associate with the dead.

This particular verb, *whetūrangitia,* which is common nowadays, does not appear at all in the Māori Niupepa Collection, suggesting it may be of comparatively recent origin. Significantly, it is also associated with language about, rather than directed to, the dead, with five out of the six examples in the corpus being indirect address.

4.   Discussion

This paper addresses some of Mühlhäusler's concerns about a certain lack of range to date in the study of endangered metaphors (2012, p. 8). Firstly, as the Māori language is a member of the Austronesian language family this study widens the hitherto major focus on metaphors in Indo-European languages. Mühlhäusler's other concern is that many studies focus on types of language involved in traditional ceremonies rather than the language of everyday interaction. While the metaphors under study arise from ceremonial use of Māori, the focus here is on how the episodic variety of *poroporoaki* has changed and adapted to new technologies in a situation of language revitalization, and in formats such as Twitter that are within the purview of everyday usage.

In Chapter six of their book which focuses on euphemisms associated with death and dying Allan and Burridge (1991, pp. 153–171), outline five fears which motivate death taboos and note that "death is a fear-based taboo". However, these fears are very removed from the Māori experience of death as, unlike other reported cultures, Māori do not have a strong tradition of euphemism with regard to death. This study has included a few phrases which are euphemisms in English and which have been incorporated into the *poroporoaki* tradition. One was an extension to the DEATH IS A JOURNEY formulae which sent the dead *tua o te ārai* ("beyond the veil"). The other two phrases compared the dead to trees or stars. Nevertheless, this study has shown that while these concepts may be euphemistic in English they lack euphemistic intent in Māori. That is, use of the phrases is not characterized by an avoidance of referring directly to death or the dying process. Instead, these phrases have become part of a repertoire of appropriate honorifics which can be called upon by a speaker to pay tribute to the dead. This is all indicative of a different perspective on death than that noted by previous commentators who have studied Indo-European and Afro-Asiatic languages.

Instead, in Māori, the linguistic resources associated with death are focused on the formulaic episode of *poroporoaki* (farewells to the dead), which has traditionally been associated with the important rituals of encounter. *Poroporoaki* can be specific (addressing the death of an individual) and general (addressing recent deaths). The largest component in *poroporoaki* given as part of the funerary rites are tributes to the deceased. This is due to the personalized nature of addressing a particular deceased person. As the *mihi* in this study contain generalized *poroporoaki* it is not surprising that they contain a relatively small number of formulaic statements which honor the dead.

In the corpus under study here, *poroporoaki* formulae are heavily dominated by the DEATH IS A JOURNEY metaphor which is attested in early reports of Māori funerary rites. Christianity and the English language also appear to have influenced *poroporoaki* with the inclusion of formulae based on the DEATH IS SLEEP metaphor. However, these formulations follow some of the linguistic formats of the DEATH IS A JOURNEY formulae such as addressing the dead and the use of repetition. English influence is apparent in the calquing of the concept of talking about the dead, rather than talking to the dead, particularly in phrases which have been adapted from English. Nevertheless, there is little overall indication that talking about the dead is supplanting the more traditional mode of talking to the dead.

Thus we find that *poroporoaki* have retained traditional metaphors and appear to have admitted new ones based on English and Christian sources with elements of both traditions blending and mixing. As a formulaic episode *poroporoaki* is able to admit new metaphors into its formulaic components while retaining its overall context and traditional concept. In talking about the importance of formulaic varieties, Kuiper and Haggo (1985, p. 167) note that "the varieties of a language define the language culturally". As we have seen, *poroporoaki* are an important part of not only Māori cultural and linguistic experience, but also have some currency and emblematic uses in wider New Zealand society.

Idström & Piirainen note that "the metaphors of a language are vulnerable. *They start to vanish at the very beginning of a language becoming endangered*"

(2012, p. 18, italics in original). Indeed, metaphors are vulnerable if they are idiomatic and not part of a formulaic episode such as *poroporoaki*. This study confirms that metaphors which are encoded in formulaic phrases and are part of formulaic genre or episodes are more resistant and adaptable to change. A formulaic episode such as *poroporoaki* therefore plays an important role in maintaining traditional forms of the language while allowing the incorporation of new ideas.

It is also of interest to note that key elements in Māori *poroporoaki* parallel clinical reports of Near Death Experiences (NDEs) (Greyson, 2003) where people who are, to all intents and purposes dead, are resuscitated. Afterwards, these people typically report a sense of being out of the physical body and awareness of an afterlife and/or awareness of other deceased family members (Parnia et al., 2001). These features of NDEs are consistent with the Māori practice of talking to the deceased and encouraging them to move on to an afterlife where other ancestors dwell. This indicates that the Māori approach to death has some grounding in human experience of the world, and, as earlier indicated, should not be seen as entirely metaphoric.

In this study we have seen how formulae used in *poroporoaki* have been adapted into post-contact written, radio and television and internet-based media. This is indicative of how important acknowledgments to the dead are. This adaption of *poroporoaki* to new media and formats of communication is a good example of what Zuckermann and Walsh call "revival linguistics" (2011). They argue that in situations of language revitalization forms of language purism should be eschewed. Instead the natural process of hybridism, where the heritage language takes on elements of the language/s it is in contact with, should be understood and embraced (Zuckermann & Walsh, 2011). Māori awareness and acceptance of hybridism are encapsulated in the words of well-known Māori orator Wiremu Parker which were recorded in a discussion about *poroporoaki*:

> [The Māori orator] fuses some ancient mythological ideas with biblical teachings and no-one takes exception. [He] plays with those ideas quite freely and from the audience point of view [that's] quite acceptable, whereas Pākehās tend to be rather squeamish when you take, you know, mythological ideas like that and link them in with biblical teachings.   (Parker, 1981, Cassette recording)

Acknowledgements

I wish to thank Caroline Syddall whose data and analysis on death notices in the Māori Newspaper Corpus was the basis of this paper; Roberta Tainui whose work as a research assistant was vital to the project; and Kon Kuiper and Ray Harlow for much valuable advice and encouragement.

References

Allan, K., & Burridge, K. (1991). *Euphemism and dysphemism: Language used as shield and weapon*. Oxford: Oxford University Press.

Aubed, M. M. (2011). A study of English death euphemisms with reference to their translations into Arabic – a case study. *Tikrit University Journal for Humanities*, 18(2), 79–91.

Benton, R. A. (1991). *The Maori language: Dying or reviving?* Honolulu, HI: East West Center. (Reprinted by New Zealand Council for Educational Research in 1997).

Best, E. (1905). Māori eschatology: The whare pōtae and its lore. *Transactions and proceedings of the New Zealand Institute*, 38, 148–239.

Best, E. (1977). *Forest lore of the Māori* (reprint). Wellington: Government Printer.

Best, E. (2001). *Notes on the art of war*. Auckland: Reed Books in association with the Polynesian Society.

Binyon, L. (1915). *The winnowing fan: Poems on the great war*. Boston, XX: Houghton Mifflin.

Boyce, M. T. (2006). *A corpus of modern spoken Māori*. Unpublished doctoral dissertation, Victoria University of Wellington, Wellington, New Zealand.

Bultinck, B. (1998). *Metaphors we die by: Conceptualizations of death in English and their implications for the theory of metaphor*. (Antwerp Papers in Linguistics 94). Antwerp: Universiteit Antwerpen.

Canagarajah, S. (2013). *Translingual practice: Global Englishes and cosmopolitan relations*. Abingdon: Routledge.

Dansey, H. (1975). A view of death. In M. King (Ed.), *Te ao hurihuri: The world moves on, aspects of Māoritanga* (pp. 173–189). Wellington: Hicks Smith & Sons.

Fernández, E. C. (2006). The language of death: Euphemism and conceptual metaphorization in Victorian obituaries. *SKY Journal of Linguistics*, 19, 101–130.

Franklin, K. J. (2012). Kewa figures of speech: Understanding the code. In A. Idström & E. Piirainen (Eds.), *Endangered metaphors* (pp. 185–204). Amsterdam: John Benjamins. DOI: 10.1075/clscc.2.09fra

Greenhill, S. J., & Clark, R. (2011). POLLEX-online: The Polynesian Lexicon project online. *Oceanic Linguistics*, 50(2), 551–559. DOI: 10.1353/ol.2011.0014

Grey, G. (1971). *Ngā mahi a ngā tūpuna* (4th ed.). Wellington: A. H. & A. W. Reed.

Greyson, B. (2003). Incidence and correlates of near-death experiences in a cardiac care unit. *General Hospital Psychiatry*, 25, 269–276. DOI: 10.1016/S0163-8343(03)00042-2

Harlow, R. (2007). *A linguistic introduction to Māori*. Cambridge: Cambridge University Press. DOI: 10.1017/CBO9780511618697

Harlow, R., Keegan, P., King, J., Maclagan, M., & Watson, C. (2009). The changing sound of the Māori language. In J. N. Stanford & D. R. Preston (Eds.), *Variation in indigenous minority languages* (pp.129–152). Amsterdam: John Benjamins. DOI: 10.1075/impact.25.07har

Head, L. (2005). Wiremu Tamihana and the mana of Christianity. In J. Stenhouse (Ed.), *Christianity, modernity and culture: New perspectives on New Zealand history* (pp. 58–86). Adelaide: ATF Press.

Higgins, R., & Moorfield, J. (2004a). Ngā tikanga o te marae - marae practices. In T. M. Ka'ai, J. C. Moorfield, M. P. J. Reilly, & S. Mosely (Eds.), *Ki te whaiao - an introduction to Māori culture and society* (pp. 73–84). Auckland: Pearson Longman.

Higgins, R., & Moorfield, J. (2004b). Tangihanga: Death customs. In T. M. Ka'ai, J. C. Moorfield, M. P. J. Reilly, & S. Mosely (Eds.), *Ki te whaiao – an introduction to Māori culture and society* (pp. 85–90). Auckland: Pearson Longman.

Horowitz, F. E. (2002). Metaphors we die by: George Lakoff's "Metaphors of terror". *Teachers College, Columbia University working papers in TESOL & applied linguistics*, 2(1). Retrieved 6 Nov 2013 from http://journals.tc-library.org/index.php/tesol/article/view/179/176

Howe, K. R. (Ed.) (2006). *Vaka Moana: voyages of the ancestors: The discovery and settlement of the Pacific*. Auckland: David Bateman.

Idström, A., & Piirainen, E. (2012). Endangered metaphors: Introduction. In A. Idström & E. Piirainen (Eds.), *Endangered metaphors* (pp. 15–19). Amsterdam: John Benjamins. DOI: 10.1075/clscc.2.02ids

Kāretu, T. (1975). Language and protocol of the marae. In M. King (Ed.), *Te ao hurihuri: The world moves on, aspects of Māoritanga* (pp. 35–54). Wellington: Hicks Smith & Sons.

Kāretu, T. (1993). Tōku reo, tōku mana. In W. Ihimaera, H. Williams, I. Ramsden, & D. S. Long (Eds.), *Te Ao Mārama: Vol. 2. Te whakaatanga o te ao =The reality* (pp. 222–229). Auckland: Reed Books.

Keegan, T. T., Apperley, M., Cunningham, S. J., & Witten, I. (2001). The Niupepa Collection: opening the blinds on a window to the past. In D. Bearman & F. Garsotto (Eds.), *Proceedings of the International Cultural Heritage Informatics Meeting Conference ICHIM01* (Vol. 1, pp. 347–356). Retrieved from: http://www.cs.waikato.ac.nz/~tetaka/PDF/OpeningBlinds.pdf.

King, J., & Syddall, C. (2011). Changes in the phrasal lexicon of Māori: *mauri* and *moe. Yearbook of Phraseology*, 1, 45–70.

Kohere, R. T. (1951). *He konae aronui: Maori proverbs and sayings*. Wellington: A. H. & A. W. Reed.

Kuiper, K., & Haggo, D. (1985). On the nature of ice hockey commentaries. In R. Berry & J. Acheson (Eds.), *Regionalism and national identity: Multidisciplinary essays on Canada, Australia and New Zealand* (pp. 167–175). Christchurch: Association for Canadian Studies in Australia and New Zealand.

Kuiper, K., King, J., & Culshaw, D. (2014). Whence Māori commentary? In A. Onysko, M. Degani, & J. King (Eds.), *He hiringa, he pūmanawa - studies on the Māori language: In honour of Ray Harlow* (pp. 149–177). Wellington: Huia Publishers.

Lakoff, G., & Johnson, M. (1980). *Metaphors we live by*. Chicago, IL: University of Chicago Press.

Mead, H. M. (2003). *Tikanga Māori: Living by Māori values*. Wellington: Huia Publishers.

Mead, H. M., & Grove, N. (2001). *Ngā pēpeha a ngā tīpuna*. Wellington: Victoria University Press.

Mühlhäusler, P. (2012). Prologue. In A. Idström & E. Piirainen (Eds.), *Endangered metaphors* (pp. 1–14). Amsterdam: John Benjamins. DOI: 10.1075/clscc.2.01muh

Nerlich, B., & Jaspal, R. (2012). Metaphors we die by? Geoengineering, metaphors and the argument from catastrophe. *Metaphor and symbol*, 27(2), 131–147. DOI: 10.1080/10926488.2012.665795

Nikora, L. W., McRae, K., Te Awekotuku, N., & Hodgetts, D. (2013). A tangi for an ariki: Mourning through print media reporting. In M. N. Agee, T. McIntosh, P. Culbertson, & C. O. Makasiale (Eds.), *Pacific identities and well-being: Cross-cultural perspectives* (pp. 174–187). Dunedin: Otago University Press.

Ngata, A. T. (1972). *Ngā moteatea: Part I.* Wellington: A. H. & A. W. Reed.

Ngata, A. T., & Te Hurinui, P. (1961). *Ngā moteatea: Part II.* Wellington: The Polynesian Society.

Ngata, A. T., & Te Hurinui, P. (1980). *Ngā moteatea: Part III.* Wellington: The Polynesian Society.

Ngata, P. (2005). Death, dying and grief. In M. Schwass (Ed.), *Last words: Approaches to death in New Zealand's cultures and faiths* (pp. 29–40). Wellington: Bridget Williams Books. DOI: 10.7810/9781877242342_3

Nyakoe, D. G., & Matu, P. M. (2012). Conceptualization of 'Death is a Journey' and 'Death as Rest' in EkeGusii euphemism. *Theory and Practice in Language Studies*, 2(7), 1452–1457. DOI: 10.4304/tpls.2.7.1452-1457

O'Carroll, A. D. (2013). An analysis of how rangatahi Māori use social networking sites. *Mai Journal*, 2(1), 46–59.

Oppenheim, R. S. (1973). *Māori death customs.* Wellington: A. H. & A. W. Reed.

Orbell, M. (1978). *Māori poetry: An introductory anthology.* Auckland: Heinemann Educational Books.

Orbell, M. (1985). *The natural world of the Māori.* Auckland: William Collins.

Orbell, M. (1995). *The illustrated encyclopedia of Māori myth and legend.* Christchurch: Canterbury University Press.

Parker, W. (1981). *Whaikoorero: Ceremonial farewells to the dead.* [Cassette recording]. Wellington: Continuing Education Unit, Radio New Zealand.

Parnia, S., Waller, D. G., Yeates, R., & Fenwick, P. (2001). A qualitative and quantitative study of the incidence, features and aetiology of near death experiences in cardiac arrest survivors. *Resuscitation*, 48, 149–156. DOI: 10.1016/S0300-9572(00)00328-2

Piirainen, E. (2012). Metaphors of an endangered Low Saxon basis dialect – exemplified by idioms of stupidity and death. In A. Idström & E. Piirainen (Eds.), *Endangered metaphors* (pp. 339–357). Amsterdam: John Benjamins. DOI: 10.1075/clscc.2.16pii

Pound, L. (1936). American euphemisms for dying, death, and burial. *American Speech*, 11(3), 195–202. DOI: 10.2307/452239

Rewi, P. (2010). *Whaikōrero: The world of Māori oratory.* Auckland: Auckland University Press.

Romaine, S. (1996). War and peace in the global greenhouse: Metaphors we die by. *Metaphor and symbolic activity*, 11(3), 175–194. DOI: 10.1207/s15327868ms1103_1

Royal, T. A. C. (2012). Te waonui a Tāne – forest mythology - sayings from the forest. *Te Ara - the encyclopedia of New Zealand.* Retrieved from http://www.TeAra.govt.nz/en/te-waonui-a-tane-forest-mythology/page-5

Salmond, A. (1974). Rituals of encounter among the Maori: Sociolinguistic study of a scene. In R. Bauman & J. Sherzer (Eds.), *Explorations in the ethnography of speaking* (pp. 192–212). London: Cambridge University Press.

Salmond, A. (1975). *Hui: A study of Māori ceremonial gatherings.* Wellington: A. H. & A. W. Reed.

Tauroa, H., & Tauroa, P. (1986). *Te marae: a guide to customs and protocol.* Auckland: Reed Methuen.

Te Puni Kōkiri. (2008). *The health of the Māori language in the broadcasting sector 2006.* Wellington: Author.

Te Puni Kōkiri. (2011). *Iwi radio achievements.* Wellington: Author.

Te Taura Whiri i te Reo Māori. (1999). *He kohinga kīwaha.* Auckland: Reed.

UNESCO Ad Hoc Expert Group on Endangered Languages. (2003). *Language vitality and endangerment*. Retrieved from http://www.unesco.org/culture/ich/doc/src/00120-EN.pdf.

Walker, R. (1975). Marae: A place to stand. In M. King (Ed.), *Te Ao Hurihuri: The world moves on: Aspects of Maoritanga* (pp. 21–34). Wellington: Hicks Smith & Sons.

Williams, W., & Williams, H. W. (1917). *A dictionary of the Māori language* (5th ed.). Wellington: Government Printer.

Wilmshurst, J. M., Anderson, A. J., Higham, T. F. G., & Worthy, T. H. (2008). Dating the late prehistoric dispersal of Polynesians to New Zealand using the commensal Pacific rat. *Proceedings of the National Academy of Sciences USA*, 105(22), 7676–7680.

Wray, A. (2002). *Formulaic language and the lexicon*. Cambridge: Cambridge University Press. DOI: 10.1017/CBO9780511519772

Zuckermann, G., & Walsh, M. (2011). Stop, revive, survive: Lessons from the Hebrew revival applicable to the reclamation, maintenance and empowerment of Aboriginal languages and cultures. *Australian Journal of Linguistics*, 31(1), 111–127. DOI: 10.1080/07268602.2011.532859

CHAPTER 3

Papua New Guinean sweet talk
Metaphors from the domain of taste

Phil King
Pacific Institute of Languages, Arts and Translation
(Ukarumpa, Eastern Highlands Province, Papua New Guinea)

People often use conceptual metaphors to understand abstract domains in terms of more directly perceptual domains, as in the English metaphor UNDERSTANDING IS SEEING. The sensory domain of TASTE is more complex and culturally conditioned than other senses. This article investigates how the TASTE domain is structured in several languages in Papua New Guinea (Dawawa, Gadsup, Gwahatike, Guhu Samane, Kamano Kafe and Tairuma) and explores how these language communities use this domain to metaphorically conceptualize more abstract experiences, particularly those of speech and interpersonal relationships. The article also compares these metaphors with those in English and Tok Pisin, the two main languages of wider communication.

Keywords: taste perception; Papua New Guinea; language, body and culture; universality and variation; conceptual metaphor; Tok Pisin

1. Introduction

It is common to find linguistic expressions where terminology from a physical sensory domain describes experiences in more abstract domains. In English, being *in the dark* uses the visual domain to describe a lack of understanding in a mental domain, and describing someone as *bitter* uses the taste domain to describe an emotion of resentment.

Conceptual metaphor research suggests these are not isolated expressions, or 'dead' metaphors, but exemplify larger conceptual structures, whereby one *target* domain is understood in terms of another *source* domain (Lakoff & Johnson, 1980). Being *in the dark* is just one realization of the mapping from SEEING to UNDERSTANDING, also evident in *I see your point, my brain is foggy,* or

DOI 10.1075/clscc.7.02kin
© 2015 John Benjamins Publishing Company

his writing is opaque. In each example, a person trying to understand something is mapped onto a person trying to see something, and hindrances in understanding map onto hindrances in vision. The scalarity of the source domain (different degrees of visibility) gives a scalar structure to the target domain, mapping onto different degrees of understanding.

These mappings mean that experiences in the perceptual domain (such as vision) are then used to reason about experiences in the more abstract domain (here, understanding). If I cannot *see* someone's point, the problem could be either in my head (with my *foggy* brain) or in their *opaque* communication. Here, logical entailments in the domain of sight are being used to draw inferences in the domain of understanding.

Such conceptual metaphors are often grounded in universal physiology, and common correlations of experience. For example, the physiology of the eye is nearly identical across the planet, and everyone experiences a limited visual field. We usually feel that items in that field are better controlled and understood than what is unseen, outside the visual field. So, it would not be surprising if many languages make a conceptual link between SEEING and UNDERSTANDING. Other universal physiological aspects of vision make it a productive source domain for intellection (Sweetser, 1990, pp. 37–39): vision can voluntarily focus on one stimulus within a multitude of input stimuli, and can perceive things at a distance (without contact), enabling multiple people to see the same thing at the same time. This supports the impression that vision is more 'objective' than other senses, and maps onto the understanding of intellection as an objective activity.

However, there is no guarantee that other languages will conceptually link vision and understanding. Such embodied conceptual metaphors are also dependent on the socio-cultural background (Kövecses, 2005; Ibarretxe-Antuñano, 2012). A source domain like VISION may structure different domains in different cultures, and these are called the *scope* of the source in that culture (Kövecses, 2002, pp. 107–120). Even if expressions from the domain of vision are used in the domain of understanding, the conceptual metaphor may differ in several ways. Conceptually, it may map different aspects of the source domain or highlight different entailments in the source domain. Linguistically, variation may be seen in the degree of elaboration (the variety of source domain terms used in the target domain); the degree of conventionalization of expressions; the transparency of the source domain; and in the kinds of syntactic expressions used (Kövecses, 2005, pp. 151–162).

Perception itself is influenced by language and culture, and these differences may affect the entailments in a target domain. For example, in Classical Hebrew, darkness is considered as an entity in itself, rather than a gradation of light. Words for darkness do not occur with degree modifiers like *very*. This influences the conceptual metaphor of DISTRESS as DARKNESS, so that distress is not readily construed as a scalar concept through this source domain (King, 2012, pp. 294–296).

UNDERSTANDING IS SEEING has been well-explored both etymologically and cross-linguistically. This paper focuses instead on how the perceptual domain of TASTE structures other experiences in Papua New Guinean languages. Although all humans have very similar anatomy for taste perception (including tongues, noses, taste buds and olfactory receptors), the tastes that are salient and those that are linguistically encoded differ from community to community and language to language. To understand the conceptual metaphors from the taste domain, we need to understand how the domain of taste itself is structured and how language and taste physiology interact in different cultures.

2. Taste perception: Physiology and language

Common human physiology means some aspects of taste perception should be fairly universal. Some of these distinguish taste perception from other senses, and will affect the linguistic structuring of taste terminology in different languages, the scope of metaphors based on this source and the entailments highlighted by any conceptual metaphors. Backhouse (1994, pp. 12–15) lists five differences between taste perception and visual perception: complexity; proximity of receptors; cultural channeling; affectivity; and individual variation.

First, taste perception is much more complex than vision. Scientific studies have often focused narrowly on the gustatory qualities of different chemical solutions perceived through the processes in different receptors within taste buds. These include the qualities known as umami (related to the concentration of monosodium glutamate or aspartate); sweet (related to the presence of sugars, sweeteners, certain amino acids or sweet proteins); bitter (related to the presence of a wide variety of toxins); sour (related to the concentration of hydrogen ions, and hence the degree of acidity); and salty, probably based on the presence of sodium (Chandrashekar et al., 2006). These different chemical tastes may vary in salience in different cultures, with some subset often being lexicalized in language. In English, *sweet, sour, bitter* and *salt* are much more common than *umami*. Some other languages only distinguish two chemical tastes, and these are often conflated with good and bad evaluation.

However, the common understanding of taste is much broader than just these chemical tastes and involves other qualities (Backhouse, 1994, pp. 1–5): olfactory qualities perceived through the nose (that make raw onion taste different from raw apple, for example); tactile qualities like heat (with mustard being hot and menthol cold) or pain (from chili peppers, for example); and the qualities of tastes that are 'metallic' or 'astringent' (rhubarb, for example). Taste words in different languages may highlight any of these kinds of qualities, or a combination of them. Studies focusing only on the tastes of solutions miss many of these qualities.

Our universal taste physiology can also discriminate differing concentrations of chemicals (be it very sweet, or slightly salty), and differing degrees of other qualities such as spiciness and astringency. This means that the taste domain potentially has natural scalarity that can be mapped to different degrees in a target domain, to describe just how *bitter* a resentful person is in English, for example.

Second, taste, smell and touch differ from vision and hearing by depending upon proximate rather than distal receptors. That is, the receptors need to be in close proximity to the object being perceived. As a result, in conceptual metaphors, the distal senses are more often associated with domains involving objectivity and intellect, whereas the closeness of the proximate senses makes them more commonly used to understand domains involving subjectivity, intimacy and emotion (Sweetser, 1990, p. 44).

Third, taste is more cultural than other senses, because the substances deemed acceptable to taste, and their evaluation, are so closely tied to the cultural activities of eating and drinking. Diet and cuisine differ from culture to culture, potentially leading to significant linguistic differences in the taste experiences that are lexically emphasized. The degree of linguistic elaboration of this domain is likely to reflect specific cultural interests. Thus, when taste is used in conceptual metaphors, different cultures may use entailments from specific culturally recognized tastes that are not salient elsewhere, as in the use of *mari* (a species of ginger) to describe someone's talk in Guhu Samane.

Fourth, taste perception involves an evaluative, affective aspect that is less significant for vision. That is, tastes are usually either categorized as pleasant or unpleasant. This perhaps has a biological basis, in the need to alert the body of positive or harmful substances being consumed. This evaluative aspect allows metaphorical entailments of positive and negative evaluation when tastes describe someone's character or speech.

Finally, taste perception exhibits more individual variation than other senses. A substance that tastes good to one person may not be appreciated by another. Thus, people generally tolerate greater variation in taste judgment for a given stimulus than they do for color judgment, for example. This makes the taste domain particularly suitable as a source domain for concepts with a high degree of subjectivity, such as whether someone's advice is good or not.

Given these aspects of taste perception, how are tastes typically described in language? Backhouse (1994, pp. 166–168) concludes that all languages have at least two words to describe tastes, one including sweet substances and another encompassing disagreeable taste qualities. However, the relation of words describing taste *qualities* (such as sour or sweet) to those *evaluating* taste (good or bad) can fit into one of three linguistic systems: a generalized system, with no separate words for *sweet* as opposed to *good*, or *bitter* as opposed to *bad*; a differentiated system in which words for taste qualities are distinguished from words for evaluation; and an intermediate system, in which words for *good* and *sweet* may be identical, but *bad* and *bitter* are distinguished.

Surveys of taste terminology in Papua New Guinean languages (cited in Backhouse, 1994, pp. 6–8) show that many have a generalized or intermediate system. That is, typically, there is one word describing good taste, whether sweet or salty. This word describes the taste of sugar cane or a salty beef cracker, for example. This is true also in Tok Pisin, the main language of wider communication (other than English), where *swit* describes many salty (non-sweet) substances. Thus, when *swit* is used in Tok Pisin metaphors, it is based on a differently structured source domain than when *sweet* is used as a metaphor in English, despite identical pronunciation.

Many New Guinea languages also do not distinguish between bitter, sour and bad tastes, using a fully generalized system which primarily distinguishes palatable from unpalatable tastes. Typically, the word for unpleasant tastes means something like 'rough' or 'biting'. Some languages in this article have this generalized system, while others do distinguish different disagreeable tastes. The degree of linguistic elaboration in the taste domain influences the variety of linguistic expressions available when used as a source domain for understanding other concepts.

3.   Metaphors from the TASTE domain in English

Before moving on to Papua New Guinean conceptual metaphors, this section considers some conceptual metaphors from the domain of TASTE in English, to demonstrate a descriptive method and to provide a reference point for comparison.

First, many conventional linguistic expressions in English describe a person's character using taste terminology: a *sweet child* (who acts kindly to others); a *sour woman* (whose face is puckered and is unpleasant to relate to); or a *bitter old man* (resentfully holding onto grudges from the past). These descriptions suggest the conceptual metaphor PEOPLE ARE FOODSTUFFS. Just as something in the chemical composition of food gives it a particular taste when someone consumes it, there is something in a person's character that affects others when they interact with them. It is much more pleasant to interact with a sweet person, than someone who is bitter. This metaphor includes the following mappings:

taste quality of food	→	character of person
someone eating food (consumer)	→	someone interacting with these people
effect of food on the consumer	→	effect of these people on those interacting with them
concentration of taste	→	'strength' of this aspect of character

The distinct tastes have different nuances when describing people's characters. For example, the difference between a *sour* person and a *bitter* person highlights aspects of the difference between these terms in the source domain. Being bitter is typically a more longstanding character trait than being sour (it is possible to be in a sour mood for an hour or so, but being bitter for an hour is less acceptable English), perhaps reflecting the fact that bitterness is an intrinsic characteristic that cannot be ameliorated, whereas sourness can often be offset by adding sugar.

Second, even more expressions reflect a mapping from taste to interpersonal communication, potentially summarized as MESSAGES ARE FOODSTUFFS. As such they may be easy or hard to *digest*, and may be *palatable* or *unpalatable*. With regard to chemical tastes, consider the sentences in (1):

(1) a.   "No," she replied *sweetly*.
     b.   "No," she replied *bitterly*.
     c.   "No," she replied *sourly*.
     d.   "No," she replied *tartly*.
     e.   *"No," she replied *saltily*.

Here, several different taste terms describe a speech act. Note, however, that the *salty* taste is rarely appropriate in conceptual metaphors to the domain of speech or character in English. In (1a), the adverb evokes a kind voice with intent to please. (1b–d) are more unpleasant to encounter, but in somewhat different ways. In (1d) the reply is short and forceful, causing pain to the hearer, whereas in (1b) and (1c) the description focuses more on the emotional state of the speaker, with *bitterly* in (1b) suggesting the most severe negative emotional condition. Whereas *sour* and *tart* denote very similar physiological tastes (both describe acidic substances, although *tart* is used more specifically for fruit and *sour* could reference vinegar, milk and cream as well), their meanings differ when used to describe speech. The use of *tart* for strongly sour fruit makes it appropriate for especially sharp, biting speech.

Many linguistic expressions reflect this conceptual metaphor in English, showing how entrenched it is. For example, someone's message may be a *bitter pill to swallow*, and easier to receive if they *sugar-coat* it. Here, source-domain reasoning (that potentially harmful substances can be digested more easily if given a sweet exterior) is used to understand the experience of accepting some-one's message more easily if it is made to sound like it will have positive effects for the hearer. Other examples pick up on prototypical foodstuffs: a *sugary* voice tries to win favor with the person addressed; whereas a *saccharin* story gives such a positive impression that it seems unrealistic, and may leave an unpleas-ant feeling.

The elements that are mapped in this conceptual metaphor include the following:

edible foodstuff	→	item of communication
eating foodstuff	→	receiving communication
person eating food (consumer)	→	person receiving communication
taste quality of food	→	aspects of the communication
effect of food on the consumer	→	effect of communication on the receiver

These mappings also allow inferences drawn from the source domain about causes and purposes. Describing a message as *sugar-coated,* for example, suggests the communicator deliberately tried to make the communication more palatable, just as a pharmaceutical company might deliberately make an unpleasant-tasting tablet easier to digest.

These two examples show a scope for the TASTE domain in English that includes character and interpersonal communication. In both examples, the effect on people is salient, whether interacting with a particular character or receiving a communication. This suggests that the positive or negative effect on others is an important aspect of the main meaning focus (Kövecses, 2002, pp. 109–110) of these conceptual metaphors in English, and fits with the affec-tive aspect of taste perception noted in Section 2. This can also be seen at higher levels of schematicity (Taylor, 2002, pp. 493–497), subsuming several conceptual metaphors in a more general expression, such as INTERACTING WITH PEOPLE IS EATING FOOD, covering both conceptual metaphors already described, but also linguistic expressions like a *sour smile* or *sweet lovemaking*. At an even higher schematic level, the conceptual metonymy PERCEPTUAL EXPERIENCES ARE TASTE EXPERIENCES, could cover further expressions like *sweet flights of jazz* (taste used in the domain of hearing), a *sour smell* (taste used in the domain of smell), or *bitter cold* (taste used in the domain of touch).[1] In every case, using the taste domain highlights the positive or negative effect of the experience on the person perceiving it.

---

1.   All examples in this paragraph are taken from the Collins Wordbank, http://wordbanks. harpercollins.co.uk.

The English data suggests the conceptual integration of taste concepts to the domain of personal interaction has reached the stage Fauconnier terms 'motivated polysemy' (1997, p. 24). At this stage, source domain terms are used automatically in the target domain, so that they feel like separate senses of words rather than giving a conscious feeling of analogy. However, the source domain is still accessible as a source of new vocabulary or ways of thinking about the target, as seen in the metaphorical use of *sugar-coating* and *saccharin*.

This section showed aspects of the well-elaborated and entrenched metaphorical system using TASTE as a source domain in English, an international language with a vast literature. The next section turns to Papua New Guinean languages, investigating how they use TASTE as a source domain for other concepts.

4.   Metaphors from the TASTE domain in Papua New Guinea

Papua New Guinea exhibits incredible linguistic diversity, having over 800 distinct living languages. With a population of roughly 7 million, most of these languages have very few speakers. The largest indigenous language has approximately 300,000 speakers, but most language communities number less than 10,000. Most Papua New Guinean languages are not in a position of sustainable literacy (with the next generation not being taught to read and write in the vernacular), and many are not even in a position of sustainable orality (since many parents are not passing on the vernacular to their children), both symptoms of linguistic endangerment.

Alongside English, the most widely spoken language is Tok Pisin, with at least 122,000 first language speakers and four million other speakers (Lewis, 2009). Where parents are not speaking indigenous languages to their children, it is predominantly in Tok Pisin that they communicate. Consequently, Tok Pisin has a huge impact on the Papua New Guinean language situation, and taste terminology and metaphors in Tok Pisin need consideration before moving to other languages.

4.1   Metaphors from the TASTE domain in Tok Pisin

Tok Pisin taste vocabulary includes the words *swit* (and *switpela*), *pait* and *saua*. Verhaar (1995, pp. 13–17) lists *swit* as one of the modifiers in Tok Pisin which can be used attributively (with the *-pela* suffix) but when used predicatively does not necessarily take the suffix. *Pait* and *saua* on the other hand, cannot be used attributively with the *-pela* suffix. The syntax is therefore asymmetrical for positive and negative tastes, as shown in (2)–(4).

(2) a. *dispela kaikai i swit*
         'This food is delicious'
     b. *switpela kaikai*
         'Delicious food'

(3) a. *dispela muli i pait*
         'This lemon is bitter'
     b. **paitpela muli*
         'Bitter lemon'

(4) a. *?dispela muli i saua*
         'This lemon is sour'
     b. **sauapela muli*
         'Sour lemon'

Tok Pisin has either a generalized or intermediate taste system, with distinct words for negative taste qualities depending on individual dialect. *Swit/switpela* always describes good-tasting, delicious food, rather than specifically sugary food. Salty crackers are regularly described as *swit*. *Saua* is much rarer than *pait*, and seems to simply borrow the English word *sour*, with a near-identical concept, prototypically describing a *muli* (lemons and other citrus fruits). *Pait* has a much broader semantic range including chemical and tactile taste qualities. Mihalic (1971, pp. 147–148) and Volker (2008, p. 60) list the following examples, encompassing substances typically described in English as bitter, sour, (excessively) salty and spicy:

(5) a. *marasin i pait*
         'The medicine is bitter'
     b. *muli i gat pait*
         'Limes have a strong sour taste'
     c. *sol i pait*
         'Salt has a sharp tang'
     d. *kari ya i gat pait*
         'This curry is really hot'

The taste word *pait* is itself a metaphorical extension from *pait* 'fight', so some speakers may still think of a substance 'fighting' with their mouth when this word is used. This etymology helps explain the wide variety of disagreeable tastes covered by *pait*.

When used in metaphor, there is again asymmetry. *Swit(pela)* is used in many different domains, but *pait* is rarely extended beyond the domain of food and no examples have been found using *saua* in other domains, as in (6).

(6) a. *dispela tok em i swit tumas!*
         'This talk is really good!'
     b. *switpela tok*
         'pleasing talk'[2]
     c. *switpela singsing*
         'pleasant/good singing'
     d. *switpela smel*
         'pleasant fragrance'
     e. *swit ya!*
         'that's great!' (common exclamation of pleasure)
     f. **dispela tok em i pait*
         'This talk is bitter/disagreeable'
     g. **dispela tok em i saua*
         'This talk is sour'

Some phrases use *pait* in conjunction with other words, but here the metaphor primarily evokes the 'fight' sense of the word rather than the taste. For example, *tok pait* 'argument' is most naturally understood as 'fighting' talk, rather than as 'bitter' talk.

These examples show very little linguistic elaboration, suggesting only very limited conceptual integration in Tok Pisin between the taste domain and other domains. It is only really *swit* which is used in multiple contexts to describe pleasant experiences. The paucity of structural mappings makes it difficult to call this a conceptual metaphor. However, the metaphorical use of this one word is very conventional and pervasive in everyday speech.

So, English exemplifies a well-elaborated, entrenched conceptual metaphor from the taste domain to domains of personal interaction, whereas Tok Pisin has a fairly impoverished metaphor from the taste domain to other experiences, although use of the word *swit* is very common. What about other Papua New Guinean languages? The remainder of this article investigates six of them. Data was collected by interviewing students and staff from across the country at the Ukarumpa Training Centre, Eastern Highlands Province. Interviews consisted of working through a questionnaire (using a mixture of Tok Pisin and English) to describe the tastes of various substances and then exploring different metaphorical uses of those tastes. As such, the examples are a result of direct elicitation rather than arising from natural contexts, and may only give a partial picture. Further informal interviews were conducted with local Gadsup speakers. Dictionaries were also consulted, where available: Frantz et al. (1996) for Gadsup; Bjorkman

---

2.   Verhaar (1995, p. 167) glosses this as 'flattery' but there is no support for this from other speakers. *Tok gris* is the equivalent of the English word 'flattery'.

& Ttopoqogo (2002) for Guhu Samane; and Payne & Drew (2005) for Kamano-Kafe. Knowledge of several of these languages is limited so morpheme breaks and linguistic conclusions are tentative.

4.2 Metaphors from the TASTE domain in Gwahatike

Gwahatike [dah] is a Trans-New Guinea language of the Finisterre-Huon sub-family spoken by approximately 1,570 speakers in the Saidor district of Madang province (Lewis, 2009). The taste system is intermediate, with one word for good/sweet tastes, but separate words for different sour and bad tastes. Separate words for good or bad, not specifically referring to taste, are: *igiŋ* 'good' and *bulun* 'bad'. Taste terminology includes the words shown in Table 1.

Table 1. Gwahatike TASTE terminology

	Taste	Examples
hapek	delicious, *swit*	sugar, beef crackers
mukuweŋ	sour	lemon, *muli*
worsak	rough, *pait*	ginger, chili pepper
urek	bad-tasting, bitter	quinine, salt water

Each of these words can occur with modifiers to express degree, such as *hapek worpo* 'very sweet'.

Despite this collection of taste words, there are very few metaphorical extensions. This is shown in (7), specifically for the domain of speech:

(7) a. *mere igiŋ*
         talk good
         'Good talk'
     b. *mere tareŋ*
         talk strong
         'Strong talk'
     c. *mere hapek*
         talk delicious
         'Delicious talk'
     d. **mere worsak*
         talk rough.tasting
         'Rough-tasting talk'
     e. **mere urek*
         talk bitter/bad-tasting
         'Bitter/bad-tasting talk'

(7c) is the only example where taste describes speech, and is itself not very common. Older mother-tongue speakers say this is a recent innovation influenced by Tok Pisin, describing very good news, for example. Traditionally, (7b) was much more common, based on a different metaphorical system, where 'strong talk' conceptualizes very powerful messages.

Taste terminology is not particularly used to describe people's character or behavior either, except in a sexual sense. When a woman is described as in (8a), this implies that a man wants to have an affair with her, and similarly for (8b).

(8) a. *bere   hapek*
         woman delicious
         'Delicious woman'
     b. *al   hapek*
         man delicious
         'Delicious man'

Thus, in Gwahatike, the TASTE domain only has very limited scope, with limited conceptual integration between the TASTE domain and other domains. Where there has been metaphorical extension into new areas, there is little linguistic elaboration, with only the word for positive taste being used.

4.3   Metaphors from the TASTE domain in Gadsup

Gadsup [gaj] is a Trans-New Guinea language from the Kainantu-Goroka subfamily, spoken by approximately 22,100 people in the Kainantu District of the Eastern Highlands Province. The taste system is a completely generalized one, with only two words to describe taste sensations, as in Table 2.

Table 2. Gadsup TASTE terminology

	Taste	Examples
ase	delicious, *swit*	sugar, beef crackers, meat, sweet potato
ika/yu	unpleasant, rough taste, *pait*	lemon, ginger, quinine, chili pepper

Tastes cannot describe behavior or character, but are being used (at least by some) to describe someone's speech. Speakers from some dialects found any taste terminology in other domains unnatural. However, speakers from more than one dialect found (9a) acceptable to describe somebody's speech when they are talking about something in which the listener is very interested. (9b) sounded unnatural to most interviewees, but one speaker explained how she used it to describe the effect of someone's talk on another, when they feel that they have been misrepresented and need to do something about it. For example, when a relative asks for something and accuses them of not reciprocating good deeds in the past (although in fact they have), this gives a rough taste spurring the hearer on, not to be angry, but to provide the help being asked for now. This would not be so appropriate if the speaker was not a relative, in that case the words would not be 'rough', the hearer could just say 'yes' or 'no' to the current request.

(9) a. *bayani ase   yemi*
         talk   delicious is.3S
         'This talk is delicious'

     b. *bena   sentim bayani yu³   ifemi*
         3S.POSS 1S   talk   rough.taste is.3S
         'His/her talk is rough-tasting to me'

Thus, there is currently very little conceptual integration between the domain of taste and other domains in Gadsup. The partial acceptability of (9a) may reflect Tok Pisin influence, but (9b) shows the creative possibilities of a potential developing mapping.

4.4   Metaphors from the TASTE domain in Tairuma

Tairuma [uar] is a Trans-New Guinea language from the Eleman sub-family spoken by approximately 4,500 people near Kerema in Gulf Province. Sweet and other delicious tastes are again conflated. There is no distinct word for sour taste as opposed to bitter or excessive salt, but there is a separate word for hot or spicy tastes, including ginger (Table 3).

Table 3. Tairuma TASTE terminology

	Taste	Examples
sirore	delicious, *swit*	sugar, beef crackers
keakea	bitter, sour, *pait*	lemon, quinine, salt water
hehea	hot, spicy	ginger, chili pepper

The words *meta* 'good' and *ea'eapo*[4] 'bad' can also describe tastes, and all tastes can be used with the qualifier *papa* 'very'.

---

3. *Yu* is a dialectical variation of *ika*.

4. The apostrophe in Tairuma represents a glottal stop.

In the speech domain, talk can be 'good', as in (10a), when someone gives a speech that the listener agrees with, or offers encouragement. Other common metaphors for speech include conceptualizing talk as *mesou* 'heavy', *lofo* 'strong/heavy', *heke* 'strong/tough', and *koko'oka'a* 'lightweight', all from the terminology of physical characteristics, as in (10b–e). Metaphors from the taste domain need to be considered in the context of these other conceptualizations. (10b) describes somebody's speech that is very urgent and serious. The listeners feel the speech's 'weight' and need to act within a specific timeframe, for example when a woman's relatives demand a bride price that must be paid to avoid the wife being taken back to her biological family. (10c) describes speech that really touches or convicts the hearer, such as warnings or advice. *Heke* in (10d) describes something that has become hard or tough in a physical setting, such as sago that has sat for a long time. In the speech context, the hearer *has* to do something in response to such a message. (10e) gives an opposite situation, for speech that has no 'weight', and is not worth talking about.

(10) a. *areve   oharo meta*
          3S.POSS word good
          'his/her talk is good'
      b. *areve   oharo meso papa*
          3S.POSS word heavy very
          'his/her talk is very heavy'
      c. *areve   oharo lofo   papa*
          3S.POSS word strong/heavy very
          'his/her talk is very strong/heavy'
      d. *areve   oharo heke   papa*
          3S.POSS word strong/tough very
          'his/her talk is very strong/tough'
      e. *areve   oharo koko'oka'a*
          3S.POSS word lightweight
          'his/her talk is lightweight'

These examples show a well-elaborated conceptual metaphor in Tairuma from the domain of physical qualities (weight and strength) to speech, with increased weight or strength mapping to increased seriousness or urgency of the message. Other linguistic examples use terminology from the taste domain to describe speech, although they are less common and less elaborated than these others. (11a) is a conventional description of someone's speech when it sounds good to the hearers, such as good preaching, a good story, or good advice. It can also describe someone who likes the sound of their own voice, who talks well but does not necessarily act on what has been said. The sentence in (11b) is not as conventional as (11a). A speaker who had spent her adult life outside of the area did not recognize it as valid, but it was familiar to another younger speaker, who described it as being used when someone has been talking angrily and using words that hurt others, words that cannot be 'swallowed'. (11c) is more conventional again, describing an unpleasant, angry, 'heated' conversation, so that discomfort is felt 'in your bones'.

(11)   a.   *areve   oharo sirore*
               3S.POSS word   delicious
               'his/her talk is delicious'
        b.   *ʔareve   oharo keakea*
               3S.POSS word   bad.tasting
               'his/her talk tastes bad'
        c.   *areve   oharo hehea papa*
               3S.POSS word   hot   very
               'his/her talk is very hot'

This conceptual metaphor emphasizes the emotional effect of someone's words on others, rather than the urgency or compulsion of the words seen in (10). Spoken words map onto ingested foodstuffs, and their emotional effect maps onto the emotional effect of eating those foods.

The word *keakea* can also describe people, as in (12a), for a bully whose words are negative and aggressive, so that they are very unpleasant to spend time with. *Sirore* does not describe character, with (12c) being used instead to describe a thoughtful, helpful person. This example is unusual, extending the word for bad taste into a new domain, but not the word for good taste. (12d) has some overlap in meaning with (12a), but can have two opposing meanings: either someone who is mean, angry, or greedy; or someone who is very daring.

(12)   a.   *a   lea   keakea   papa*
               that person bad.tasting very
               'That person tastes very bad'
        b.   **a   lea   sirore   papa*
               that person delicious very
               'That person is very delicious'
        c.   *a   lea   meta papa*
               that person good very
               'That person is very good'
        d.   *a   lea   eaʔeapo*
               that person bad
               'That person is bad'

Thus, Tairuma shows limited scope of taste vocabulary into other domains, being used primarily in the speech domain. In this domain it is not very well elaborated, with conventional expressions only using the positive taste attribute.

4.5   Metaphors from the TASTE domain in Guhu Samane

Guhu Samane [ghs] is a Trans-New Guinea language from the Greater Binanderean sub-family, spoken by approximately 13,000 people in Morobe and Oro Provinces. The taste terminology is well elaborated, but still classifies as an intermediate system since sugary (sweet) taste qualities are not separated from other good taste qualities (Table 4).

Table 4. Guhu Samane TASTE terminology

	Taste	Examples
meke/mekenoma	delicious, *swit*	sugar, beef crackers, sweet potato
tobaira	sour	lemon, some pineapple
qaa	rough, *pait*	ginger, chili pepper
togo/togonoma	bad, bitter	quinine, salt water
mari	taste that becomes bitter once inside your body	a particular type of wild ginger (*mari*) which can burn soft parts of your body (such as lips or eyes) if you touch them after handling this

Bagenoma and *qidza*[5] both mean something like 'good' and can also be used to describe foods. The difference is fairly subtle: a *bagenoma* sweet potato tastes good; whereas if it is *qidza,* it is good as opposed to rotten. When applied to people, *bagenoma* could describe someone who looks attractive, whereas *qidza* would describe someone with good character. Thus, *bagenoma* is used to describe perceived goodness, whereas *qidza* describes more intrinsic goodness. Conversely, *qanga* is the most general word for 'bad'. All the evaluative and taste qualities can take the suffix *nipamu* to express greater degrees of the quality, so that *mekenomanipamu* corresponds to 'very sweet', and *tobairanomanipamu* to 'very sour'.

The scope of the taste domain includes speech, emotions and evaluation of people and places. In the speech domain, taste terminology is used to evaluate a person's speech, and specifically the effect it has on others. First, though, (13a) and (13b) show the use of general positive words to describe speech. Just as *bagen-oma* describes physical objects that look good, but may not necessarily be good

---

5.   The *q* in Guhu-Samane represents a glottal stop.

throughout, it can describe speech that just sounds good, as in (13a). The following sentence in a discourse could begin with *onihe* 'but', to give a concession. (13b) could not easily be followed by *onihe*, describing talk that is particularly helpful. (13c) describes speech that demeans another person, or swearing. Bad advice would not be described in this way, since it attributes something negative to the character of the speaker.

(13) a. *noho   nooi   bagenoma*
          3S.POSS word perceived.good
          'his/her word is good'
      b. *noho   nooi   qidza*
          3S.POSS word good
          'his/her word is good'
      c. *noho   nooi   qanga*
          3S.POSS word bad
          'his/her word is bad'

All of the taste words can also describe someone's speech. In (14a), the use of *meke* 'sweet/delicious' is very similar to (13a) and (13b), but the positive effect penetrates deeper, as when someone hears very good news with significant personal impact, such as news of a relative's recovery from sickness, or on reading a Bible passage that speaks into someone's life. The use of *tobaira* 'sour' in (14b) is more idiomatic, used when making fun of someone to describe someone who does not really know what they are talking about, so that their talk does not make sense. In (14c), when someone's talk tastes like ginger or chili pepper (*qaa*), their words make others very angry. By contrast, in (14d), words described as bad-tasting like quinine or salt water (*togo*) make people concerned or sad, evoking more of an internal emotion (which may be similar to resentment) than outward anger. Finally, (14e) and (14f) show how the specific taste of *mari* ginger conceptualizes speech. This ginger can taste reasonable at the point of ingesting, but turns bitter in your stomach. When describing speech, these may be words that sound good, but are actually unhelpful, or that the hearer disagrees with.

(14) a. *noho   noo   oi   mekenoma*
          3S.POSS word that delicious
          'that speech of his/hers was delicious'
      b. *noho   nooi   tobaira*
          3S.POSS word sour
          'his/her word is sour'
      c. *noho   nooi   qaa   eete*
          3S.POSS word *pait*/rough makes
          'his/her word is rough-tasting'

(14) d. *noho   nooi   togo   eete*
          3S.POSS word bitter makes
          'his/her word is bitter/bad-tasting'
      e. *noho   nooi   mari   eete*
          3S.POSS word *mari*.ginger makes
          'his/her word tastes like *mari* ginger'
      f. *noho   nooi   bagenoma   onihe   mari   eete*
          3S.POSS word perceived.good but   *mari*.ginger makes
          'his/her word seemed good, but is really like *mari* ginger'

These sentences demonstrate a well-elaborated conceptual metaphor from the taste domain to the speech domain in Guhu Samane, including a wide variety of tastes, and highlighting the emotional effect of words on others. (14e) also shows the use of a cultural prototype (the *mari* ginger) to conceptualize a particular scenario in the speech domain.

Most of these taste terms can also describe emotional states when used with the insides or 'heart'. (15a) describes someone who is very happy, feeling particularly touched, blessed or encouraged by another. (15b) describes an angry emotion directed at someone else, whereas (15c) describes someone who has been emotionally hurt, perhaps through sad news or as a result of an unintentional offence. In Tok Pisin, (15b) corresponds most closely to *bel kros* 'angry insides', whereas (15c) corresponds to *bel hevi* 'heavy insides'. In Guhu Samane, the word *bame* 'heavy' can also describe the heart, evoking an emotion of sadness, without the element of repressed anger or resentment that is still present in (15c). (15d) shows the unnaturalness of using the word *tobaira* 'sour' with the heart. In (15e), the taste of *mari* ginger is again used, describing an emotional state that is somewhat 'heavy' and cross, as a result of a disagreement with someone.

(15) a. *naho   qupa   meke   eete*
          1S.POSS heart delicious   makes
          'my heart is delicious/sweet'
      b. *naho   qupa   qaa   eete*
          1S.POSS heart *pait*/rough makes
          'my heart tastes *pait*'
      c. *naho   qupa   togo   eete*
          1S.POSS heart bitter makes
          'my heart is bitter/bad-tasting'
      d. **naho   qupa   tobaira eete*
          1S.POSS heart sour   makes
          'my heart is sour'
      e. *naho   qupa   mari   eete*
          1S.POSS heart *mari*.ginger makes
          'my heart tastes like *mari* ginger'

Again, these examples show a well-elaborated use of the taste domain in another domain, and once again the use of *qaa* (the rough taste of ginger or chili) is associated with a more visible anger than the repressed resentment or sadness evoked by the *togo* taste of quinine. This may arise from the hot taste of chilies and ginger mapping to the heat of visible anger.

A more limited set of taste terms can be extended into other domains. (16) shows *togo* and *meke* conceptualizing whether the people living in a certain location are enemies or friends. They might be the response given when someone asks about a nearby village.

(16) a. *abi   ma nagapa togo*
          people and village bad-tasting
          'the people and their village are bad-tasting (i.e. enemies)'
      b. *abi   ma nagapa meke*
          people and village delicious/sweet
          'the people and their village are delicious/sweet (i.e. friends)'

A similar pair of expressions is shown in (17). Here, a young man might be asking about some young girls he sees, to discover how to relate to them. If the girls are *meke* 'sweet' as in (17a), they are safe to approach and relate to as sisters. If they are *togo* 'bitter/bad-tasting' as in (17b), they could be a potential wife for the enquirer, because they come from the appropriate clan (with which good relations need to be maintained), so the young man needs to be cautious and keep his distance.

(17) a. *paimane oi   meke*
          girls   those sweet/delicious
          'Those girls are sweet/delicious'
      b. *paimane oi   togo*
          girls   those bad-tasting/bitter
          'Those girls are bitter/bad-tasting'

Finally, the word *togo* can also describe places, as in *haba togo* 'bitter place'. This describes a sacred place associated with particular spirits, usually somewhere muddy or swampy. People who enter have to be very careful, to avoid negative things happening. They might wear something around their neck to protect them; any talk must be quiet; they cannot defecate or urinate there; and they should not use the real names of their companions.

All these examples show significant scope for the taste domain in Guhu Samane, being used to conceptualize speech, emotions, people and places. The main meaning focus from this domain is the positive (beneficial or safe) or negative (harmful or dangerous) effect on others. The metaphors are also generally well-elaborated and conventional.

4.6   Metaphors from the TASTE domain in Dawawa

Dawawa [dww] is an Oceanic Austronesian language from the Papuan Tip sub-
family, spoken in the Rabaraba district of Milne Bay Province by approximately
2,500 speakers. This is the only language in the survey which has a somewhat differentiated taste system, distinguishing different positive tastes (Table 5).

Table 5. Dawawa TASTE terminology

	Taste	Examples
din	pleasant tasting	sugar, sweet potato, meat, coconut cream
ḡaroro	delicious, sweet, pleasantly salty	sea water, beef crackers, milk, juicy fruits, sugar cane
yairuru	sour	lemon
karati	biting	ginger, chili pepper
ḡora	bitter/bad tasting	quinine, overly salty food
toma	bad-tasting	coffee without sugar in it

The root *din* covers a wider range of substances than *ḡaroro*,[6] being a more
general word for good tasting food. A mother-tongue speaker suggested that
ḡaroro was particularly suited to good-tasting liquids (milk, juicy fruits, sugar
cane) whereas *din* could describe solids too. However, salty beef crackers are
appropriately described as *ḡaroro*. The most general word for 'good' (not just
for tastes) is *vere*, and the equivalent for 'bad' is *gewagewa*. These two words can
be used to describe someone's speech, as in (18). Example (18a) could describe
good advice, a good speech or someone's encouragement. Example (18b) could
describe bad advice.

(18) a. *Alan na   giuma yavere*
          Alan POSS talk   good
          'Alan's talk is good'
      b. *Alan na   giuma yagewagewa*
          Alan POSS talk   bad
          'Alan's talk is bad'

When taste terminology describes someone's speech, it particularly emphasizes
the effect it has on the hearers. In (19a), using the root *din* to describe speech
classifies it as more positive than the general term *vere*, such as someone tell-
ing a good story, offering encouragement or comfort, giving meaningful advice,
or in other situations where the talk will benefit the hearer. In (19b), the more

---

6. *ḡ* in Dawawa is a voiced velar fricative.

specific positive taste *ḡaroro* describes a more specific positive situation, such as when someone gives an official speech that really benefits the good living of the community, and which will leave a very lasting impression. Whereas any talk could be *din*, the word *ḡaroro* is only really appropriate for special events or big meetings, where what is said gives you something special to remember. Example (19c) can describe the effect of someone's talk that would also be classified as *gewagewa* 'bad', such as swearing, insults or dirty jokes. Such talk makes you screw up your face as you do when eating a *yairuru* 'sour' lemon. The use of *ḡora* in (19d) describes an even more unpleasant taste than *yairuru*. When describing speech, this would not include dirty jokes, but rather specifically mean insults or bad swearing. Example (19e) gives a final acceptable case using taste terminology, where the word *tomatoma* (used for coffee without sugar in it, for example) describes someone's speech that is not helpful, offers no benefit to the listener, or is meaningless. It is not worth listening to such a person speaking. The example in (19f) is not acceptable, though the root *karati* can describe the state of the insides being 'bitten' after hearing sad news.

(19)   a.   *Jino na   giuma yadina*
            Jino POSS talk   pleasant.taste
            'Jino's talk tastes pleasant'

       b.   *Jino na   giuma yaḡaroro*
            Jino POSS talk   delicious
            'Jino's talk tastes delicious'

       c.   *Jino na   giuma yairuru*
            Jino POSS talk   sour
            'Jino's talk tastes sour'

       d.   *Jino na   giuma yaḡorana*
            Jino POSS talk   bitter
            'Jino's talk tastes bitter/bad'

       e.   *Jino na   giuma yatomatoma*
            Jino POSS talk   bad-tasting
            'Jino's talk tastes bad'

       f.   **Jino na   giuma yakarati*
            Jino POSS talk   biting.taste
            'Jino's talk bites'

These examples show taste terms being used to understand the intensity of the benefit or harm of someone's words. Just as something *ḡaroro* is more delicious than something *din*, so words described this way are even more special, and at the opposite end, words that are *ḡorana* are more harmful than those that are *yairuru*, just as is true for the corresponding foods.

Speech is the main domain to which taste terminology is extended. However, in recent years some of these words are being used to describe people's characters. In (20a), a *din* person has good character: giving to others; sharing; speaking well and caring for people. By contrast, in (20b) a *ḡora* person is one who is bad-tempered or may steal things from others. Just like people do not want to eat quinine, they do not want to be near such a person. Other taste words cannot be used in collocation with *banaga*.

(20) a. *banaga dinama*
          person   good-tasting
          'sweet/good-tasting person'
      b. *banaga waiḡoranama*
          person   bad-tasting/bitter
          'bitter/bad-tasting person'

Thus, Dawawa has a well-elaborated conceptual metaphor from the taste domain to that of interpersonal communication, but a much less well-elaborated metaphor into the domain of character. As in other languages, the domain of taste is used to express positive or negative evaluation of effect in other domains.

4.7   Metaphors from the TASTE domain in Kamano-Kafe

Kamano-Kafe [kbq] is a Trans-New Guinea language from the Kainantu-Goroka sub-family, spoken by at least 80,000 people in the Kainantu and Henganofi districts of the Eastern Highlands Province (Payne & Drew, 2005). Only three words are used to describe distinct tastes (Table 6).

Table 6. Kamano-Kafe TASTE terminology

	Taste	Examples
haga	delicious, sweet	sugar, sweet potato, meat, beef crackers
ka	bad tasting, *pait*	ginger, chili pepper, salt water, quinine
ta	sour	lemon, unsweetened coffee

Payne and Drew (2005, pp. 9, 20) claim that *ta* and *ka* are variants of the same taste,[7] but respondents to the questionnaire classified them as separate tastes. Further, the example sentences in Payne & Drew use *ta* in conjunction with lemon and *ka* with ginger, lending support to the distinction given here.

---

7. They are cited as *aka* and *ata*.

There are also general words for evaluating things: *kanare* 'good' and *haviza* 'bad'. The sentences in (21) are common ways of describing speech. Example (21a) might be used after someone has given a sermon or a good speech, or offered encouragement or advice, whereas (21b) evaluates talk as bad, such as wrong advice, or talk about fighting others.

(21) a. *ke*   *amo'a*[8] *kanare* *hu'ne*
          word 3S.poss   good   is
          'his/her word is good'
      b. *ke*   *amo'a* *haviza* *hu'ne*
          word 3S.poss bad   is
          'his/her word is bad'

Words from the taste domain can also be used in this frame, giving more specific entailments. Sentence (22a) could be used when someone is speaking politely or offering good advice, whereas (22b) could also be used for advice, but advice that is not really helpful. Example (22c) is much more negative, describing someone who is swearing or saying other strong bad words.

(22) a. *ke*   *amo'a* *haga*   *hu'ne*
          word 3S.poss good.tasting is
          'his/her word tastes good'
      b. *ke*   *amo'a* *ta*   *hu'ne*
          word 3S.poss sour is
          'his/her word tastes sour'
      c. *ke*   *amo'a* *ka*   *hu'ne*
          word 3S.poss bad.tasting is
          'his/her word tastes bad'

When these taste words describe someone's behavior or life situation they have very similar meanings. Example (23a) again gives a general description of someone with a good life, perhaps in good health, and with substantial material wealth. By contrast, when using a word from the taste domain in (23b), the meaning is that this person may be in the same situation but also loves people, shares what they have, and gives good advice to others. That is, the person described as *haga* has a positive effect on others, not just a good situation for themselves. The person described in (22c) is less admirable, being generally a good person but sometimes falling short of appropriate moral standards, perhaps getting angry or hitting his wife. However, the most serious situation is the person described in (23c), who causes severe problems for the community, by taking someone else's wife, for example.

---

8. The apostrophe represents a glottal stop in Kamano-Kafe.

(23) a. *mani'za ma'amo'a kanare hu'ne*
          life   3S.POSS   good   is
          'his/her life is good'

      b. *mani'za ma'amo'a haga   hu'ne*
          life   3S.POSS   good.tasting is
          'his/her life tastes good'

      c. *mani'za ma'amo'a ta   hu'ne*
          life   3S.POSS   sour   is
          'his/her life is sour'

      d. *mani'za ma'amo'a ka   hu'ne*
          life   3S.POSS   bad.tasting is
          'his/her life tastes bad'

When taste terminology is used in the domain of speech and behavior, it provides a way of expressing the degree to which a person or their speech has a positive or negative effect on others. In both domains the 'sour' taste, *ta*, is considered unpleasant, but considerably less harmful than the bad-tasting *ka* quality. This shows a reasonably well-elaborated mapping from taste terminology into two different domains.

5.   Conclusions

Having surveyed metaphors from the taste domain in English, Tok Pisin and six Papua New Guinean vernaculars, several things can be noted. First, there is considerable variety in the way the taste domain is conceptualized in these different languages, ranging from just two taste terms in Gadsup to at least six terms in Dawawa. The sets of items classified as having the same taste differs from language to language, especially for items considered in English as sour, spicy and bitter (lemons, chili and quinine). Every language apart from English classified pleasantly salty substances in the same category as pleasantly sweet substances.

Second, every language showed some metaphorical extension of at least some of the taste terms, into other domains. Specifically, every language has a metaphorical extension of the word for delicious (sweet) taste to the domain of speech, even if this is the only metaphorical usage of the taste domain. This may reflect Tok Pisin, in which this is so common. Time will tell whether this remains the only metaphorical extension in these languages or whether they will develop new metaphors reflecting the same conceptual mapping, as is perhaps happening in Gadsup.

Third, however, there is considerable variety in the scope, elaboration and conventionalization of these metaphors. Table 7 shows some of this variety.

Table 7. Comparison of taste metaphors

Language	Number of taste words	Scope	Conventionality	Elaboration	Highlighted elements
English	5+	Character, communication, wide range of perceptions	High	Significant	Positive/negative effect on perceiver Nature of perceived stimulus
Tok Pisin	2–3	Character, communication, range of perceptions	High	Very limited	–
Gwahatike	4	Speech	Low	Very limited	–
Gadsup	2	Speech	Very low	Very limited	–
Tairuma	3	Speech	Reasonable	Limited	Benefit/harm to perceiver
Guhu Samane	5	Character, speech, places	High	Significant	Benefit/harm to perceiver Emotional response of perceiver
Dawawa	6	Speech	High	Significant	Benefit/harm to perceiver Intensity of experience Emotional response of perceiver
Kamano-Kafe	3	Character, speech	High	Significant	Benefit/harm to perceiver

There is a general correlation that languages with more conventional expressions also have greater elaboration of the conceptual metaphor (that is, more terms from the taste domain used in the target domain). This supports the claim that when one word from a domain is metaphorically extended to a new domain, closely related words, such as antonyms, are also usually available for extension into that domain (Backhouse, 1994, p. 170). However, Tok Pisin is a very noticeable exception, with highly conventional use of the word *swit* in metaphorical extensions, but very limited use of any other taste words in other domains.

There is no special correlation between the variety of taste terms and the scope or degree of conventionalization and elaboration of metaphors. Kamano-Kafe with only three taste terms has equally conventional, elaborated metaphors in more than one domain as languages with more taste terminology. Conversely, Gwahatike, with more taste terms has very limited conventional metaphors into other domains.

Table 7 also captures some different aspects of the TASTE source domain highlighted by the conceptual metaphors in different languages. In every language, the evaluative aspect of taste is highlighted in metaphors to the speech domain, providing entailments concerning positive or negative evaluation of someone's speech, and the benefit or harm it causes to the hearer. The emotional response to eating good or bad tasting food (linked to the proximity of receptors in Section 2) is also highlighted in some languages, as in Guhu Samane where *qaa* (the spicy taste of ginger or chili) talk generates an angry emotional response, or in Dawawa where *ḡora* (bad taste of quinine or salt water) talk creates a negative emotional reaction.

Different entailments from the same domain in different languages can be seen, for example, when someone's talk is described as tasting like a lemon. In Guhu Samane, using *tobaira* means someone does not really know what they are talking about; in Dawawa, *yairuru* talk makes you screw up your face like eating a lemon; and in Kamano-Kafe, talk described as *ta* is not really helpful. In English, a *sour* comment is unpleasant and perhaps sarcastic. This shows the way that Dawawa highlights emotional response, whereas Kamano-Kafe highlights positive and negative effects of taste. The use of *tobaira* in Guhu Samane is more idiosyncratic.

Finally, is there evidence that the generalized or intermediate structure of the source domain in these Papua New Guinean languages (contrasted to the differentiated structure of English) affects the entailments when used in conceptual metaphor? Specifically, does the fact that the word for 'good' tastes includes both 'sweet' and 'salty' qualities in Papua New Guinean languages mean that metaphors using 'sweet' in English have different entailments to those using *swit* in Papua New Guinea? Since in English the chemical *sweet* quality is not identical to *good* tasting, we might expect to see differences where *sweet* in English describes things that are not unequivocally good, but not in the Papua New Guinean examples. This is indeed the case. In Tok Pisin and the other Papua New Guinean languages, describing a person or their communication as *swit* (or the equivalent word) is uniformly positive, describing something that is beneficial. Only the *sirore* example in Tairuma describes someone who likes to speak, but what they say might not actually be good. By contrast, in English, describing anyone (especially male) beyond childhood as 'sweet' is somewhat insulting; describing movies as 'sweet' suggests they may be naïve or idealistic (closer to 'saccharin'); and referring to 'sweet talk' or 'sweetening' a message suggests the communicator does not have totally good motives.

This has implications for studying the spread of metaphors into these endangered languages. Where metaphors using sweet/*swit* are entering Papua New Guinean vernaculars, they usually maintain the completely positive association, as in Tok Pisin, rather than the more ambivalent English associations. Noticeably, the one counterexample (in Tairuma) comes from the southern part of the country, where English was the language of wider communication for many years, rather than Tok Pisin. It is clear from these examples that Tok Pisin *swit* metaphors are spreading into the vernaculars, and in some cases (notably Gwahatike) taking over from more traditional metaphorical conceptualizations. In other cases, however, these metaphors may actually enrich the vernaculars, providing stimulus to think of new ways of conceptualizing the domain of speech and character as other prototypical tastes and substances are brought into use to conceptualize life experiences. Certainly Tok Pisin will play a very significant role in the future linguistic scene in Papua New Guinea. Whether its metaphors will sweeten Papua New Guinean vernaculars, or vice versa, remains to be seen.

References

Backhouse, A. E. (1994). *The lexical field of taste: A semantic study of Japanese taste terms.* Cambridge: Cambridge University Press. DOI: 10.1017/CBO9780511554322

Bjorkman, D., & Ttopoqogo, M. (Eds.). (2002). *Noo Supu: A Triglot Dictionary.* Ukarumpa: Summer Institute of Linguistics.

Chandrashekar, J., Hoon, M., Ryba, N., & Zuker, C. (2006). The receptors and cells for Mammalian taste. *Nature,* 444, 288–294. DOI: 10.1038/nature05401

Fauconnier, G. (1997). *Mappings in thought and language.* Cambridge: Cambridge University Press. DOI: 10.1017/CBO9781139174220

Frantz, C., Frantz, M., Amosima, N., & Iyama, M. (1996). *English-Gadsup School Dictionary.* Ukarumpa: Summer Institute of Linguistics.

Ibarretxe-Antuñano, I. (2012). The importance of unveiling conceptual metaphors in a minority language: The case of Basque. In A. Idström & E. Piirainen (Eds.), *Endangered metaphors* (pp. 253–273). Amsterdam: John Benjamins. DOI: 10.1075/clscc.2.12iba

King, P. D. (2012). *Surrounded by bitterness: Image schemas and metaphors for conceptualizing distress in Classical Hebrew*. Eugene, OR: Pickwick Publications.

Kövecses, Z. (2002). *Metaphor: A practical introduction*. Oxford: Oxford University Press.

Kövecses, Z. (2005). *Metaphor in culture: Universality and variation*. Cambridge: Cambridge University Press. DOI: 10.1017/CBO9780511614408

Lakoff, G., & Johnson, M. (2003 [1980]). *Metaphors we live by (with a new afterword)*. Chicago: University of Chicago Press.

Lewis, P. (2009). *Ethnologue: Languages of the World* (16th ed.). Dallas: SIL.

Mihalic, F. (1971). *The Jacaranda dictionary and grammar of Melanesian Pidgin*. Boroko: Jacaranda Press.

Payne, A., & Drew, D., updated by Mattocks, R., Mattocks, J., & Banala, N. (2005). *Kamano-Kafe' Kemofo Agafa'e Dictionary for Kamano-Kafe' English Tok Pisin*. Ukarumpa: Summer Institute of Linguistics.

Sweetser, E. (1990). *From etymology to pragmatics: Metaphorical and cultural aspects of semantic structure*. Cambridge: Cambridge University Press. DOI: 10.1017/CBO9780511620904

Taylor, J. R. (2002). *Cognitive grammar*. Oxford: Oxford University Press.

Verhaar, J. W. M. (1995). *Towards a reference grammar of Tok Pisin*. Honolulu: University of Hawai'i Press.

Volker, C. A. (Ed.). (2008). *Papua New Guinea Tok Pisin English Dictionary*. South Melbourne, Vic.: Oxford University Press.

CHAPTER 4

Towards a taxonomy of metaphors of a curtailed language

The case of Waray

John Ivan V. Palagar
Leyte Normal University / Bahrain Training Institute, Philippines

Waray is one of the spoken languages in the Philippine archipelago. It is spoken mainly in the provinces of Samar and in some municipalities of Leyte – islands in the eastern part of the country. The use of this language is curtailed due to government policy formulation, colonial consciousness, and cultural inferiority (Sugbo, 2003). This paper provides a taxonomy of Waray metaphors through the documentation of its occurrences in selected compilation of idioms, proverbs, narratives, folk songs, popular songs, lyric poetry, and internet blogs that are representative samples of linguistic data from the first few decades of the 20th century (1914–1920) to the onset of the 21st century (2000–2011). Analysis of metaphors was primarily based on the description of its vehicles (cosmological, geographical, zoological, botanical, somatic, social relation, and general tangible/intangible) and tenors (emotion, time, space, and other abstract domains). In exploring the source domains or vehicles, the properties attached to these domains were elaborated by looking into its structural aspects, positive-negative dichotomy, locative and locomotive features, causative and productive attributes, and abstract-concrete qualities. The analysis of tenors was primarily based on the neutrality, positivity, and negativity of the values carried by these domains. In the sectional analysis, the paper offers a mollifying proposition on the applicability of the four major metaphor theories: Conceptual Metaphor Theory, Context-Limited Simulation Theory, Lexical Concepts and Cognitive Models Theory, and Discourse Dynamics Theory.

Keywords: metaphor analysis, metaphors in different domains, metaphors of Waray language

DOI 10.1075/clscc.7.03pal

1.   Introduction

The status of Waray. Waray is one of the spoken languages in the Philippine archipelago. It is spoken mainly in the provinces of Samar and in some municipalities of Leyte – islands in the eastern part of the country. As a member of the Visayan language family, it is considered to be distinct from Cebuano because of its harsh phonological characteristics, but it shares close features with Hiligaynon and Masbatenyo.

The use of this language is curtailed due to government policy formulation, colonial consciousness, and cultural inferiority (Sugbo, 2003). In a report during the last decade, Waray ranked last among the six major languages in the Philippines in terms of the number of its language users: Tag-alog, Cebuano, Ilocano, Binisaya, Hiligaynon, Bikol, and Waray-waray (Mansueto, 2013). Although there have been sporadic and uncoordinated attempts in resuscitating the language in the region, its vitality remains debilitated by other factors such as prestige attribution, employment opportunities, and migration. Waray usage continues in several limited contexts such as in pedagogy, formal social transactions, and written discourse, where it also shows decline.

On the analysis of metaphors. The significance of metaphor analysis is an acknowledged premise in the field of linguistic research because of the extensive existential potential it offers across disciplines. Information processing, tacit knowledge, representation of realities, understanding of social and cultural processes can all be accessed through the exploration of metaphors (Moser, 2000). Theorization of concepts and relationships can be tackled using the attribution and association of categories inherent in this figurative genre (Andriessen & Gubbins, 2009). Some metaphoric perspective can tackle detailed cognitive and political dimensions of cultural processes (Vaara, Tienari, & Santti 2003). Taking this perspective of metaphor pervasiveness, researchers like Schmitt (2005) summarized the possible social and psychological significance of metaphor analysis by looking into transcultural metaphors, culture-specific metaphors, and individual occurrences of metaphors among others.

Previous analyses of metaphorical vehicles have been conducted in various cultural contexts, but most of these endeavors are limited to the exploration of animal metaphors or zoomorphs that represent human personality (Sommer & Sommer, 2011). Also, the methodological design used, for example in Sommer & Sommer's (2011) study, does not make use of natural language use; that is to say that the vehicles were just pre-determined by the researchers and the respondents were just required to formulate generalizations regarding the correspondence between the tenors and the animal vehicles.

In other studies, researchers have approached metaphor analysis by measuring the level of the concreteness and abstractness of the vehicles. Turney et al. (2011) devised an algorithm of abstractness and concreteness of metaphor vehicles. This algorithm proved to be very limited for various reasons in the area of metaphor analysis. Metaphoric vehicles, in some experiments, were subjected to reversal with the tenors to test the interpretability of a reinvented canonical set of figurative expressions (Campbell & Katz, 2009). Generation of semantic domains of metaphorical tenors and vehicles, and the comparison of these categories proved to be a practical procedure in studying metaphors (Bremer & Lee, 1997).

Metaphorical vehicles are also analyzed using the concrete and abstract dichotomy. Discourse goals are considered to be major variables in the production of metaphors and in the decision of the language user to use concrete or abstract tenors (Harris, Friel, & Mickelson, 2006). The concreteness or abstractness of the topic and the vehicle of a metaphor is seen to affect the extent of figurativeness of an expression in the study of Gineste (2007). In other studies, the concrete-abstract dichotomy is tackled as means of studying the structural aspects of metaphors (Perrin, 1987). Comparison on the occurrence of concrete metaphors versus abstract metaphors is one of the methodological schemes commonly used in some studies involving visual metaphors such as in the empirical work of Pop (2008) which highlighted the predominance of abstract elements in most visual metaphors related to "Information Technology" (IT).

Analysis of metaphors is not limited to its elements (tenor and vehicles). The conventionality and novelty of the metaphoric expression has been one of the emphases in the past decades. Neurological studies on metaphor processing are not new in metaphor research; for example, Lai, Curran, & Menn (2009) utilized the amplitudes of the "N400 Event Related Potentials" (ERP) component to confirm the occurrences of novel and conventional metaphors, while Mashal & Faust (2009) used the brain lateralization principle to provide an empirical evidence on the processing of novel and conventional metaphorical expressions.

Cognitive studies on metaphor conventionality and novelty have used time-based methods to confirm the processing period among subjects and to affirm the hypothesis on the role of conventional metaphors in the comprehension of novel metaphors (Thibodeau & Durgin, 2007). Observation on the occurrence of novel metaphors in academic essays has led to the formulation of certain typology focusing on the common first language interference issues and the classification of deliberate and non-deliberate production of novel metaphors (Nacey, 2009). Such empirical endeavors have extended to researches involving metaphors in cultural mapping (Takada, Shinohara, Morizumi, & Sato, 2000); its routing effects (Liang & Heywood, 2002); its usage and application in colors (Shabani, 2008), infectious diseases (Downing & Mujic 2009), and marketing (Bremer & Lee, 1997); and its explanatory values (McGlone, 2007).

Metaphor classification, as an approach in metaphor analysis, received important attention in recent years. One approach in metaphor taxonomy formulation is the identification of single and multiple metaphors, simple and complex metaphors, pure and mixed metaphors, and restricted and extended metaphor occurrences in written discourse (Crisp, Heywood, & Steen, 2002). Determining the mutually distinct characteristics between culturally adapted metaphors and conventional metaphors is a practical methodology in classifying metaphors related to the field of immunology (Downing & Mujic, 2009). Classifying metaphor production on the basis of rhetorical usage is an area already explored by Lukes (2005) who outlined the cognitive, interpersonal, and textual usage of metaphors. In some studies, metaphors have been classified in terms of their triteness and genuineness (Kemertelidze & Manjavidze, 2012). Categorization of the same included poetic and non-poetic metaphors (Lei, 2007); ad-hoc and conventional metaphors (Hanks, 2004); referential metaphors and collocational metaphors (Huang et al., 2011); extinct metaphors, dormant metaphors, and active metaphors (Black, 1962); radical metaphors and derivative metaphors (Zhang, 2008); foundational metaphors, coherence metaphors, and philosophical metaphors (Thagard & Beam, 2013). Shelestiuk's (2006) work on metaphor analysis is worthy to mention because of the nomenclatures of metaphors from the available corpus data such as metaphoric personification, animalification, metaphoric antonomasia, metaphoric allusion, metaphoric periphrasis, synesthesia, allegory and metaphoric symbolism. Semantic, structural, and functional classifications of metaphors are also outlined in Shelestiuk's (2006) work.

Theoretical directions. The verity of the major theories of metaphor is examined in this paper. One important theoretical doctrine is Lakoff and Johnson's (1980) "Conceptual Metaphor Theory", which highlights the premise that metaphor production is influenced by the conceptual system inherent in a particular culture. Hence, metaphor is conceptual in nature and this conceptual system plays a vital role in understanding everyday realities. In the analysis of Waray metaphors, the tenets of the Conceptual Metaphor Theory are used as paradigm of interpretation. These tenets utilized as the parameters of the discussion schema include the following: (1) The two conceptual domains – source domain and target domain – are connected by metaphors wherein the former "consists of a set of literal entities, attributes, processes and relationships, linked semantically and apparently stored together in the mind" (Lan & MacGregor, 2009, p. 16); (2) Metaphors both hide and highlight aspects of the target domain (Lakoff & Turner, 1989); and (3) "Abstract concepts are defined metaphorically in more concrete [...] terms-concepts; however, no single, concrete, non-metaphorical concept is ever structured in exactly the right way to completely [...] define any single abstract concept" (Lakoff, 1985, p. 60). Albeit the aforesaid assumptions of the Conceptual Metaphor Theory are valuable in the analysis of metaphors, Deignan (2005) asserts its expedient pitfalls in terms of the generalizability of its application. This gives countenance in the corroboration of appositeness of other metaphor assumptions.

Ritchie's (2006) "Context-Limited Simulation Theory" provides a more specific perspective of metaphors than the precepts of the "Conceptual Metaphor Theory" (CMT). Instead of just viewing metaphor processing in the domain of cognition as embodied in the conceptual systems, the "Context-Limited Simulation Theory" postulates the primacy of nuances, expression, perception and feeling in meta-phor understanding. Such model of metaphor meaning construction rivets on the premise that thoughts and emotions attached to the vehicle of source concept and language are pivotal in metaphorical meaning. A broader understanding of this model can be traced back to the "Simulation Theory", which explains how individuals attribute mental states to others through an activity in which mental states represent other mental states (Shanton & Goldman, 2010). In the analysis of the metaphors in Waray, the pertinence of this theory is deemed cogent, not-withstanding its modality which is more appropriate in the comprehension than the production aspect. Despite this issue on the modality of the theory applica-tion, its assumptions can be subjected to a critical inquiry using the metaphors of a curtailed language.

The "Lexical Concepts and Cognitive Models" (LCCM) is acknowledged to be a useful scheme in analyzing metaphors, both conventional and non-conventional ones. It views metaphor production and comprehension as a function of the lan-guage user's activation of cognitive models which leads to the conceptualization and interpretation of the corresponding lexical concept (Evans, 2010). This means that metaphoric expressions carry with them a vehicle lexical concept that clarifies characteristics about a target lexical concept. The collision in the cognitive models between the target and the vehicle constructs produces occurrences of metaphoric language use.

From the aforementioned theories of metaphorical language use, it is valid to formulate an integrative theory of metaphor analysis – a framework that consid-ers the limitations, assuages the issues, and exploits the potentials of the plausible constructs. This is operationalized in the "Discourse Dynamics Theory" (DDT), which considers linguistic, cognitive, affective, physical and cultural dimensions of metaphor as completory (Cameron, 2007). On a critical point of view, it is impera-tive to examine the valid points of this model, to pinpoint the unresolved areas of metaphorical language use, and to contend imminent theoretical trajectories based on the context of the Waray metaphor analysis.

2. Methodological framework

Data source. This paper provides a description of the metaphors observed in the available corpus data obtained from the first few decades of the 20th century (1914–1920) to the onset of the 21st century (2000–2011). Conventional metaphorical occurrences were obtained from an available compilation of Waray idioms, proverbs, and metaphors of Tamayo (1990) whose anthology of the same is considered to be the most comprehensive since it covers previous collections from 1914 to 1990. Other types of metaphorical data, including novel metaphors, were obtained from various literary types that range from narratives, folk songs, popular songs, lyric poetry, and internet blogs. Textual data obtained from selected Waray writers such as Sugbo (2008), Oyzon (2008), Alunan & Pundavela (1997), Lucente (1922), De Veyra (2007), Macabasag (2007), and Dino (2005).

Scheme of analysis. Framework of analysis was based on the categories of the domain of tenors and vehicles used in a metaphorical occurrence. Cosmological, geographical, zoological, botanical, somatic, social relation, and general tangible/intangible vehicles were identified to probe the nature of Waray metaphors. Regardless of the type of source domain or vehicle being analyzed, the property attached to these domains was described. The simplicity or singularity as opposed to complexity and compound nature of the vehicles was one of the dimensions used in vehicle analysis. Positive-negative dichotomy was another method of describing the various source domains. The locative, locomotive, causative, and productive properties of these vehicles serve as an alternative descriptive framework. It was imperative to use the abstract and concrete classification in describing the last group of Waray vehicles. Identification of the source domain's primary cognitive models and secondary cognitive models provided a useful dimension in exploring the nature of Waray vehicles.

Tenors of emotion, time, space, and other abstract concepts of Waray metaphors were also explored in terms of the conventionality-novelty dimension. Description of tenors was primarily based on the neutrality, positivity, and negativity of the values and attributes carried by these domains. Determining the instances of concrete and novel tenors was an approach that complemented the holistic description of metaphors, avoiding incidence of redundant documentation of linguistic data. In the sectional analysis, the paper offers a mollifying proposition on the applicability of the four major metaphor theories: Conceptual Metaphor Theory, Context-Limited Simulation Theory, Lexical Concepts and Cognitive Models Theory, and Discourse Dynamics Theory.

3.   Load of the Waray metaphorical vehicles

Cosmological vehicles. Cosmological vehicles of Waray metaphors include *adlaw* or 'sun' to represent REMINISCE or REMEMBER; and *langit ug tuna* or 'earth and sky' to represent CONFLICT or MISUNDERSTANDING. These cosmological vehicles signify abstract concepts in Waray. These vehicles are formed using a simple lexical term pertaining to the elements of the cosmos. Using these constructs of the universe as association to the abstract ideas of reminiscing and misunderstanding is a function of the activation of the Waray speaker's cognitive models. Since these vehicles are considered to be novel metaphorical vehicles, generalizability of this pattern in relation to the understanding of how Waray speakers access target vehicles in their conceptual systems can be inconclusive. If there is a valid abstraction from these observed metaphorical expressions, the singularity of these target attributions can only be emphasized.

In the preceding vehicles, SUN and EARTH and SKY are cosmological concepts that represent singularity for the former and aggregation for the latter. The ontological nature on the relationship between the vehicles and the tenors involving the cosmological constructs are based on the abstractness of the tenors. As seen in the tenors represented by the cosmological vehicles, MISUNDERSTANDING and REMINISCE are both abstract concepts, but the question on the singularity of the vehicle chosen to represent these target topics remain to be a fertile ground for critical inquiry.

A careful examination of other cosmological vehicles indicates that Waray people attribute the elements of the universe to the concept of TIME. For example, *nagsasaklang nga adlaw* 'climbing sun' is used as a vehicle for MORNING; *langit nga namumuhaypuhay* or 'AWAKENED SKY' is used as another vehicle for MORNING; *nasusunog nga sidsid han langit* 'burning peripheries of the sky' is used as a vehicle for DUSK; and *pinutos nga kabiton-an* 'wrapped stars' is used as a vehicle for NIGHT.

In the representation of time, Waray temporal vehicles are used in a participial phrase. The object of the participial phrase in these vehicles of time is either active or passive. It is passive in the /WRAPPED STARS/ vehicle. The /SUN/ and /SKY/ are cosmological vehicles of time that are active in orientation. The dominance of the active object in the participial phrase remains to be inconclusive in the absence of other metaphorical occurrences reflecting this structure, but the high frequency of these active objects demonstrates that Waray culture views time as a moving entity with the propensity of being constant. The use of cosmological vehicles to represent temporal constructs in Waray suggests that albeit time is moving, its presence is perennial and eternal like the elements of the universe such as the sky, stars, moon, and sun.

In some vehicles of time, the cosmological element is used as the object of the preposition such as the 'burning peripheries of the sky'. Instead of using a compound vehicle, few of the Waray vehicles of time use a simple vehicle such as *kadayaw* 'full moon' as a vehicle for LONG TIME. Inasmuch as the available corpus is concerned, there exists no pattern of vehicle choice of temporal concepts in terms of the compoundness-simplicity dichotomy of the same. One logical generalization from the analysis of Waray metaphors is that cosmological elements are not used as metaphorical vehicles for the concept of spatial and social relationships. The scarcity of the cosmological vehicles denoting spatial and social ideals is a focal point of future inquiry.

Geographical and spatial vehicles. Geographical and spatial vehicles observed in Waray metaphors mostly have abstract tenors. The vehicle *harayo* 'long distance' is used to represent *pulong* or WORDS; *balud* 'waves of the sea' is used to represent LOVE and REALITY; *dagat* 'sea' is used to represent ARGUMENT; *burabod* 'deep well' is used to represent TEARS or SADNESS; *katutnga* 'middle' is used to represent LONELINESS; *kadulunutan* 'slippery turns' is used to represent LIFE; *linaw* 'depths' is used to represent UNCERTAIN FATE; *dagat* 'sea' is used to represent the HEART; and *dalan* 'road' is used to represent GAMBLING. The aforementioned geographical and spatial vehicles have abstract tenors that are mostly related to emotions such as LOVE, LONELINESS, and SADNESS. Some of the aforesaid vehicles are used to represent negative concepts in Waray such as TALKATIVENESS, GAMBLING, and POVERTY. The singularity of the geographical and spatial vehicles representing abstract concepts is pervasive in the corpus data. Unlike the cosmological vehicles of time, this group of vehicles obtained in Waray metaphorical expressions are not used in a participial phrase. Attribution to these geographical and spatial concepts is made directly and explicitly during the production of figurative expressions. In the framework of the Conceptual Metaphor Theory, it can be argued that most geographical and spatial concepts in Waray are directly accessed in the process of providing meanings to the abstract concepts such as SADNESS, GAMBLING, and other related terms.

There seems to be few vehicles in Waray that utilize phrasal structure to convey the essence of the connection. This includes the following: *makigbisog ha kalawdan* 'fight at the depths of an open sea' is used to represent SHAME; *dalan han libot-libot* 'circular road' is used to represent POVERTY; and *baba han sapa* 'mouth of a stream' is used to represent TALKATIVENESS. Such usage of geographical and spatial vehicles is based on the access of the periphery of the same. Instead of using the central core of the geographical and spatial concepts, the source is accompanied by other characteristics that are lexicalized in order to reinforce the association of the latter to the target domain.

In the aforesaid example, 'sea' is a geographical source of SHAME; but it is only when the source is accompanied by the phrase /fight at the depths/ that the association of the two is clearly established. The spatial category /road/ is joined with the modifier /circular/ to combine the characteristics of the two concepts of space and shape signifying the target /POVERTY/. Without the aggregate concept of shape, the spatial vehicle could not possibly be a metaphor for the said abstract construct. In such case, the periphery characteristics of the spatial vehicle, which is strengthened by adding features using another semantic domain, are essential elements in the activation of association between the vehicle and the tenor. In the third metaphorical occurrence containing a compound geographical source, the vehicle /stream/ is combined with the lexicon in the somatic category. To conceptualize this linguistic metaphor, the language user needs to have access to both the conceptual systems of geographical and somatic domains. Using the periphery characteristics of /stream/ and the core features of /mouth/, the language user generates a unique source for /TALKATIVENESS/ as target domain – a process that is based on the idiosyncratic linguistic, cognitive, affective, physical, and cultural (Cameron, 2007) dimensions available.

Few geographical vehicles are used to signify the concept of time in Waray. This includes *dagat nga guindadalait* 'flaming sea' which is used to represent DUSK. In this metaphorical occurrence, the geographical vehicle /sea/ is used in a phrasal structure. This time the geographical concept is combined with a verbal lexicon /flaming/. Producing this type of vehicle in signifying a time element involves a complex process. Visual and kinesthetic properties of the /sea/ from the speaker's target conceptual system need to be generated during the initial phase of the metaphoric conceptualization. The complexity of this process is based on the hierarchy of representation. The speaker needs to find connectivity between two domains for claiming that a /sea/ is /flaming/ before he/she is able to make possible association with the target domain. Unlike singular vehicles, compound vehicles are formulated using different levels of representation.

Zoological vehicles. Most conventional metaphorical expressions in Waray contain zoological elements as vehicles. This includes *huni han kalaw* 'sounds of birds' to represent REMINISCE or REMEMBER; and *pagkalpad han maya* 'flying of the birds' to represent REMINISCE or REMEMBER also. In the metaphorical expressions containing these zoological vehicles, an implicit association is made between the target and the source. The target /REMEMBER/ is not directly mentioned in this metaphorical occurrence, and this presents another complexity in the access of this semantic category from the conceptual system of the Waray language user. From the point of view of the Discourse Dynamics Framework, it can be argued that this expression is a form of a linguistic metaphor since two distinct ideas are linked metaphorically in order to establish lucidity in the context of discourse, and the identification of its occurrence can be made through logical argument of the association of its elements (Cameron, 2007). A thorough examination of the load of this metaphorical source can be drawn from the Context-Limited Simulation Theory (Ritchie, 2006), wherein it can be deduced that the simulators of perception related to the vehicles /sounds of the birds/ and /flying of the birds/ are activated. What is interesting to note in this example is that instead of activating the secondary simulators, the primary simulators are activated as reflected in the emphasis of the literal and natural characteristics of the /birds/ which includes /flying/ and /sounds/. Through the activation of these context-relevant simulators for the concept of /birds/, the target concept of /REMEMBER/ in the metaphorical expression is established.

The representation of /birds/ in Waray conventional metaphors is important to consider since this is the only animal vehicle that is not associated with a negative tenor. For example, *pako han tamsi* 'wings of a bird' is used to represent MONEY; and *limukon ug punay* 'pigeon and dove' is used to represent LOVE. In both zoological vehicles, the animal source is combined with another semantic category. In the first metaphorical occurrence, the zoological vehicle is the object of the preposition that is connected to a somatic category, that is /wings/. Access to this somatic category is reinforced when the zoological categorical concept is presented since the latter is the most concrete embodiment of an entity with wings. Hence, /TIME/ as a target concept is better expressed by using the aforesaid somatic source, but its expressive quality is strengthened when another immediate synecdochic connection is established. In the second metaphorical expression, the zoological vehicle is paired with another zoological element to signify the concept of /LOVE/. Access to both animal vehicles is necessary to exhibit the target concept. It is evident that the use of these two zoological vehicles involves another implicit cognitive process based on the conceptual system of the Waray language user. The /pigeon/ and /dove/ vehicles do not only entail access to the peripheral and core characteristics and attributes of their zoological nature, but also present certain relational characteristics manifested in both elements.

Fowls and other poultry animals are used to represent negative tenors in Waray conventional metaphorical expressions. For example, *bukaw* 'owl' is used to represent LACK OF SLEEP; *manok* 'chicken' is used to represent a LIGHT SLEEPER; *patikarol* 'oriole' is used to represent BEING WARY; *kurambitsi manok* 'cock' is used to represent PRESUMPTUOUSNESS; *putik hin manok* 'anus of a chicken' is used to represent TALKATIVENESS; *iti* 'chicken dung' is used to represent SHAME; and *mata hin sikop* 'bird's eyes' is used to represent VOYEURISM. Singular zoological vehicles are used to signify negative human attributes in the aforementioned instances. The said generalization shares the same claim with Sommer & Sommer (2011) who argued that majority of animal metaphors related to human behavior and attitude are pejorative and derogatory, which supports the assumption of the perceived distance between animals and humans. On an important emphasis, the aforementioned fowl and poultry animals do not single out a particular gender group as the object of its target concept in Waray. This is contrary to the findings of Rodriguez (2009, p. 82) which highlighted the pervasiveness of poultry animals such as "*chick, bird, kitten, pollita*" to refer to women, while four-legged animals such as "*studs, bucks, wolves, toros* (bulls), *zorros* (foxes) and *linces*" are used to refer to men.

Four-legged animals and other crawling creatures constitute another group of zoological vehicles that are used to signify derogatory human personality as reflected in conventional Waray metaphorical occurrences. This includes *hayop nga waray agaron* 'wild beast' to represent an UNLOVING CHILD; *lakat hin halas* 'snake walk' to represent SLOWPOKES; *nagdudugmon nga baboy* 'sow' to represent a MESSY PERSON; *kamatay hin ayam* 'death of a dog' to represent a TRAGIC DEATH; *mata hin ayam* 'dog's eyes' to represent BEING; *gusok han bugsok* 'deer's ribs' to represent DISGUISE; and *kiyaw* (animal) to represent DISORDER. Similar to other zoological categories used as vehicular concepts, this group can be classified into two classes: singular zoological vehicles and compound zoological vehicles. In the aforementioned conventional metaphors, only /*kiyaw*/ (a type of animal) has a singular vehicle, while the rest have compound vehicles. The dominance of compound vehicles involving four-legged and crawling zoological entities is a premise worthy to note. This high frequency of compound vehicles supports the perceived need of the Waray language user to utilize attributes of other conceptual domains in order to hide or highlight aspects of the target domain (Deignan, 2005) focusing on negative human behaviors.

In the available corpus data of Waray metaphors, insects comprise a special group of zoological vehicles that denote pejorative and negative forms of human personality. For example, *marungparong* 'moth' is used to represent A PERSON IN DANGER; *naikid nga liring* 'long-legged ant' is used to represent a HYPOCRITE PERSON; *bungkog hin haniban* 'back of a beetle' is used to represent FLAMBOUYANCE; *langaw* 'flies' is used to represent OVERSTAYING GUESTS; and *guintitirok nga tubak* 'ants being gathered' is used to represent IMPOSSIBILITY. These Waray connotations of insects are also consistent with the summary of insect metaphors outlined by Goatly (2006) from the *Melatude* database, which enumerates the insect vehicles signifying the following target domains of human behavior: a person who enjoys social pleasures, unproductive member of society, person who deliberately annoys or challenges people in authority, dishonorable person, stupid person, idiot, and self-important woman. In concepts involving technological dimensions, these entomological elements represent a positive meaning. For example, White (2002) used ant behavior as a metaphor for distributed algorithms in the management of mobile systems. It must be considered that the said study did not involve natural language but a framework of algorithm as a target concept.

Finally, marine zoological vehicles are also found to serve as source domains for negative human characteristics. This is manifested in the following examples: *isda nga nalilibunan* 'trapped fish' to represent BEING CONCERNED; *pawikan* 'sea turtle' to represent IRRESPONSIBLE PARENTS; *kagang* 'crab' to represent WILD PERSON; and *bungol nga pating* 'dumb shark' to represent STUBBORNNESS. It is cogent to stipulate that these marine zoological vehicles contain both singular and compound elements like the other categories of animal metaphors in Waray. In all of the above metaphorical occurrences, the zoological element has passive characteristics such as being dumb or trapped. This reinforces the assumption that Waray culture presupposes these aquatic creatures to be remote from their physical realities. It can also be conjectured that marine animal behavior is something that Waray people has domination – a premise that gains validation based on the coastal topographical nature of the Waray territory. These suppositions about the ontological relationship between the marine zoological source and the said target domains are framed by the Discourse Dynamics Theory, which asserts that the language user's language, cognition, emotional states, physicality, and culture influence the production of metaphors and other forms of figurative language (Cameron, 2007).

Botanical vehicles. Botanical elements are also used as vehicles in Waray metaphorical expressions related to human personality. This includes *nangangaslom nga bahalina* 'bad coconut wine' to represent LOVE; *binuklad nga uhong* 'sprouted mushroom' to represent an OVERNIGHT SUCCESS; and *bagol nga naglalaga* or 'flaming coconut shell' to represent FURY. It is evident from these vehicles that the elements related to plants are used in phrasal structure, making it conform to a group of compound vehicles. These botanical concepts are presented as active objects of the operational image reflected in the metaphorical occurrence. The /coconut shell/ is viewed to be flaming, the /mushroom/ is assumed to have sprouted, and the /coconut wine/ is said to be having an unsuccessful fermentation process resulting to its bad taste. In gaining route to these botanical vehicles, the Waray language user highlights the active characteristics of these elements to institute a plausible access to the target domains of LOVE, FURY, and OVERNIGHT SUCCESS.

Some conventional metaphors in Waray involving botanical vehicles contain phrasal structures wherein the source domain is a passive object. For example: *ibinutang nga tilad* 'betel nut thrown aside' is used to represent DEEP SLEEP; *hinuyop nga laburo* 'a laburo that is blown away' is used to represent QUICK

DISAPPEARANCE; *linuunan nga lahing* 'smoked coconut' is used to represent a
DARK-SKINNED PERSON; and *nagsamsam hin layuan* 'masticating a layuan' is used
to represent a MESSY PERSON. As shown in these metaphorical occurrences in
Waray, /betel nut/ is a passive object of the action of throwing; /laburo/ is a passive
entity of being blown by a natural or human force; /coconut/ receives the action
of being smoked that is assumed to have been performed by a human agent; and
/layuan/ receives the action of masticating that is also performed by a human
agent. Regardless of the passivity of the botanical objects used in the aforesaid
phrasal vehicles, the endemic qualities of these elements must be significantly
noted since the presence of these realities constitutes a primary function in the
production of these metaphors in Waray.

There are some botanical vehicles in conventional Waray metaphorical statements that are used with a locative element in order to convey the meaning of
the target concept. *Nagtungtung ha tuud* 'standing on a tree stump' to represent a
DANGEROUS SITUATION; and *kaamyaw nga bunot* 'coconut husk neighbor' to represent USELESSNESS are some examples of the said claim. The vehicle /tree stump/
provides information on the location of standing, while /coconut husk/ receives
locative information by presenting the concept of neighbor. Inherent in both vehicles are their synecdochic qualities in that they represent a part of the entire entity;
the husk is an incidental product from a coconut tree, while stump is the part a
tree that remains attached to the root after the trunk is cut. Like most botanical
vehicles, both synecdochic and locative vehicles are used to signify negative states
of human activity in Waray.

In some botanical vehicles, presentation and description of its somatic parts
are apparent. This includes *bukad nga waray liso* 'seedless flower' to represent
LOQUACIOUSNESS; and *bukad hiton hasmin* or 'blossoms of jasmine' to represent
a LONG TIME. In the first vehicle, the absence of the seeds of a flower reinforces
the process of highlighting the attributes of loquaciousness which is the target
concept. The plant /jasmine/ gains better access to the language user's expressive
intent by using it as the object of its somatic parts.

Singular or simple botanical vehicles also exist in conventional Waray metaphors. Examples of these are *bukad* 'flower' to represent LIFE; *dabong* 'bamboo
shoot' to represent RAPID GROWTH; *burunganon* 'burunganon grass' to represent
SUPERFICIALITY; *dalairo* 'water plant' to represent BEING EASILY CARRIED AWAY
or INDECISIVENESS; *binlad* 'rice grain' to represent LIFE; and *pinya* 'pineapple' to
BEING BLIND. Most of these vehicles signify either negative or neutral tenors, but
the frequency of their neutral representation is dominant. The presence of the
synecdochic quality is apparent in bamboo shoot, flower, and rice grain.

Somatic vehicles. Somatic elements are used in conventional Waray metaphorical expressions. This includes *kasing-kasing* 'heart' to represent FEELINGS; *tuhod* 'knees' to represent ACTION; and *dila* 'tongue' for LOQUACIOUSNESS. In these metaphorical samples, the somatic vehicles are simple in that they are used singularly to highlight the aspects of the target domain. Compound somatic vehicles in conventional Waray expressions include *turo han agtang* 'sweat on the forehead' to represent WORK; *nasirong nga dila* 'curled tongue' to represent TAKING REFUGE UNDER A LEAKING ROOF; *patay nga simod* 'dead lips' to represent UNHEEDED COUNSEL; and *hilaba nga dila* 'long tongue' to represent TALKATIVENESS.

In the aforesaid metaphor samples, the /heart/ is used to signify the construct of feeling as a target domain. Aschale (2013) explains that the heart is the elemental organ of the human body that is responsible for the cognitive, affective, and psychomotor dimensions of human behavior, which supports how the Waray people consider the heart as a source domain for feelings. Related attributes of the heart analyzed by Aschale (2013) are significant to mention, and these include various metaphorical pragmatic extensions which are inherently wired to tolerance, thought and wisdom, loss of the mind, and moral values – conceptual dimensions related to feelings. The centrality of the heart in the representation of feelings finds strong empirical claim in the study of Berendt & Tanita (2011) who used /HEART IS THE LOCUS OF EMOTIONS AND ATTITUDES/ as one of the conceptual metaphor models in analyzing the heart as a source domain in Thai and Japanese discourse.

/Tongue/ is a prominent somatic vehicle in conventional Waray metaphors that is used to highlight the aspects of LOQUACIOUSNESS, UNHEEDED COUNSEL, and other negative abstract constructs. These attributes of tongue as a somatic vehicle has been subjected to critical analysis by Pauwels & Simon-Vandenbergen (1995) who documented metaphors for actions related to language behavior using the somatic parts as source domains. Mouth, tongue, and throat are considered to be present in metaphors referring to HUMAN COMMUNICATION. Aschale (2013) explained that the tongue and the mouth are common vehicles used to show oratorical prowess, skills in deception, nagging behavior and talkativeness of the people, being deceived, and offensive conversations or dialogues. This Waray concept of the /tongue/ as a source domain for human communication, either negative or positive in nature, is seen to be universal across languages. Goossens (2002) mentioned 49 English expressions containing somatic categories providing reference to human speech, while Schmidt (2008) reported that the 1996 Duden Universal Dictionary enumerates 20 tongue-related source domains in German signifying human communication as the target domain. Similar to the Waray concept of tongue as a source domain, Schmidt (2008) described the pejorative load of mouth and tongue in Chinese discourse, which is reinforced when the size characteristics are presented such as in the example *hilaba nga dila* 'long tongue' to represent TALKATIVENESS.

The /forehead/ is another somatic vehicle that is found in Waray metaphor samples. Its related elements are head and brain which have been a focal point of study in various cultural settings. Aschale (2013) elaborates that head metaphors represent pieces of advice or counsel that are important to be followed by a certain individual. The importance of forehead as an element of the head is universal across cultures. For example, embellishing the forehead with extraordinary markings and imprinting idiosyncratic colors is a symbol of worship to some deity (Revelation, 13:16). In the vehicle /*turo han agtang*/ or /sweat on the forehead/ representing the concept of WORK, the somatic element is combined with another bodily element, which is /sweat/. The production of this compound vehicle involves the transition from the primary cognitive model to a secondary cognitive model as explained in the context of Lexical Concepts and Cognitive Models (Evans, 2010). The primary cognitive model involves a lexicon related to the main body part, which is /forehead/, while the secondary cognitive model that is created from the latter involves a lexicon related to a by-product of a physical activity which is manifested in the forehead. Thus, the /sweat/ vehicle signifies a product of a process observed and experienced in the said somatic category /forehead/. This manifestation of the product provides an access route to the concept of /WORK/ as the target domain.

/Knees/ is a Waray somatic vehicle that is used to represent the construct of /WORK/. In the work of Aschale (2013) knees, as a related component of feet and legs, is connected to the target domain of fear, length, movement and luck in English language. This contains bearing to the concept of /WORK/ as a target domain in Waray. The causative property of this somatic element is the ground for both the concrete vehicle and the abstract tenor. Knees are somatic parts that are perceived by the Waray culture to be the causality of action and movement.

The present analysis of Waray somatic vehicles contrasts with the findings of Charteris-Black (2004) who claimed a high frequency of metaphors related to the body that represents the concept of nations, cities, and political communities. As reflected in the preceding discussion, none of the somatic vehicles represent geographical concepts and political communities or bodies. But what is more important to consider is the centrality of these somatic elements in Waray metaphorical expressions denoting abstract concepts of human states, emotion, and personality. Aschale (2013, p. 1.) noted that "… body experiences are the ones the brain experiences first and keeps experiencing all the time. It is very palatable and logical that the body takes center stage among the multifaceted tokens of conceptual metaphors." Like any other culture, Waray people's utility of somatic elements in metaphoric expressions is anthropocentric as observed in the previous descriptions in that the somatic elements have primary salience in describing human behaviors. Perekhvalskaya (2013, p. 1) maintained that "any existing language is anthropocentric, and in any language there are metaphors which perceive objects, animate or inanimate, as persons." This gains support in the proposition of Skara (2004), which gives merit to the idea that the high frequency of body metaphors is a consequence of human being's propensity to give central importance to their physical bodies. Metaphorical occurrences involving the bodily parts are manifestations of man's attempt to express his internal paradigm or the way he sees himself, using the elements that are already inherent and familiar to him, to the external and more abstract realities. Despite these cognitive elaborations of how a language user in a particular culture constructs metaphorical statements, selects appropriate vehicles, and establishes a ground between the source and the target domains, it is still important to consider various empirical data from other branches of inquiry (Goschler, 2005) in order to formulate valid claims about the nature of metaphors involving somatic vehicles.

Social relation vehicles. Most social relation vehicles are used to signify geographical and spatial concepts, while some are used to represent abstract ideas of human behavior. This includes *malutas hini nga kapisot* 'free from infancy' to represent the PESO CURRENCY; and *karaslon* 'getting married' to represent the state of being UNDULY EXCITED. In these vehicles pertaining to social relations, a phrasal structure is used making the entire vehicle compound in nature. Creation of more than two cognitive models is required in order to establish the ground between the vehicle and the tenor. In the first example, /infancy/ is a social relation characterized by being small in size, one who cannot perform complex human activities. Another related *attribute* of the said source is immaturity and dependency, which becomes a ground for establishing the intended meaning of the target domain. A secondary cognitive model is created when the language user uses the immaturity and dependency attributes of the source, creating a resonance. A third cognitive model is accessed when the language user introduces another attribute of the source concept. As seen in the phrasal structure, a locomotive property is attached to the vehicle when the concept of being /FREE/ is presented. Related to the locomotive property affixed in the third cognitive model, the social relation element /infant/ now receives a spatial property; that is, a place, location, or state wherein someone must be liberated from. That being said, the state of vehicular elements in this novel Waray metaphor is interesting to note since it demonstrates the idea that vehicles can possess various properties along the process of creating various routes to different cognitive models in an effort to establish the ground between the source and the target domains.

In the second example, /getting married/ is a vehicle denoting a social process rather than social relations. The primary cognitive model of the said lexical concept involves the semantic potential pertaining to a union between two persons of legal age that is made possible through a contract acknowledged by law (Haviland et al., 2011). In formulating this metaphorical statement, the language user makes use of a secondary cognitive model wherein the non-conventional information related to marriage is activated. In such case, the emotive property of being married provides an access route resulting to the said association between the vehicle and the tenor. From the case presented, the Waray emotive property attached to the process of marriage is that of excitement, and this results to the creation of the metaphor.

Dominant in Waray metaphorical expressions are simple or singular social relation vehicles such as *riko* 'rich person' which is used to represent the SEA; *uripon* 'slave' which is used to represent PHILIPPINES; *iroy* 'mother' which is used to represent NATIVE LAND; and *bugto* 'brother' which is used to represent GOOD-NESS, THRIFTINESS, and INDUSTRY. In the aforementioned instances, the vehicles related to social status and relations are used to highlight aspects of a geographical tenor such as the country Philippines, sea, and native land. A common pattern is exhibited in these examples wherein the language user makes use of a more specific and immediate domain in expressing the concept of an abstract, remote, or general target domain. The vehicle /brother/ is a social relation vehicle that is used to represent positive human personality traits such as thriftiness, industry, and goodness. The use of a concrete and specific vehicle in signifying an abstract tenor is again evident in this scenario.

General tangible and intangible vehicles. Waray metaphors often contain tangible objects as vehicles. This includes *puthaw nga batobarani* 'metal and magnet' to represent DESIRE; *mabug-at nga butang* 'heavy object' to represent JUDGMENT; *maburuong nga butang* 'fragile thing' to represent WORDS; *tubig* 'water' to represent DROWSINESS; *butang* (implied) or 'object' to represent LONELINESS; *sunit* 'splinter' to represent LOVE; *bugsay* 'oars' to represent RESPONSIBILITY; *kalamay* 'sugar' to represent PLEASURE; *bangkaw* 'sword' to represent a DANGEROUS SITUATION; *lais* 'pointed weapon' to represent DANGER; *bunay* 'eggs' to represent a DELICATE SITU-ATION; *baga* 'embers' to represent SECRETS; *ispiho* 'mirror' to represent UTTER-ANCES; *hablon* 'hand loom' to represent WORK; *huraw* (implied) 'after the rain' to represent HOPE; *makausa kaguguba* (implied) 'fragile thing' to represent REPUTA-TION; *asin* 'salt' to represent FEAR OF RAIN; *nahunaw hin bura* 'washing in soap-suds' to represent FAILURE; *salsalon* 'sword' to represent WORDS; *tubig* 'water' to represent MONEY; *bato* 'stones' to represent THOUGHTS; and *naglilinakat* (implied) 'an entity with feet' to represent TIME.

From the previous enumeration of general tangible vehicles used in Waray metaphors, it can be asserted that regardless of the properties attached to these source domains, the target concept is at all times a domain possessing abstract qualities. This linguistic description confirms the assumption that language users tend to utilize the available concrete and specific realities in expressing the hypothetical, abstruse, and abstract experiences.

The aforesaid principle is not always universal. There are some Waray metaphoric instances that exploit intangible elements as vehicles in expressing another intangible domain. This includes *katurog* or *sleep* to represent *death*; *kamatayon* or *death* to represent *sleep*; *hangin* or *wind* to represent *debt* or *debtor*; and *aso* or *smoke* to represent *money*. By stating this, one of the tenets of Conceptual Metaphor Theory is put to test: "abstract concepts are defined metaphorically in more concrete […] terms-concepts" (Lakoff, 1985, p. 60). Such theoretical limitation is compensated by the Discourse Dynamics Theory, which asserts the idea that metaphor is a function of the endless interaction of language, thinking, affect, physicality, and culture of the language user (Cameron, 2007). In other words, the choice or preference of the language user to employ a vehicle in the representation of an abstract domain is not only a function of the immediacy, specificity, and concreteness of available realities, but a product of the interaction among the linguistic situation, emotional salience, cognitive predispositions, and sociocultural prominence that are idiosyncratic in nature.

4. Representation of the Waray tenors

Emotional and other abstract tenors. Emotional tenors reflected in Waray metaphorical expressions utilize various categories of vehicles. The concept of LOVE as a positive emotional tenor is attributed to the image of metal and magnet, waves of the sea, pigeon and dove, action, splinter, bad coconut wine, and sea – categories which encompass all the physical and psychological realities of the Waray culture.

Negative emotional tenors such as LONELINESS, NERVOUSENESS, SADNESS, and DROWSINESS are represented by concrete metaphors (water, object, explosive things, deep well, and space). Neutral abstract tenors in Waray metaphorical expressions such as thoughts, words, reputation, utterances, work, life, secrets, action, sleep, labor, reality, argument, feelings, judgment, dream, action, and reminisce utilize a combination of concrete vehicles (stones, sword, fragile things, mirrors, hand loom, rice grain, embers, knees, sea, knees waves, heart, chicken, betel nut, heavy object, flying birds, shining of the sun) and abstract vehicles (distant road, death, written text, and space). Positive abstract tenors reflected in Waray metaphorical expressions such as rapid growth, overnight success, and pleasure have botanical vehicles (bamboo shoot, mushroom, and sugar). INDUSTRY and GOODNESS are positive abstract tenors of Waray metaphors that utilize social relations as vehicle.

The social construct of LIFE in Waray metaphorical expressions is represented by negative, neutral, and positive vehicles. Rice grain, flower, and slippery turns are representations that can be categorized in the botanical and spatial domains. DEATH is represented by sleep which is an abstract vehicle. The concrete metaphors used to represent LIFE, in contrast with DEATH, suggest that Waray people regard the latter as a remote experience, while the former is an experience that they undertake in their daily lives, making the concept of this experience a concrete and tangible one.

In Waray, MONEY is commonly attributed to vehicles with elusive characteristics such as water, smoke, and the wings of the birds. It is interesting to argue that Waray people view money as something that is beyond their reach – an entity that has the propensity to vanish or to be beyond their physical realities.

A few negative abstract tenors such as shame, poverty, conflict, uncertain fate, gambling, and hopeless waiting have spatial and tangible metaphors (an open sea, circular road, earth and sky, fire, depths, road, and rain). The yearning of Waray people to fathom the causal aspects of these experiences could have led them to establish the relationship between these domains. Most negative human characteristics in Waray such as being an unloving child, wild person, slowpoke, quitter, messy person, a person in danger, a person lacking of sleep, hypocrite, talkative, flamboyant, presumptuous, peeping tom, angry, overstaying guest, cornered, wild, irresponsible parent, and stubborn have zoological vehicles (wild beast, crab, snake, earthworm, sow, moth, owl, ant, chicken, beetle, cock, bird, dog, flies, fish, harrow, sea turtle, and shark). Some negative human characteristics such as being a messy person, easily carried away, useless, furious, loquacious, deceitful, superficial, and blind have botanical elements as vehicles (layuan, water plant, coconut husk, flaming coconut shell, seedless flower, guava, burunganon grass and pineapple).

Temporal and spatial tenors. Tenors of time in Waray metaphors such as morning, dusk, long time, and night commonly use geographical and cosmological vehicles (climbing sun, awakened sky, burning peripheries of the sky, flaming sea, full moon, and scattered stars). Time tenors are rarely associated with botanical and human persona vehicles (blossoms of jasmine, an entity with feet, and person). Spatial and geographical tenors such as native land, Philippines, and sea in Waray metaphorical expressions use social relations as vehicles (mother, slave, and rich person).

5. Conclusion and recommendations

Formulating a taxonomy of metaphors in Waray based on an objective methodological framework provided meaningful insights on how the Waray culture encodes and decodes their physical, cultural, social, and psychological realities. Based on the description of the properties and attributes of the vehicles, certain patterns of the language-user's choice of source domain were reflected. The presence of cosmological vehicles was evident across all target domains such as those that denote abstract concepts of human feelings, state, and personality, but these vehicles were mostly dominant in expressing temporal tenors, while its utility has not been documented in target domains related to space and social relationships.

Geographical and spatial source domains are pervasive in conveying abstract tenors of human behavior. Only novel metaphorical occurrences utilize geographical and spatial vehicles in suggesting the target domain referring to time. In both novel and conventional metaphors, the said source domain was not used in denoting social relationships. Zoological vehicles have high frequency of usage in conventional metaphorical expressions about negative human personality, behavior, and state. Regardless of the target domain being referred to, zoological vehicles come in varied structures (from simple to complex structures); this is also true with botanical, somatic, social relationship, and the general tangible and intangible vehicles.

In all of the samples of metaphorical expressions in Waray, none of the domains in the vehicles were used to convey the target construct having the same domain. That is, if the domain of the vehicle is botanical, the target domain does not belong to the elements of the plant concept. This generalization is important to emphasize since it validates a novel principle in metaphor processing: the "Principle of Domain Non-Transmissibility". Such principle is based on the assumption that a language user does not duplicate the usage of domains in a given metaphorical expression. But, similar to other general truths, some exemptions to its tenets are present. This is reflected in the use of general intangible vehicles to represent a target domain in the abstract domain. Just like other models and theoretical underpinnings, this newly-conceived hypothesis must be subjected to further verification by using other methods of data collection, classification, and interpretation. Examining the specific differentia that created the exemption to the aforesaid principle is a challenge for future researchers concerned with metaphors processing.

Documentation of metaphors in Waray texts provides corporeal evidence in the affirmation of theoretical claims contained in the previously acknowledged assumptions of figurative language. First, it provides assertion that Waray language users construct their physical and psychological realities based on an anthropocentric mentality as reflected in their perceived reference to their own being as the center of all the positive things. One credible manifestation to this claim is the prevalence of negative attributes associated to plants and animals in Waray metaphorical occurrences since the said domains are perceived to have unknown experiences and realities to them. The use of somatic domain to convey a more abstract target domain is another demonstration on the applicability of the anthropocentric nature of Waray language users.

Second, through the juxtaposition of varied frames of description of the source domains, the assumptions of the major theories of metaphor (Conceptual Metaphor Theory, Context-Limited Simulation Theory, Lexical Concepts and Cognitive Models, and Discourse Dynamics Theory) were subjected to relevant application. In some cases, two or more theoretical assumptions were found to be relevant in elaborating the properties and attributes attached to the vehicles of Waray metaphorical occurrences. The complementary nature of these theories, as depicted in the main discussion section of this paper, supports the supposition that metaphor processing involves an operation that is based on the idiosyncratic linguistic, cognitive, affective, physical, and cultural (Cameron, 2007) dimensions available to the language user – a principle contained in the Discourse Dynamics Theory.

Third, the verity of Conceptual Metaphor Theory was examined and affirmed with the use of the available taxonomy of Waray metaphors. In one of the sections of the nomenclature, an important observation was drawn, which presents a contrary fact to one of the tenets of the CMT. There are some Waray metaphoric instances that exploit intangible elements as vehicles in expressing another intangible domain. As such, this poses limitations to CMT's assertion that concrete concepts define abstract domains (Lakoff, 1985, p. 60). Although this has been a notable observation, future investigations should consider the probing of the strengths and weaknesses of this claim using other language data.

The comprehensive categories of the domains covering the various vehicles and tenors in the description of Waray metaphors make it almost impossible to cross-tabulate the identification of componential properties of the same. For example, in one source domain, the element is described in terms of its passivity and locative properties, while in other categories of the same source domain, another dimension of its vehicle is utilized as a framework of analysis. In the discussion contained in this inquiry, it is apparent that the location of the vehicle in the phrasal structure is used as one of the bases in the linguistic description of the metaphoric elements in the cosmological source domain, but other dimensions are used in the description of botanical and somatic vehicles. This is true to other vehicles documented in this paper. Applying this scheme was a logical approach to ascertain equal sampling of the possible dimensional properties as bases of analysis for both the source and target domains.

Data on Waray metaphors and other related concepts obtained from the early decades of the 20th century to the recent years of the 21st century do not necessitate a solid ground for longitudinal comparison. The limited recorded archive of Waray text poses to be one of the challenges in achieving a valid and reliable framework of analysis. The combination of novel and conventional metaphors used in the analysis of vehicles and tenors constitutes both a limitation and asset to the overall inquiry. One of its limitations is related to issues of data dispersion and distribution since the standard deviation for both types of metaphors was not ascertained because of the qualitative nature of data. The advantage of combining these two types of metaphors is that cross-sectional comparison of Waray source and target domains was effectively implemented – an approach which has not been sought in previous studies. As a final statement, it is important to consider that with the comprehensive and multifaceted nature of Waray metaphors, it is impossible to address all the aforesaid issues given the predetermined size of this manuscript. Thus, a more specific cross-tabular analysis of individual vehicles in Waray maybe promulgated in the future to qualify the claims asserted in this paper.

References

Alunan, M., & Pundavela, E. (1997). *Susumaton of Leyte: Transcript and analysis of oral narratives in five towns of Leyte: Palo, Tanauan, Tolosa, Dulag, and Carigara*. Iloilo, Philippines: Office of Research Coordination, UP in the Visayas.

Andriessen, D., & Gubbins, C. (2009). Metaphor analysis as an approach for exploring theoretical concepts: The case of social capital. *Organization Studies*, 30(8), 845–863.

Aschale, A. (2013). The human body metaphors: A critical analysis of the metaphoric extensions vis-a-vis Amharic and English languages. [pdf] Retrieved from http://www.academia.edu/3658757/The_Human_Body_Metaphors_The_Metaphorical_Extensions_of_the_Human_Body_Parts_in_English_and_Amharic_Languages_Series_1

Black, M. (1962). *Models and metaphor: Studies in language and philosophy*. Ithaca, NY: Cornell University Press.

Berendt, E. A., & Tanita, K. (2011). The 'heart' of things: A conceptual metaphoric analysis of *heart* and related body parts in Thai, Japanese and English. *Intercultural Communication Studies*, 20(1), 65.

Bremer, K., & Lee, M. (1997). Metaphors in marketing: Review and implications for marketers. *Advances in Consumer Research*, 24, 419–424.

Cameron, L. (2007). Patterns of metaphor use in reconciliation talk. *Discourse and Society*, 18(2), 197–222. DOI: 10.1177/0957926507073376

Campbell, J. D., & Katz, A. N. (2009). On reversing the topics and vehicles of metaphor. *Metaphor and Symbol*, 21(1), 1–22. DOI: 10.1207/s15327868ms2101_1

Charteris-Black, J. (2004). *Corpus approaches to critical metaphor analysis*. Basingstoke: Palgrave Macmillan. DOI: 10.1057/9780230000612

Crisp, P., Heywood, J., & Steen, G. (2002). Metaphor identification and analysis, classification and quantification. *Language and Literature*, V11(1), 55–69. DOI: 10.1177/096394700201100105

Deignan, A. (2005). *Metaphor and corpus linguistics*. Amsterdam: John Benjamins. DOI: 10.1075/celcr.6

De Veyra, V. S. (2007). Mga siday hin ka-Waray. [Blog post] Retrieved from http://waraypoems.vicentesoriadeveyra.com/an_mga_siday/index.html

Dino, M. (2005). *Norte Samar*. [Blog] Retrieved from http://sidaykultura.wordpress.com/2007/

Downing, L. H., & Mujic, B. K. (2009). Infectious diseases are sleeping monsters: Conventional and culturally adapted new metaphors in a corpus of abstracts on immunology. *IBERECA*, 17, 61–82.

Evans, V. (2010). Figurative language understanding in LCCM theory. *Cognitive Linguistics*, 21(4), 601–662. DOI: 10.1515/cogl.2010.020

Gineste, M. (2007). [Research article] Retrieved from Emergence of figurative and non-figurative features in poetic metaphors. [online] Retrieved from http://www.jcss.gr.jp/iccs99OLP/o2-07/o2-07.htm

Goatly, A. (2006). Humans, animals, and metaphors. *Society & Animals*, 14, 1. DOI: 10.1163/156853006776137131

Goossens, L. (2002). Metaphtonymy: The interaction of metaphor and metonymy in expressions for linguistic action. In R. Dirven & R. Porings (Eds.), *Metaphor and metonymy in comparison and contrast* (pp. 349–378). Berlin/New York: Mouton de Gruyter.

Goschler, J. (2005). Embodiment and body metaphors. [Journal article] Retrieved from http://www.metaphorik.de/sites/www.metaphorik.de/files/journal-pdf/09_2005_goschler.pdf

Hanks, P. (2004). The syntagmatics of metaphor and idiom. *International Journal of Lexicography*, 17(3), 245–274. DOI: 10.1093/ijl/17.3.245

Harris, R. J., Friel, N. R., & Mickelson, N. R. (2006). Attribution of discourse goals for using concrete- and abstract-tenor metaphors and similes with or without discourse context. *Journal of Pragmatics*, 38(6), 863–879. DOI: 10.1016/j.pragma.2005.06.010

Haviland, W. A., Prins, H. E. L., McBride, B., & Walrath, D. (2011). *Cultural anthropology: The human challenge* (13th ed.). Wadsworth Cengage Learning.

Huang, X., Huang, H., Xu, C., Chen, W., & Wang, R. (2011). A novel pattern matching method for Chinese metaphor identification and classification. *Lecture Notes in Computer Science*, 7(4), 104–114. DOI: 10.1007/978-3-642-23896-3_13

Kemertelidze, N., & Manjavidze, T. (2012). Classification of the metaphors according to the degree of unexpectedness. *European Scientific Journal*, 8(2). [Journal article] Retrieved from http://www.eujournal.net/index.php/esj/article/viewFile/37/37

Lakoff, G. (1985). Metaphor, folk theories, and the possibilities of dialogue. In M. Dascal & H. Cuyckens (Eds.), *Dialogue: An interdisciplinary approach* (pp. 60–71). Amsterdam: John Benjamins. DOI: 10.1075/pbcs.1.07lak

Lakoff, G., & Johnson, M. (1980). *Metaphors we live by*. Chicago: University of Chicago Press.

Lakoff, G., & Turner, M. (1989). *More than cool reason: A field guide to poetic metaphor*. Chicago: University of Chicago Press. DOI: 10.7208/chicago/9780226470986.001.0001

Lai, V. T., Curran, T., & Menn, L. (2009). Comprehending conventional and novel metaphors: An ERP study. *Brain Research*, 1284, 145–155. DOI: 10.1016/j.brainres.2009.05.088

Lan, L., & MacGregor, L. (2009). Colour metaphors in business discourse. In V. K. Bhatia, W. Cheng, B. Du-Babcock, & J. Lung (Eds.), *Language for professional communication: Research, practice & training*. Hong Kong: The Hong Kong Polytechnic University.

Lei, Q. (2007). Nature and classification of poetical metaphor. *Canadian Social Science*, 3(4), 47–50.

Liang, S., & Heywood, M. I. (2002). The effect of routing under local information using a social insect metaphor. [Research article] Retrieved from https://web.cs.dal.ca/~zincir/bildiri/cec02-snm.pdf

Lucente, I. (1922). *Mga kali-awan*. Tacloban, Philippines: n.p.

Lukes, D. (2005). Towards a classification of metaphor use in text: Issues in conceptual discourse analysis of a domain-specific corpus. [Research article] Retrieved from http://metaphorhacker.net/files/2013/04/Luke%C5%A1-2005-Towards-aclassification-of-metaphor-use-in-text-.pdf

Macabasag, M. T. (2007). Ha mga Waray nga intelektuwal. [Blog post] Retrieved from http://sidaykultura.wordpress.com/2007/10/27/ha-mga-waray-nga-intelektuwal/

Mansueto, T. D. (2013). Preserving Cebuano and other languages. *Inquirer Visayas*, 1 September 2013. [Online news] Retrieved from http://newsinfo.inquirer.net/479137/preserving-cebuano-and-other-languages-2

Mashal, N., & Faust, M. (2009). Conventionalisation of novel metaphors: A shift in hemispheric asymmetry. *Laterality: Asymmetries of Body, Brain and Cognition*, 14 (6), 573–589. DOI: 10.1080/13576500902734645

McGlone, M. S. (2007). What is the explanatory value of a conceptual metaphor? *Language & Communication*, 27, 109–126. DOI: 10.1016/j.langcom.2006.02.016

Moser, K. S. (2000). Metaphor analysis in psychology – Method, theory, and fields of application. *Forum: Qualitative Social Research*, 1(2), Article 21. [Journal article] Retrieved from http://www.qualitative-research.net/index.php/fqs/article/view/1090/2388

Nacey, S. (2009). Novel metaphors and learner English. [Journal article] Retrieved from http://www.academia.edu/1643664/Novel_Metaphors_and_Learner_English

Oyzon, V. Q. (2008). *An maupay na mga Waray ug iba pa nga mga siday*. Philippines: National Commission for Culture and Arts.

Pauwels, P., & Simon-Vandenbergen, A. (1995). Body parts in linguistic action: Underlying schemata and value judgements. In L. Goossens, P. Pauwels, B. Rudzka-Ostyn, A. Simon-Vandenbergen, & J. Vanparys (Eds.), *By word of mouth: Metaphor, metonymy and linguistic action in cognitive perspective* (pp. 35–69). Amsterdam: John Benjamins. DOI: 10.1075/pbns.33.03pau

Perekhvalskaya, E. (2013). Body parts and their metaphoric meanings in Mwan and other South Mande languages. [Research article] Retrieved from http://llacan.vjf.cnrs.fr/PDF/Mandenkan44/44perexvals.pdf

Perrin, S. G. (1987). Metaphorical revelations: A description of metaphor as the reciprocal engagement of abstract perspectives and concrete phenomena in experience. *Metaphor and Symbol*, 4(2), 251–280. DOI: 10.1207/s15327868ms0204_3

Pop, A. (2008). The nature of visual metaphors in IT advertising. *Acta Linguistica*, 2, 55–60.

Ritchie, L. D. (2006). *Context and connection in metaphor*. Basingstoke, UK: Palgrave Macmillan Ltd. DOI: 10.1057/9780230286825

Rodriguez, I. L. (2009). Of women, bitches, chickens and vixens: Animal metaphors for women in English and Spanish. *Culture, Language and Representation*, 7, 77–100.

Schmidt, Z. (2008). Much mouth much tongue: Chinese metonymies and metaphors of verbal behaviour. *Cognitive Linguistics*, 19(2), 241–282.

Schmitt, R. (2005). Systematic metaphor analysis as a method of qualitative research. *The Qualitative Report*, 10 (2), 358–394.

Shabani, A. (2008). A comparative study of the translation of image metaphors of color in the Shahnameh of Ferdowsi. [Online article] Retrieved from http://www.translationdirectory.com/articles/article1701.php

Shanton, K., & Goldman, A. (2010). Simulation theory. *Wiley Interdisciplinary Reviews: Cognitive Science*, 1(4), 527–538.

Shelestiuk, H. V. (2006). Approaches to metaphor: Structure, classifications, cognate phenomena. *Semiotica*, 161(1/4), 333–343. DOI: 10.1515/SEM.2006.069

Skara, S. (2004). Body metaphors – reading the body in contemporary culture. *Collegium Antropologicum*, 28(1), 183–189.

Sommer, R., & Sommer, B. (2011). Zoomorphy: Animal metaphors for human personality. *Anthrozos*, 24(3), 237–248. DOI: 10.2752/175303711X13045914865024

Sugbo, V. (2008). *Initokan*. Diliman, Quezon City, Philippines: The University of the Philippines Press.

Sugbo, V. N. (2003). Language policy and local literature in the Philippines. [Online article] Retrieved from http://www-01.sil.org/asia/ldc/parallel_papers/victor_n_sugbo.pdf

Takada, M., Shinohara, K., Morizumi, F., & Sato, M. (2000). A study of metaphorical mapping involving socio-cultural values: How woman is conceptualized in Japanese. [Journal article] Retrieved from http://aclweb.org/anthology/Y/Y00/Y00-1030.pdf

Tamayo, N. G. (1990). *Waray proverbs*. Tacloban City Philippines: Divine Word University Publications.

Thagard, P., & Beam, C. (2013). Epistemological metaphors and the nature of philosophy. [Journal article] Retrieved from http://cogsci.uwaterloo.ca/Articles/epistemological.html

The Holy Bible. (2006). *Revelation. The Holy Bible*, King James Version. 1611 Edition. Peabody, MA, USA: Hendrickson Publishers.

Thibodeau, P., & Durgin, F. H. (2007). Productive figurative communication: Conventional metaphors facilitate the comprehension of related novel metaphors. *Journal of Memory and Language*, 58(2), 521–542. DOI: 10.1016/j.jml.2007.05.001

Turney, P. D., Neuman, Y., Assaf, D., & Cohen, Y. (2011). Literal and metaphorical sense identification through concrete and abstract context. [Proceedings article] Retrieved from http://aclweb.org/anthology//D/D11/D11-1063.pdf

Vaara, E., Tienari, J., & Santti, R. (2003). Identity-building in cross-border mergers. *Human Relations*, 56 (4), 419–451. DOI: 10.1177/0018726703056004002

White, T. (2002). Management of mobile agent systems using social insect metaphors. [Proceedings article] Retrieved from http://citeseerx.ist.psu.edu/viewdoc/download?doi=10.1.1.95.3837&rep=rep1&type=pdf

Zhang, Q. (2008). The cognition and image preservation in the translation of metaphor from English to Chinese. *Asian Social Science Journal*, 4(8), 84–89.

CHAPTER 5

Hot eyes, white stomach

Emotions and character qualities in Safaliba metaphor

Paul Schaefer
GILLBT and SIL, Ghana

With a population of only about 7000, the Safaliba are one of the least numerous ethnic groups in Ghana that still use a distinct language as their primary means of communication with one another as well as with many outsiders. Many Safaliba metaphors are similar to those of other Ghanaian languages: to TELL LIES in Safaliba, you "cut" (ŋma) them, while to MAKE A GOOD EFFORT, you "wrestle" (mɔbɛ); metaphors like this are linguistically and geographically wide-spread and have even made their way into registers of Ghanaian English. However, there are also types of metaphorical usage where there is a fair amount of cross-language variation. Emotions and character-qualities are sometimes lexicalized but are also regularly conveyed by compound words or phrases with a strong metaphorical component. In these cases an image used to convey a particular quality in one language may convey a different quality in another language: for example, in Safaliba the expression po-pɛɛlǫŋ "white stomach" is used to refer to the quality of KIND-NESS, while in the related language Farefare the equivalent expression is used to refer to the emotion of HAPPINESS. Working within the general framework of Lakoff and Johnson (1980 and later developments), this paper gives an overview of selected Safaliba metaphors relating to emotions and character-qualities. It also compares these to similar constructions in four other north-ern Ghanaian languages, Waali, Farefare, Sisaala, and Chumburung.

Keywords: Safaliba, Gur, Oti-Volta, body metaphor, emotions, literacy, Ghana

DOI 10.1075/clscc.7.04sch

1.   Introduction

Ɛ̰ *bee niŋŋe togiliye geni!* "Your child's eyes are very hot!" Our eldest son was born six weeks after we moved to the Safaliba area; he never really crawled but was determined to run (not walk!) from a very early age, and he loved to wake up before the crack of dawn and would go anywhere and do anything without the least fear or hesitation. Our first conscious exposure to Safaliba metaphor was in our neighbors' descriptions of the sort of child we had: one with "hot eyes", a term used exclusively for children who rush headlong into whatever they can get into. As time went by we learned more of the language, and realized that many character qualities and emotions were conveyed by similar constructions. Eventually we learned that a child who was careful and cautious is described as *Q niŋŋe maaya* "His eyes are cool" – but nobody ever said that about our son (or any of his siblings for that matter).

When words or word groups are used to convey something quite different from their basic denotative meaning, it is easy to identify the presence of a metaphor. However, in *Metaphors We Live By* (and subsequent works) Lakoff and Johnson (1980) introduced the idea that the presence of "metaphor" in human language goes far beyond the occasional creative use of words by a gifted speaker trying to make a rhetorical point. In fact, the use of metaphor pervades natural language, so that a great deal of human communication can be seen as metaphorical. For example, the first sentence of this paragraph uses the terms "convey", "identify", and "presence" in a metaphorical sense, because these terms actually have their basic meaning in relation to physical objects, and their use with abstract concepts is necessarily metaphorical. This type of metaphorical usage is termed a "conceptual metaphor" by Lakoff and Johnson.

Does each language and culture create its own conceptual metaphors, or are there some conceptual metaphors that are common to all languages and cultures? This question appears in Kövecses (2002), and it would seem that the answer should be "yes", since the "cognitive science" which forms much of the grounding for Lakoff and Johnson's work involves physical studies of brain function which should be independent of human culture. However, at the same time Lakoff and Johnson stress the real arbitrariness of certain conceptual metaphors, and show that to a great extent the metaphors used in a particular language constrain the perspectives of those people immersed in that particular language and culture. They give the example that, in English, a predominant conceptual metaphor for "argument" is ARGUMENT IS WAR; but in a language where argument was not conceptualized as war, but as something different, how would this affect public and private discourse? My own experience working among minority language groups has been that while there are certainly many commonalities in metaphor between unrelated languages and cultures, still the predominant and most typical metaphors used in a particular language are often significantly different from those used in a different language and culture.

This book is offered on the assumption that lesser-studied languages are likely to make use of metaphors that are not the same as those known from majority languages. The only way to even begin to consider the question of universal metaphors is through empirical research of lesser-studied languages. And in fact, data from endangered and lesser-studied languages seem to indicate that few if any true universals exist in metaphor, and further that ideas and methods developed primarily from study of well-known European languages should not be relied upon uncritically in the study of "disappearing metaphors and shifting conceptualizations."

In my doctoral research on Safaliba grammar and pragmatics, I was continually running into aspects of the Safaliba language that did not align well with the supposed "linguistic universals". I found that many of the high-profile claims of "universality" for particular grammatical features or pragmatic categories are based almost solely on analyses of well-known languages, usually Indo-European. Theories and explanations are frequently constructed without consideration of data from non-majority languages. Although the situation continues to improve, it seems prudent not to adhere too strongly to proposed "universals" unless they are supported by field research from diverse language families worldwide. Until a great many studies of conceptual metaphors are done on lesser-known languages, we will not even know what questions to ask about what such "universals" might really look like.

2.   The Safaliba in their linguistic and cultural environment

The Safaliba are a very small ethnic group, defined primarily by their distinct language. They are traditionally located directly west and south of the town of Bole (on the western border edge of Ghana's Northern Region), though Safaliba communities also exist in a number of larger nearby towns, such as Sawla, Kalba, Bole itself, and the towns of Vonkoro and Bouna (Gbonaa) across the river in Cote d'Ivoire. Bole is the administrative capital of the Bole District, which extends from just south of the town of Sawla to the north, as far as to the town of Bamboi to the south. The Bole District is a highly multilingual area, with at least 7 languages being spoken (including at least the following: Gonja, Vagla, Safaliba, Deg a.k.a. Mo, Choruba, Nafaanra, Kamara, Birifor, and Dagaare). Gonja and Waali are used in the northern part of the district as LWCs.

The cultures represented in Bole district are more homogeneous than the multiplicity of languages would suggest. Culturally, the Safaliba are very similar to the Vagla, Gonja, and Choruba in the northern part of the Bole District. Linguistically, however, Safaliba is quite distinct from its cultural neighbors and is actually closest to Waali and the central dialect of Dagaare, which are languages spoken in and around the city of Wa about 100 km to the north. Safaliba, Waali and Dagaare are all members of the Northwestern Western-Oti-Volta subfamily of the Gur languages; Birifor, Farefare, and Moore are the other members of this group, all of which are spoken in northern Ghana except for Moore, which is the majority language in Burkina Faso. Vagla and Deg are members of the linguistically quite different Grusi branch of Gur, while Choruba and Gonja are members of the Guang branch of the Kwa family; none of these is inherently intelligible with Safaliba to any degree.[1]

The Safaliba people therefore share many similarities with other ethnic communities in northern Ghana. The ethnographic studies by Fortes (1945, 1949) on the Tallensi subgroup of Farefare, Jack Goody (1956, 1962) on some of the Dagaare-speaking communities, and Skinner (1964) on the Mossi (speakers of Moore) all describe aspects of social structure and customs shared to a great extent by the Safaliba people. Geographically, the Safaliba live in a part of the ancient Gonja kingdom, and as such hold many customs in common with other inhabitants of Gonja, as presented in Esther Goody's studies in social anthropology (1973, 1982, among others). In nonlinguistic research the Safaliba themselves have usually not been presented as a distinct ethnic group; one notable exception is Christiana Oware Knudsen's study of female circumcision in Ghana, which devotes a full page to the Safaliba (1994, pp. 100–101).

It is important to remember that the peoples of this area have a long and complex history, one which is intimately tied to the history of West Africa over the last 1000+ years. In the 1500's as the historical empire of Mali was collapsing, a Malian warlord was sent to secure the sources of the empire's gold, and after doing so "he defected and moved eastwards to found the kingdom of Gonja in the lower Black Volta" (Wilks, 2000, p. 99). According to local oral traditions, the Safaliba, Vagla, and Choruba were already living in the area at the time of the founding of the Gonja kingdom. Amazingly there are written records that refer to these events: in the 1700's the imams of the king of Gonja compiled records of the kingdom in Arabic script (Wilks, 2000, p. 99; see also Wilks et al., 1986).

---

1.   However there are a number of words that are shared between these otherwise-unrelated languages, due to the linguistic borrowing that occurs when language communities exist in comparative proximity to each other.

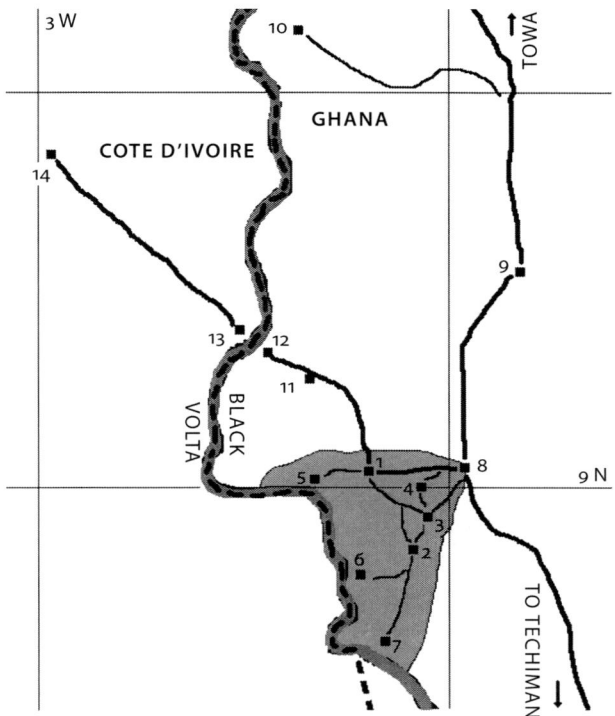

The detailed map shows the location of the Safaliba towns and villages, as well as those towns in Ghana and Cote d'Ivoire where sizable Safaliba-speaking populations live. These have been numbered according to the key below:

Safaliba-speaking towns and villages:	*Towns which have Safaliba-speaking minorities:*
1. Mandari	8. Bole
2. Gbenfu	9. Sawla
3. Manfuli	10. Kalba
4. Tanyiri	11. Zantige
5. Nsunua	12. Chache
6. Chorubawala	13. Vonkoro (Cote d'Ivoire)
7. Ntereso	14. Bouna (Cote d'Ivoire)

Map taken from Schaefer and Schaefer (2003)

The history of the Safaliba people is therefore very much a part of the history of the rest of the area.[2]

Although today the effects of globalization affect even the remotest villages (Piot, 1999), there is still much continuity with the past in current Safaliba cultural practices and worldview. The traditional activities of Safalibas are subsistence farming and trading, though many farmers farm cash crops as well. Farms are usually a mile or more from the village, and the area is forested and hilly so much of the cultivation is done using hand tools; a tractor can be hired for initial plowing if the farm area is accessible enough. Most food is grown locally, with some flavoring ingredients like garlic and ginger brought in from other areas of the country.

Houses are often still built of the traditional mud balls or bricks with flat solid roofs, although most people now prefer to build with cement blocks and roof with galvanized metal sheets when they have the resources to purchase the materials. People still walk within and even between towns and villages, though motorcycles, bicycles, and other vehicles are much more prevalent than ever before. Local weaving among the Safaliba has virtually died out, though it is maintained in other towns in the area for the purpose of making certain traditional garments that are still popular and are worn on special occasions. There are tailors in every town who make clothing of all sorts from commercially-woven cloth; for farming and daily use people purchase used clothing from the weekly market in Bole.

Educational facilities are more prevalent than before, and the majority of children are enrolled in the public schools[3] instead of engaging in the traditional activities of their parents, as occurred in former times. According to Ghanaian educational policy, children are to be taught in their mother tongue for the first three years of primary school, and a Ghanaian language is to be taught as a subject

---

2.   I would like to note here three other books which, while not directly related to the Safaliba, are nevertheless very helpful in understanding the cultural milieu in which the Safaliba live. Wilks (1989) details some of the history of the Wala people as Islam became part of their cultural identity. Allman and Parker (1995) describe the history and ritual practices of the Farefare people, particularly as these were affected by the relations of the Tongnaab god's keepers with the colonial administrators during the century before Ghana's independence. Kirby (1986) gives an ethnography of the society and world view of another typical traditional society in northeastern Ghana. The Safaliba share many cultural forms and perspectives with the peoples who are the subjects of these books, including both the Islamic and the traditional African background.

3.   However the number of classrooms and teachers has not grown proportionally – many primary school classrooms, usually designed to contain 30 to 40 students, have anywhere from 50 to 90 students under a single teacher.

thereafter. However, the diversity of languages in the area makes effective schooling difficult to implement. There are not always teachers who speak the local language of the students to whom they are assigned, and educational materials in the appropriate language are not always in stock or even in existence.

3. Safaliba revitalization efforts

Safaliba's ongoing existence as a separate language is threatened. Until recent decades it has been comparatively isolated from related languages, and this isolation has helped it to remain distinct. However, improvements in road infrastructure, access to electricity and mobile phone networks, and television are all bringing Safaliba speakers into contact with many more languages than before. Older people say that younger speakers do not always learn the right Safaliba words, and that some are mixing in words from other languages. Many of the inhabitants of smaller villages are moving to Bole or other large towns, for education, work, or trade, and this also creates more opportunities for contact with majority languages. In Bole this effect is somewhat mitigated as Safaliba has become one of the LWC's in Bole, however this has come with a price as the variety of Safaliba spoken in Bole often contains borrowed words and other differences, since it is spoken by many as a second language.

There are efforts in several corners to revitalize the Safaliba language, however. A group of concerned educated elders have made some of the higher-profile efforts. In the late 80's Mr. Edmund Kungi Yakubu wrote to the Ghana Institute of Linguistics, Literacy and Bible Translation (GILLBT), who at that time was operating an effective literacy program in Vagla villages near the Safaliba area. Mr. Yakubu, a graduate of the School of Ghana Languages – Ajumako, requested GILLBT's assistance to develop the language, and proposed an orthography.

Several years later, GILLBT sent my wife and I to undertake development of the Safaliba language (at that time still almost completely an unwritten language). We moved to the largest Safaliba town, Mandari, and began study of the phonology and grammar (Schaefer & Schaefer, 2003, 2004). We proposed an orthography based on those findings, and published some books of stories. We worked with some of the younger educators to prepare a set of reading primers for adult-education classes. I later completed a doctoral dissertation on aspects of the pragmatics and discourse structure of the language (Schaefer, 2009), and improved the analysis of the phonology and grammar. Needless to say, it was the Safaliba people themselves who were persistent enough to keep correcting the analysis until it became more representative of actual language structure, so that the orthography could be revised to the point of widespread usability. A number of people, including Mr. Yakubu, began to compose and write short stories and other works in Safaliba; GILLBT published these as booklets to encourage community literacy, though the idea of Safaliba as a written language was still novel to most of the population.

However, many Safaliba people were familiar with the idea of literacy in local languages through GILLBT's Vagla literacy program and through the government-sponsored Non-Formal Education (NFED) program in the Gonja language. NFED regularly trains interested people as community literacy facilitators, and several Safaliba people had gone through this training. One of these, Mr. Iddi Bayaya, became exceedingly passionate about transferring those literacy skills to his own language. He began by writing down a number of stories, songs, and other texts in Safaliba. Once he had proven to himself the practicality of writing his own language, he started meeting with a group of interested adults in the town of Mandari to teach them also to read and write Safaliba during the evenings after the workday was over. It is largely through his efforts over a period of 10 years, through regularly teaching literacy classes in three different Safaliba villages (Mandari, Nsunua, and Gbenfu) that the practicality of Safaliba as a written language has been proven to the larger community.

Although these "night classes" are oriented towards adult participants, Mr. Bayaya has always accepted children as students as well. These children have learned literacy skills which have markedly improved their performance in the formal school system. This effect has come to the attention of the community at large, and their local government representative has made the case to the Bole District Assembly that Safaliba should be used to teach reading and writing skills in the primary schools in the Safaliba-majority villages. If the Safaliba language is formally taught as part of the education program of the local schools it will not only help individual children in improving their literacy skills but will be a major step towards a more secure future for the Safaliba language.

4.   Aspects of Safaliba phonology and grammar

Before digging into Safaliba metaphor, it is necessary to have a little background on Safaliba linguistic structure. Safaliba is in many ways a typical example of a Western Oti-Volta language. Phonologically and morphologically it is more conservative than some of its linguistic relatives, maintaining nine distinct vowel phonemes and a comparatively transparent morphological structure.

Like many of its linguistic relatives, Safaliba has an active cross-height vowel harmony system based on the phonological feature commonly described as "advanced tongue root" or ATR.[4] In most non-compound words, the vowels come from one or the other of two sets: the first set of vowels are represented by the traditional Roman characters /e/, /i/, /o/, /u/, and are all pronounced with the +ATR voice quality; each of these has a –ATR counterpart in the second set of vowels /ɛ/, /ẹ/, /ɔ/, /ọ/.[5] The vowel /a/ is also pronounced with –ATR voice quality but does not have a +ATR counterpart.

Vowel harmony effects are most clearly seen the variation of various suffixes, which must agree in harmony with the ATR value of the root morpheme: for example, *pẹsẹga* "sheep-singular", *pẹsẹsẹ* "sheep-plural"; but *kokke* "stool-singular", *kogisi* "stool-plural". Because the /a/ vowel does not have a +ATR counterpart, an /a/ in a suffix changes to /e/ when the suffix is attached to a +ATR root.

Safaliba nouns are formed by the addition of a nominal suffix[6] to a root. In the examples above, the root for "sheep" is **pẹs**- and the root for "stool" is **kog**-. The nominal suffix for singular nouns in this class is **-gA**, which surfaces as **-ge** with +ATR words and **-ga** with –ATR words; similar the plural suffix **-sI** emerges as **-si** or **-sẹ**.[7]

Safaliba verbs also have several forms: the unmarked or basic form has no suffixes, but there are two derived forms which indicate something about the "aspect" or type of action expressed. The form expressing completed aspect is shown by a -**yA** suffix, and the form expressing ongoing or continuous aspect is shown by a -**rA** suffix. Variants of these appear on actual words, again according to the principles of ATR vowel harmony: -**ya** and -**ra** appear on –ATR words, while -**ye** and -**re** appear on +ATR words.

Compound nouns are made by attaching roots together and adding an appropriate suffix at the end. For example, **po**- "stomach" can be joined to **pɛɛ**- "be white", and with the addition of the -**lɔŋ** suffix (used to indicate certain abstract

---

4. Standard analysis proposes that the physiological factor behind the separation of the 9 vowels into two distinct sets is the position of the tongue root; one set is pronounced with an "advanced tongue root" and one pronounced without it.

5. "ẹ" is the orthographic representation of the high front –ATR vowel represented by IPA [ɪ], while "ọ" is the orthographic representation of the high back –ATR vowel represented by IPA [ʊ]. These orthographic characters were chosen to maintain some continuity with the orthographies of Gonja, Akan, and many other Ghanaian languages which are under-representational with respect to vowels, using "o" and "e" to represent two vowel sounds each, i.e. 7 symbols for 9 phonemes.

6. There are different sets of suffixes, based on the class of noun represented by the root: different classes of noun represent singular and plural by different suffixes.

7. A different phonological process changes **kog-ge** to *kokke*, and yet another process inserts an /ẹ/ so that **pẹs-ga** emerges as *pẹsẹga*.

concepts) this creates the word *popεεlɔŋ* "kindness". The same idea can also be expressed in a sentence, "He is kind," using the same elements: **ɔ** "3rd person pronoun", **po-** "stomach" **-o** (noun class singular marker), **pεgele̱**-[8] "be white" **-ya** (completive aspect), which give us *Ɔ poo pεgele̱ya,* "He is kind" (literally, "His stomach is utterly white"). In compounds, roots maintain their inherent ATR value, while suffixes agree in ATR with the nearest root.

As the presence of the verb *pεgele̱* "be white" suggests, modifiers in Safaliba do not necessarily fall in an "adjective" word class as is the case in English. In fact many concepts expressed by adjectives in English are conveyed through verbs in Safaliba, and true "adjectives" are less common. Nouns also frequently serve as modifiers in a compound structure, such as **po-** "stomach" with *likke* "darkness" to give *polikke* "evil-scheming" (literally, "dark-stomach"). There are also a few true adjectives, such as *kpεεne̱* "hard", which can occur in stative constructions such as *A yala be kpεεne̱,* "The matter is hard" (i.e. it is a difficult situation). There are also a small number of bound adjectives which can only occur as part of a compound word: for example, *-ze̱aŋ* "red", as in *nimbize̱aŋ* "trouble" (literally, "eyes-red").[9]

5.   Safaliba metaphors for emotions and character qualities

Like English as well as many languages around the world, Safaliba uses the human body as one of the "most common images for comparison in surface realizations of metaphor" (Hansford, 2005, p. 137). Such "body metaphor" is one of the most common ways to express emotions and character qualities in Safaliba, as is also the case in many of its linguistic neighbors in Northern Ghana. In the rest of this paper, I explore the similarities and differences in the metaphors used for emotions and character qualities in Safaliba and other languages.[10]

---

8.   The words *pεε* and *pεgele̱* "white" are actually variants of the same root; in some contexts (i.e. *popεεlɔŋ* "kindness") a root like *pεgele̱* is usually simplified to *pεε* in most people's speech, though in the careful pronunciation of some people the longer form can be distinctly heard. In this paper some details of morphological derivation are not made explicit as they are not relevant to the present topic.

9.   However with the verbal root *mɔɔ* "be red" is used, the metaphorical meaning changes: *Ɔ niŋŋe mɔɔya* is literally "Her eyes are red," but it means "She is serious about her work."

10.   My understanding of meaning in language is guided by the cognitive approach of Lakoff and Johnson (Lakoff, 1987; Johnson, 1987; Lakoff & Johnson, 1980, 1999), who credit Merleau-Ponty (1962) as an early proponent of embodied philosophy. I have also found Kövecses (2002) helpful as a general survey.

In the metaphors presented below, the following Safaliba body-part terms occur:

body-part	eye[11]	chest	stomach	body
word	*niɲɲe*	*nyea*	*poo*	*eɲɲa, eɲganne*[13]
in compounds	*nimbi-*	*nyɛ-*	*po-*	*eɲ-, eɲgam-*

These body-part terms are described by the following qualifiers:

hot	cool	white	dark	red[14]	(others)
togili (v)	*maa* (v)	*pɛgɛlɛ* (v)	*likke* (n)	*mɔɔ* (v)	*birii* "whole" (adj)
tooligu (n)	*maasɛgo* (n)	*pɛɛlɔŋ* (n)		*-zɛaŋ*[15] (adj)	*kpɛɛnɛ* "hard" (adj)
					baaŋsɛ "pain" (n)

There are other qualifiers, of course; the selection above shows one apparently binary set (hot-cool) and a set of colors (white, dark, red) in addition to some other modifying concepts.

First, consider the following metaphorical descriptions, which all refer to the eyes:

o niɲɲe togiliye	"his eye is hot"	HE IS FEARLESS
o niɲɲe maaya	"his eye is cool"	HE IS CAREFUL
nimbitooligu	"eye-heat"	FEARLESSNESS
nimbimaasɛgo	"eye-cool"	CAREFULNESS

---

11. The eye can be referred to either by the same word used for the face, *niɲɲe*, or more specifically by *nimbigɛllɛ* "eyeballs" (literally "eye-eggs").

12. This is literally "body-skin", but seems to be generally used as an alternative way to refer to the entire body.

13. It will be noted that color words are quite productive, and that the three colors are white, dark, and red. This is in accordance with predicted language universals that "all languages have foci for 'black' and 'white'; if a language has three basic colour terms, then the third has the focus of 'red' (Comrie, 1989, p. 37).

14. As noted above, *-zɛaŋ* is one of the bound adjectives; it does not occur except as part of a compound.

There appears to be a binary opposition between heat and cold: the "cool eye" is careful, while the "hot eye" is careless or fearless. The image of heat or cold, and its implication, remains the same whether the metaphor is packaged in a compound noun or presented in a sentence. But the eye can also be red or hard:

nimbimɔɔ[15]	"eye-red"	SERIOUSNESS or HARDWORKING
nimbizɛaŋ	"eye-red"	TROUBLE

As can be seen above, what a "red eye" signifies is further dependent on the specific word used for "red". As noted above, *mɔɔ* is a verbal root which means "to be red" while *-zɛaŋ* is a bound adjective with the same basic meaning. The metaphorical meanings SERIOUSNESS and TROUBLE could possibly be related (the word for "eye" by itself is often used to refer to what is called in English the root, crux, or core[16] of a problem).

nimbikpɛɛnɛ	"eye-hard"	PITILESS

A PITILESS person has a "hard eye". Although there does not seem to be a contrasting expression for PITY which uses the metaphor of "soft eyes", a contrasting metaphor is conveyed to some degree by the phrase *kaatɔ nɛmbagelɛba*, "look on us as soft people", which is a request for PITY or MERCY. Perhaps the conceptual metaphor that could be generalized from all these cases is THE EYE REVEALS HOW A PERSON RELATES TO THE WORLD AROUND HIM.

Next, consider the following metaphorical descriptions, which refer to the chest and to the stomach (or more specifically, the interior of the abdomen):

nyɛbirii	"whole-chest"	BOLDNESS

The literal meaning here is that the person's chest is whole or undivided. The meaning BOLDNESS has a more generally solemn and positive connotation than the FEARLESSNESS of a person with "hot eyes." The person with *nyɛbirii* might show BOLDNESS in war, hunting, or speaking publicly on potentially dangerous topics, whereas the connotation of *nimbitooligu* has more to do with acting without considering the consequences; such a person is indeed fearless, but is perhaps not as intentional about it as the person with *nyɛbirii*.

---

15. This metaphor can also be carried in a sentence: *ɔ niŋŋe mɔɔya* "his eye is red" (he is) SERIOUS or HARDWORKING.

16. All these are of course metaphorical usages; as Lakoff and Johnson point out, metaphor is pervasive.

popɛɛlɔŋ[17]	"stomach-white"	KINDNESS or OPENNESS
polikke	"stomach-dark"	EVIL-SCHEMING or SECRETIVE
potɔɔŋ[18]	"stomach-bitter"	WICKEDNESS

The first two kinds of stomach seem to indicate a contrast between transparency and hiddenness: the KIND person has nothing to hide but does good to those around him, whereas the person who hides things is certainly doing so because he has EVIL SCHEMES planned against others. The metaphor for WICKEDNESS once again relates to what is inside a person: in this case, a taste (bitter) instead of a color. The conceptual metaphor here might be that THE WAY A PERSON RELATES TO THOSE AROUND HIM SHOWS WHAT HE IS LIKE IN HIS INMOST PARTS.

The next example uses the image of coolness in the same positive sense seen in the first examples.

| *ọ nyẹa maa* | "his chest is cool" | HE IS HAPPY |
| *nyɛmaarẹ* | "chest-coolness" | HAPPINESS |

Here, however, the metaphor of coolness seems to include more than just the absence of (possibly negative) heat but seems to be seen a characteristic of WELL-BEING, or more specifically HAPPINESS. Furthermore, the chest image in this case seems similar to the use of the stomach in the examples above, in that it seems to stand for the whole person.

The state of the "whole person" is also referenced in Safaliba body metaphors using the image of the whole physical body (*ẹŋgannẹ* in Safaliba):

| *ẹŋgammaasẹgo* | "body-coolness" | PEACE, WELL-BEING |
| *ẹŋgambaaŋsẹ* | "body-pain" | ENVY |

Like a cool chest, a cool body is a description of general WELL-BEING. But whereas *nyẹamaarẹ* tends more towards HAPPINESS, *ẹŋgammaasẹgo* seems to have more of a connotation of PEACE. The word *ẹŋtooligu*, "body-heat", is used literally refers to fever such as accompanies malaria, and as such is not a good candidate for metaphorical usage. But a lack of internal peace is captured in *ẹŋgambaaŋsẹ*, which is literally "body-pain" and describes JEALOUSY or ENVY.

The entire body is also referenced in the following metaphors:

---

17. This metaphor can also be carried in a sentence: *ọ poo pẹgẹlẹya* "his stomach is white" (he is) KIND.

18. Tony Naden reports (p.c.) that in languages further north and east this expression connotes CRUELTY.

ọ ɛŋŋa kpɛŋŋeya	"his body strengthens"	HE IS HAPPY
ɛŋkpɛŋŋẹ	"body-strength"	HAPPINESS, JOY
kpɛŋŋera ẹ ɛŋŋa	"be strengthening your body"	BE ENCOURAGED

Like some other Safaliba words, *kpɛŋŋẹ* has a restricted usage. It occurs only in metaphorical constructions of this type and is no longer used in non-metaphorical constructions. By comparison with its cognates in related languages, and by looking at the meanings that occur in the metaphorical instructions, it appears that its original meaning was something like "strengthen." The meanings of the metaphorical constructions above are similar, but distinct. The first two constructions clearly connote the feeling of being HAPPY. However the third is somewhat different and means to BE ENCOURAGED. This may be in some way attributable to the *-ra* ending on the verb which indicates ongoing or continuous aspect.

ɛŋsunni	"body-pardon"	MERCY
sunne ọ ɛŋŋa	"pardon his body"	(show) MERCY (to him)

The word *sunne* is like *kpɛŋŋẹ* in that it occurs only in collocation with *ɛŋŋa* "body". The word itself may literally mean to "pardon" or to "forgive", but the constructions above refer specifically to the quality of MERCY.

6.   Comparison with metaphorical constructions in other area languages

To what extent then are the above metaphors particularly endangered? This depends to some extent on the degree to which they are shared with other languages in the area. In fact it appears that many of the metaphorical constructions documented above do not have exact parallels in other languages of Northern Ghana: either a different image is used to convey the same meaning, or else the same image is used convey a different meaning.

The following examples present some of the more clear examples of similarity and difference. Examples are taken from the following languages: Waali (which, along with the dialect of Dagaare spoken near Wa, is Safaliba's closest linguistic relative), Farefare (also closely-related language), Sisaala (distantly related), and Chumburung (from a completely different language family). The approximate location of these languages is indicated on the following map:

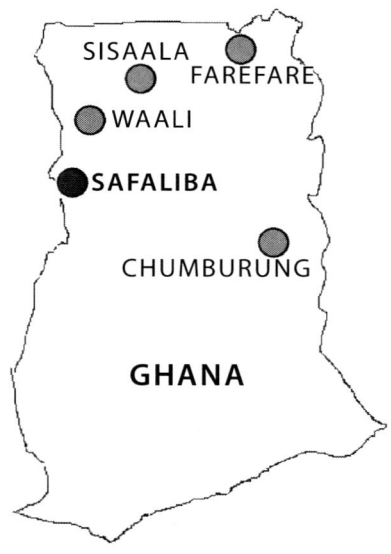

6.1   Metaphors with eye imagery

In Safaliba metaphorical usages of eye-imagery include the following:

nimbitooligu	"eye-heat"	FEARLESSNESS
nimbimaasego̱	"eye-cool"	CAREFULNESS
nimbimɔɔ	"eye-red"	SERIOUSNESS or HARDWORKING
nimbize̱aŋ	"eye-red"	TROUBLE
nimbikpɛɛne̱	"eye-hard"	PITILESS

Three of the comparison languages also use eye-imagery, however only one image, that of red eyes, is used consistently with the Safaliba and also has similar meaning. In Farefare, to have *nini mɔgere* "red eyes" means to be SERIOUS. In Waali, a *nimbijıa daana* "owner of red eyes" is SERIOUS about his work. It is interesting that, of the two Safaliba words for "red", Farefare uses the *mɔɔ* cognate in the same way as Safaliba, while Waali uses the *-ze̱aŋ* cognate to indicate SERIOUS rather than TROUBLE as in Safaliba. Finally, Sisaala has *sii-duoŋ* "eye-strong" which seems comparable (though not cognate) to Safaliba *nimbikpɛɛne̱* "eye-hard", however the meaning in Sisaala is PRIDE rather than PITILESS.

6.2 Metaphors with stomach and chest imagery

In Safaliba metaphorical usages of stomach-imagery include the following:

popɛɛlǫŋ	"stomach-white"	KINDNESS or OPENNESS
polikke	"stomach-dark"	EVIL-SCHEMING or SECRETIVE
potɔɔŋ	"stomach-bitter"	WICKEDNESS

Three of the comparison languages also use stomach-imagery, but with significant differences from Safaliba. In this case Waali shows the most similarity, having a very similar metaphor for KINDNESS or OPENNESS as Safaliba, the image of a white stomach: *o ɛ la popɪelaa daana* "he is a plain, honest, kind person" (though the emphasis seems slightly more towards plain and honest, rather than kind). In Farefare the same image occurs in the word *popeelom* "stomach-white" but it means HAPPINESS. Sisaala has a number of examples of stomach-imagery.[19] The only close parallel to Safaliba metaphor is *tuɔ-hɛɛŋ* "stomach-hard/bitter" which means WICKEDNESS, like Safaliba *potɔɔŋ*. For GRACIOUSNESS (a form of KINDNESS) Sisaala has *tuɔ-bala* "stomach-one", while the "white-stomach" image occurs as *tuɔ-pula* and means RIGHTEOUSNESS or GOODNESS.

The Safaliba metaphorical usages of chest-imagery include the following:

nyɛbirii	"whole-chest"	BOLDNESS
nyɛmaarẹ	"chest-coolness"	HAPPINESS

Only in the Waali data is there a similar construction: *sikirimaahʋ̃* apparently has the same literal and metaphorical meanings as Safaliba *nyɛmaarẹ*. However when the image is put in sentence form it becomes *ye bia maahʋ̃* "be in coolness", meaning be HAPPY. This loses the body-imagery and results in a simpler metaphor, TO BE COOL IS TO BE HAPPY. Sisaala has *bɔi-duoŋ* "chest-strong" for COURAGE or BOLDNESS, but it also has *nyu-duoŋ* "head-strong" and *tuɔ-doluŋ* "stomach-strong" for the same metaphorical meaning. Chumburung has *yee kẹkaŋ* "press chest" for WEEP IN SORROW (Hansford, 2005, p. 163), which is similar to but also rather different from Safaliba *dibi ẹ nyẹa* "press your chest" as a metaphor meaning BE CONSOLED (said to someone who is weeping in sorrow).

---

19. The Sisaala-English dictionary (Blass 1975) actually glosses *tuɔŋ* as "body-inside, emotions, character". I include Sisaala compound words with *tuɔŋ* with stomach-metaphors since *tuɔŋ* seems to be analogous to the words that literally mean "belly" or "abdomen" in other languages.

6.3   Metaphors with whole-body imagery

For the whole-body imagery metaphors, there is only limited similarity with other languages in the data. Only Waali keeps the imagery of the "body", for one construction, but with a different meaning: Safaliba ɛŋgambaaŋsɛ "body-pain" indicates ENVY and is similar in image to Waali ɪmbãahɪ daana "body-pain owner", but the Waali metaphor refers to a LAZY person.

Parallels to the other Safaliba constructions are only partial. Safaliba kpɛŋŋɛra ɛ ɛŋŋa "strengthen your body" meaning BE ENCOURAGED finds something of a parallel in Farefare kpɛ ho mɛŋa "strengthen your self", which means TRY HARDER. The related Safaliba sentence ɔ ɛŋŋa kpɛŋŋɛya "his body strengthens" meaning HE FEELS JOY is also partially paralleled by Waali m bia kpɛɛhʋ poo "I am in rejoicing"[20] – both are metaphors for JOY, but the word for "body" is missing in the Waali expression.

The Safaliba metaphor for PEACE or WELL-BEING (ɛŋgammaasegɔ "body-coolness") has parallels in other languages, but none uses the "body" part of the image. For WE ARE AT PEACE, Waali can say, tɪ bi la maahʋ poo "we are in coolness". PEACE is associated with coolness in particular body parts in other languages: in the stomach for Sisaala (tuɔ-fiɛla "stomach-cool"), and in the heart for Farefare (sumaahom "heart-cool") and Chumburung (kakpɔnɔ-yuri "heart-cool") (Hansford, 2005, p. 165). Thus the main consistency seen across these various metaphors and languages is TO BE COOL IS TO BE AT PEACE, but this metaphorical use of coolness is not consistently associated with a particular part of the body.

7.   What do these data suggest for "universals" in metaphor?

The "universal metaphors" listed by Kövecses do not appear to be very salient for Safaliba and the other languages examined for this study. Rather than HAPPINESS IS UP or any of the other suggested universals, for the people of northern Ghana it is more like HAPPINESS/PEACE/WELL-BEING IS BEING COOL. Hansford found similar results for Chumburung (2005, p. 64), stating that happiness, sadness, and anger were not typically represented by the suggested universal metaphors. In fact, judging by the diversity of metaphorical expression found within a comparatively small (but still linguistically diverse) set of data; it appears that conceptual metaphors are potentially very open-ended. Even among a few of the languages and

---

20. This is another possible piece of evidence suggesting that Safaliba kpɛŋŋɛ and its cognate in Waali at least are not preserved in non-metaphorical language.

cultures of northern Ghana, there seems to be great diversity of expression and metaphor-creation. Therefore it seems likely that any in-depth comparison among typologically different languages and diverse cultures is likely to reveal far more diversity than similarity.[21]

In this brief survey of a few metaphors on a limited semantic area there appear to be only a few points of consistency of metaphor imagery or meaning across the various languages considered. The one thing that seems consistent is that in this part of the world, body parts and various qualifications (color, temperature, etc.) are commonly used to express emotions and characteristics. It would be possible to do a more exhaustive study and determine more clearly if any clear patterns exist. However, such patterns would be mainly applicable to languages which use a similar type of metaphor for concepts in a similar domain. This suggests that in other parts of the world there may be equally great diversity in images and patterning principles, which would suggest that any truly "universal" tendencies in metaphor would be difficult to capture except in the most abstract (and hence less "interesting") formulations.

A note on the data

The Safaliba data presented have been extracted from data collected over a number of years. Though it is impossible to list all the other Safaliba people who have at one time or another contributed insights into their language, I must specifically mention the late Mr. Amaaliya Mbatumwine who did more than any other single person to convey to me something of the richness and breadth of the Safaliba language. I would also like to thank Mr. Eden Kosiaku, a schoolteacher who has been instrumental in developing Safaliba written materials and encouraging community literacy classes, for doing a final check to confirm the forms and meanings of the Safaliba words and expressions documented in this paper.

For comparative data I have mostly made use of work done by my colleagues in GILLBT: for Chumburung I used Hansford's (2005) article on Chumburung body metaphor; for Sisaala, the Sissaala-English dictionary compiled by Blass (1975); and for Farefare, data collected by my parents, Robert and Nancy Schaefer. For Waali, which remains fairly undocumented, I collected data from an adult L1 speaker of Waali from the city of Wa.

---

21. For example, in Safaliba a PITILESS person has "hard eyes", but in English he has a "hard heart". However in Classical Hebrew, to have a "hard heart" means that a person is STUBBORN; which in English metaphor is called having a "stiff neck" but in Safaliba having *tokpɛɛŋsɛ* or "hard ears".

References

Allman, J., & Parker, J. (2005). *Tongnaab: The history of a West African god*. Bloomington, Indiana: Indiana University Press.

Blass, R. (Ed.). (1975). *Sisaala-English/English-Sisaala Dictionary*. Tamale, Ghana: Institute of Linguistics.

Comrie, B. (1989). *Language universals and linguistic typology* (2nd ed.). Chicago: University of Chicago Press.

Fortes, M. (1945). *The dynamics of clanship among the Tallensi: Being the first part of an analysis of the social structure of a Trans-Volta tribe*. London: Oxford University Press for the International African Institute.

Fortes, M. (1949). *The web of kinship among the Tallensi: The second part of an analysis of the social structure of a Trans-Volta tribe*. London: Oxford University Press for the International African Institute.

Goody, E. (1973). *Contexts of Kinship: An essay in the family sociology of the Gonja of Northern Ghana*. (Cambridge Studies in Social Anthropology, 7). Cambridge: Cambridge University Press.

Goody, E. (1982). *Parenthood and social reproduction: Fostering and occupational roles in West Africa*. Cambridge: Cambridge University Press.

Goody, J. (1956). *The social organization of the LoWiili*. (Colonial Research Studies, 19). London: Her Majesty's Stationery Office.

Goody, J. (1962). *Death, property, and the ancestors: A study of the mortuary customs of the Lodagaa of West Africa*. London: Tavistock Publications.

Hansford, G. (2005). Body metaphor in Chumburung. *Journal of West African Languages*, 32(1–2): 135–180.

Kirby, J.P. (1986). *Gods, shrines, and problem-solving among the Anufɔ of northern Ghana*. (Collectanea Instituti Anthropos, 34). Berlin: Deitrich Reimer Verlag.

Johnson, M. (1987). *The body in the mind: The bodily basis of meaning, imagination, and reason*. Chicago: University of Chicago Press.

Kövecses, Z. (2002). *Metaphor: A practical introduction*. Oxford University Press.

Lakoff, G. (1987). *Women, fire, and dangerous things: What categories reveal about the mind*. Chicago: University of Chicago Press. DOI: 10.7208/chicago/9780226471013.001.0001

Lakoff, G., & Johnson, M. (1980). *Metaphors we live by*. Chicago: University of Chicago Press.

Lakoff, G., & Johnson, M. (1999). *Philosophy in the flesh: The embodied mind and its challenge to Western thought*. New York: Basic Books.

Merleau-Ponty, M. 1962. *Phenomenology of perception*. London: Routledge.

Oware Knudsen, Ch. (1994). *The falling dawadawa tree: Female circumcision in developing Ghana*. Højbjerg, Denmark: Intervention Press.

Piot, Ch. (1999). *Remotely global: Village modernity in West Africa*. Chicago: University of Chicago Press.

Schaefer, P. (2009). *Narrative storyline marking in Safaliba: Determining the meaning and discourse function of a typologically-suspect pronoun set*. PhD dissertation, University of Texas at Arlington.

Schaefer, P., & Schaefer, J. (2003). *Collected field reports on the phonology of Safaliba*. (Collected Language Notes, 25). Legon, Ghana: Institute of African Studies, University of Ghana.

Schaefer, P., & Schaefer, J. (2004). Verbal and nominal structures in Safaliba. In M. E. Kropp Dakubu & E. K. Osam (Eds.), *Studies in the languages of the Volta Basin II* (pp. 183–201). Legon, Ghana: Department of Linguistics, University of Ghana.

Skinner, E. (1964). *The Mossi of the Upper Volta: The political development of a Sudanese people.* Stanford: Stanford University Press.

Wilks, I. (1989). *Wa and the Wala: Islam and polity in northwestern Ghana.* (African Studies Series, 63). Cambridge: Cambridge University Press.

Wilks, I. (2000). The Juula and the expansion of Islam into the forest. In N. Levtzion & R. L. Pouwels (Eds.), *The history of Islam in Africa* (pp. 93–115). Athens/Ohio: Ohio University Press.

Wilks, I., Levtzion, N., & Haight, B. (1986). *Chronicles from Gonja.* Cambridge: Cambridge University Press.

CHAPTER 6

Literacy and language instruction

Flathead Salish metaphor and a task-based pedagogy for its revitalization

Ari Sherris, Tachini Pete and Erin Haynes

Texas A&M University-Kingsville / Confederated Salish and Kootenai Tribes / American Institutes for Research

Flathead Salish, a critically endangered language spoken by dwindling numbers of first language speakers from the Confederated Salish and Kootenai Tribes in Montana, USA, is the object of collaborative efforts at language revitalization. Often such efforts rely on traditional categories of language from which to base dictionaries, pedagogical grammars, and language textbooks for heritage learners, both children and adults. Missing from most revitalization efforts is the analysis of conceptual metaphors that could support language and literacy revitalization by supporting the semantic and pragmatic underpinnings of the language and potentially reducing calquing by heritage learners, or at the very least, alerting learns to its occurrences. Consequently, this study fills a gap by describing 19 metaphors, comparing them to English, and illustrating possible task-based language teaching approaches for their use.

Keywords: Flathead Salish, Conceptual Metaphor Theory, task-based language teaching, Montana Salish, language revitalization

1. Introduction

Flathead Salish is part of a large and growing group of languages that are classified as endangered, or restricted in use and inter-generational transmission (see Fishman, 2001). It is a critically endangered language with dwindling numbers of first language speakers ($N < 50$). Lexical, morphological, phonological, and syntactic studies of the Salishan language family, comprising 23 languages (Kiyosawa & Donna, 2010), have been produced (for a review see Kroeber, 1999). Absent from this corpus of scholarly endeavor is the study of Salish

DOI 10.1075/clscc.7.05she

metaphor. The purpose of this chapter is to add to the body of work on Salish with an exploration of everyday metaphor (Lakoff & Johnson, 1999, 2003) in Flathead Salish, comparing it with English language metaphor, and suggesting pedagogical applications for youth and adult curricula in community language revitalization efforts among English speakers for whom Salish is a heritage language (Sherris et al., 2013). Our methodology is the exploration of the role of metaphor as it resonates from concrete human experiences (e.g. movement, proximity) to abstract experiences (e.g., affection, importance, happiness), with attention to the cultural differences between English and Flathead Salish (after Lakoff & Johnson, 1999). Flathead Salish metaphors are compared to English metaphors along the same dimensions and task-based interactive activities (Ellis, 2003; Long, 2015; Van den Branden et al., 2009) discussed as a way to facilitate Flathead Salish second language everyday metaphors among language learners.

However, before we undertake an analysis of metaphor, it is necessary to sketch some background. Hence, in the next section, we briefly discuss the tribes for whom Flathead Salish is a heritage language as well as an encapsulated sense of their history.

2. Flathead Salish people

Archeological evidence demonstrates First Peoples occupied areas of British Columbia, Canada 12,000 years ago, and they were most likely the early ancestors of the Flathead Salish. As they grew and prospered, the Salishan people moved northward and also southward to what is currently the US state of Washington, eventually crossing the Cascade Mountain range to settle what is today northern Oregon, Idaho, and eventually Western Montana. Regional dialects eventually developed due to geographic challenges and contact with different ambient languages (Thompson & Egesdal, 2008).

Fast-forward to 1800 and we find Interior Salish people lived in forested mountain and semi-desert landscapes, experiencing colder winters than their relatives along the Northwest Coast, which was temperate by comparison. Nevertheless, culturally, there were many similarities among Coastal and Interior Salish people during the 1800s, including feasts for first fruits (bitterroot and other plants) and first salmon (with the sacred return of salmon bones to the rivers to guarantee plentiful salmon in the future). Cultural rituals for Coastal and Interior Salish youth reaching puberty provided opportunities for them to seek guardian spirits, whereas throughout their lives healing, bewitching, and blessing were additional spiritually life-sustaining rituals. Moreover, both Coastal and Interior

Salish people participated in sweathouse activities for cleansing and psychic health (Thompson & Egesdal, 2008).

These cultural traditions continue today, though they were severely interrupted in the 1800s through a growing presence of European settlers, traveling salesman, and gold-miners, who introduced disease that took the lives of many in the Salish communities of Montana and elsewhere. Forced re-settlement disrupted tribal life for the Bitterroot Salish, the Pend d'Oreille and the Kootenai, three Montana Salish tribes who were forced to settle on the Flathead Reservation (Confederated Flathead and Kootenai Tribes, 2004). Perhaps more disruptive to Salish culture, Salish youth were forced to attend US government-founded boarding schools. These youth were torn from their families, culture, and language as was the fate for indigenous youth throughout the US as government officials enacted a relentlessly aggressive, horrific, and racist assimilationist ideology to squelch indigenous cultures (Reyhner & Eder, 2004). Nonetheless, the Flathead Salish prevailed. Though the language is now endangered, it is still spoken, and a new generation is learning it in an immersion environment. In the next section, we briefly discuss the Flathead Salish language, followed by a description of Flathead Salish immersion schooling.

2.1   Flathead Salish

The variety of Salish spoken today by the Confederated Salish and Kootenai Tribes of the Flathead Reservation in Montana is a highly agglutinative language of the Interior Salish branch in the Salishan language family (Thomason, 2006). The language developed from contacts among Bitterroot Salish, Pend d'Oreille, Spokane, and Kalispel speakers. It has extended suffixation encoding semantic and syntactic import (e.g., affixes demonstrate transitivity, voice, aspect, and number, with many being reduplicative) (Thomason, 1994). While not as prevalent as suffixes, infixes – for locative purpose – and prefixes also play a role in the language. Flathead Salish grammar generally divides vocabulary into two parts – words that can be predicated and verbs that cannot. Verbs are usually found in the initial position in utterances and sentences, making VSO (verb-subject-object) the default word order, but not the only one as there is, indeed, some flexibility.

Some linguists represent Salish as a language that lacks clearly articulated distinctions among word-class types such as nouns, verbs, and adjectives (Thompson & Egesdal, 2008; Kroeber, 1999), but this is not universally agreed upon. Other researchers argue against this position (Eijk & Hess, 1986; Kinkade, 1983). This is a language that remains of great interest to linguists. The next section introduces revitalization efforts.

2.2   Flathead reservation immersion education

Today, Flathead Salish children can attend the Snq̓ʷiiq̓ʷo Salish language immersion school (also called the Nk̓ʷusm Language Institute), which was established in 2002 as a preschool, but which today serves twenty-five students in pre-kindergarten through Grade 8 (data from the 2012–2013 school year; Nk̓ʷusm Language Institute, 2013). Students receive instruction through the medium of Flathead Salish, a polysynthetic language of the Interior Salish branch in the Salishan language family (see Sherris et al., 2013, for a full description of the school's history and Pete, 2010, for a pedagogical discussion of the Flathead Salish language). Other schools have less intensive community, heritage, and after school and after work programs for children and adults, also on the Flathead reservation (e.g., St. Ignatius Elementary School, Arlee, Flathead). A sustained effort at tertiary course offerings in Salish has been designed and maintained by the Salish Kootenai College, also on the Flathead Reservation. Finally, there are some online materials that can be accessed, though none of these, nor any of the educational programs have specific metaphor development as a component to our knowledge.

For the continued vitality of this language, it is crucial to discover effective ways to teach it to the younger generation, especially those whose home language is English. In this paper, we explore a method for strategically utilizing Salish metaphors to this end. In the next section, we briefly describe a construct of everyday metaphor that informs our research.

3.   Metaphor studies

Lakoff and Johnson (1980) were the pioneers in the field of linking metaphor to the basic components of language. They identified and analyzed the everyday uses of metaphor – its prosaic permeation of cognition and its ubiquitous, "mostly unconscious" (Lakoff, 1993, p. 247), resonance in abstract and conceptual systems. They have also been keen on pointing out that the novel use of metaphor in poetry, for instance, is based on the understandings between conceptual domains of knowledge not unlike the everyday use (Lakoff, 1993, p. 248). Basing work on that of Reddy (1979), who showed that the conduit metaphor influences literal thought, Lakoff (1993) further dispelled the notion of hard and fast boundaries between literal and figurative thought in his subsequent research. He argues that, "A sentence like 'the balloon went up' is not metaphorical, nor is the old philosopher's favorite 'the cat is on the mat.' But as soon as one gets away from concrete physical experience and starts talking about abstractions or emotions, metaphorical understand is the norm" (1993, p. 205).

According to Lakoff and Johnson (1980), human sensory-motor experiences are categorized through language, giving rise to the use of metaphor to tie our concrete experiences to more complex concepts. In this conceptualization, also adopted in this paper, the concrete, experiential aspect is the source domain, and the complex concept it embodies is the target domain. Lakoff and Johnson also introduce the notion that culture plays a role in this categorization of language, because it shapes our subjective experience beyond the sensory experiences common to all humans: "Try to imagine a culture where arguments are not viewed in terms of war, where no one wins or loses, where there is not sense of attacking or defending, gaining or losing ground. Imagine a culture where an arguments is viewed as a dance [...] In such a culture, people would view arguments differently, experience them differently, and talk about them differently" (1980, p. 125). According to their theory, metaphors may create realities.

Sidestepping the essentialism that this view may give rise to, it is worth considering that some experiences are so fundamental to human experience that they will result in the same linguistic patterns in a multitude of unrelated languages. Kövecses (2002) shows that metaphors are rooted in human experience and argues that they result in the same linguistic patterns in a variety of otherwise unrelated languages. However, these theories have not been widely tested, especially with languages indigenous to North America.

Intriguingly, Palmer (1998), a scholar of Native American languages, began to look at the conceptual semantics of endangered languages, including interior Salish languages, but did not explore conceptual metaphor, although he did cite Lakoff & Johnson's (1980) seminal text on conceptual metaphor in passing recognition, and he suggested the field of conceptual semantics be expanded as a future research direction for Salishan languages. While this research has not yet been conducted in the Salishan languages, a small amount of research has been conducted on other endangered languages from the Americas. Rice (2012) analyzes figurative expressions in Dene Sųłiné, an Athapaskan language. She concludes that metaphor mappings of target and source domains hold great promise for linguists willing to move beyond an isomorphic treatment of meaning and beyond the cataloguing of "items on the basis of the free gloss", encouraging "a more open-minded posture that looks for literal and figurative" mappings within the semantic analyses of endangered languages (p. 72). Rice illustrates this by analyzing how sets of items share root stems or constructions, such as between the following three sets of terms from her analyses: (1) 'blood clot' and 'cheese curds'; (2) 'snow' and 'toothpaste'; (3) and with respect to 'waking up', 'aging', and 'dying' in Dene Sųłiné") (Rice, 2012, p. 72).

Intriguingly, Rice's fluent speakers characterize their language as literal and are often not aware of these correspondences, whereas in Pasamonik's (2012) research, albeit in a different endangered Canadian language, metalinguistic insights from her cohort of fluent speakers "unveil crucial meaning components which are extracted as departing points for prototypical meanings to create further sense through elaboration" (Pasamonik, 2012, p. 78). Pasamonik (2012) analyzes metaphoric and metonymic mappings from body parts to abstract emotions and personal traits in Beaver Athabascan. The work of both Rice (2012) and Pasamonik (2012) provide important seminal claims for their respective endangered languages. Finally, Lovick's (2012) recent study of animal idioms in Upper Tanana, an Alaskan Athabascan language, concludes that "colloquial speech is getting lost even more quickly than the more formal genre used for narratives" (p. 119) and that "idioms seem to be disappearing even faster" (p. 119). We understand this as is a clarion call for documentation of not just animal idioms, but all such subtle semantic and pragmatic aspects of talk, especially among very critically endangered languages including conceptual metaphor.

Conceptual metaphor theory assumes that metaphor and even more broadly, the structure of language, reflects the structure of cognition, which we contend is only partly the case. It is also true that metaphor and the structure of language reflect culture and environmental stimuli. While there are numerous critiques of CMT (e.g., Kövecses identifies five and addresses them, 2002), the most profound, perhaps, is that any theory, such as CMT, that is focused fundamentally on a better understanding of cognition will less adequately address links to culture and environment. While this might be true if it is accompanied by ideological blinders, it is not intrinsic to a CMT perspective. Cultural perspectives only add, rather than detract from CMT. We explore these notions in more detail in the next section with a comparison of English and Salish source domains for a sample set of target domains.

3.1   Montana Salish metaphors

The following is a brief catalogue of nineteen Montana Salish metaphors. Each metaphor characteristically has a source domain and a target domain. Source domains are less abstract than target domains. For instance, with respect to the English metaphor LIFE IS A JOURNEY, the source domain is *journey*, a concrete concept vis-à-vis LIFE, an abstract target domain. The source domain helps us better understand the target domain (Lakoff & Johnson, 1980). Following the presentations of Salish target and source domains, we also provide the closest English source domain to serve as a point of comparison for each target. Then, we discuss similarities and differences in Flathead Salish and English source domains. Our inspiration for this work derives from Matsuki's (1995) analyses of the similarities and differences between English and Japanese metaphors. We conclude our work by taking a pedagogical turn, squarely positioning our voices in the critically important domain of language revitalization. In the final section of this paper, we present task-based language teaching ideas with some Flathead Salish examples that we believe will support metaphor development among L2 and heritage Flathead Salish learners.

ACHIEVING IS MOVING TO A STANDING POSITION
Salish example: tešlš łu qł ilmixʷm
Gloss: "rose to be the leader"
Translation: 'His/her achievements are great such that s/he can be the leader'
English source domain: ARE REACHING A DESIRED LOCATION/OBJECT (Lakoff, 1992)
English example: He reached his sales goal.

AFFECTION IS BEING IN CLOSE PROXIMITY
Salish example: łʔem-ncut
Gloss: "Close-one's self"
Translation: 'S/he is close (has a close relationship)'
English source domain: BEING IN CLOSE PROXIMITY
English example: Over time, we became very close.

ATTENTION IS FITTING TIGHTLY
Salish example: č-q̓ʔ-els-mn
Gloss: "purpose-fit tightly-feel-I"
Translation: 'I pay attention to it.'

Salish example: s-n-q̓ʔ-els
Gloss: "NOMINAL-within-fit tightly-feeling/fitted within"
Translation: 'business'
English source domain: AN OBJECT OF VALUE
English example: Pay attention
English example: Give me your attention

CATEGORIES ARE NARROWING
Salish example: n-k̓ʷnš-aqsm
Gloss: "inside-how-many-narrow.some"
Translation: 'how many kinds are there?'

Salish example: n-kʷtn-aqsm
Gloss: "inside-large-narrow.some"
Translation: 'important/expensive' (type)
English source domain: containers (Lakoff, 1992)
English example: They moved from the first category to the next category. [e.g., games]

CONTROL IS PRESSURE
Salish example: ṗič̣-mstn
Gloss: "pressure" TRANS.I
Translation: 'I control someone'
English source domain: pressure
English example: I pressured him into doing it.

DEATH IS TO BECOME MOTIONLESS
Salish example: x̣l-il
Gloss: "non.movement"-REDUPLACATIVE.become
Translation: 'die'
English source domain: departure (Lakoff, 1992)
English example: He left us last year.

DIFFICULTIES ARE BURDENS
Salish example: x̣emt łu ispuús
Gloss: "heavy DET my.heart"
Translation: 'My heart is heavy'. [I am much on my mind.]
English source domain: burdens (Lakoff, 1992)
English example: Our difficulties weighed on us heavily.

EXTREME IS AT THE TOP
Salish example: es-ya-p-qin
Gloss: STATIVE-"gather"-INCHOATIVE-top
Translation: 'powwow or celebration'

Salish example: q̣sp-qin
Gloss: "long time-top"
Translation: 'a very long time, live to old age'
English source domain: <u>extremely good</u> is at the top
English example: She's a top strategist.

FEELINGS ARE SUBSTANCES
Salish example: i łppeš łu aspuús
Gloss: "light DET your.heart"
Translation: 'Your heart is light'

Salish example: kʷ in-x̣m-enč
Gloss: "you mine-weighty-stomach"
Translation: 'I love you'.
English source domain: have physical weight
English example: His death weighs on me heavily.

IMPORTANCE/SIGNIFICANCE IS BIG
Salish example: kʷtunt sx̣lx̣alt
Gloss: "big day"
Translation: 'holiday'

Salish example: kʷtn-aqsm
Gloss: "big-kind"
Translation: 'important'
English source domain: big (Lakoff & Johnson, 1980)
English example: He's a giant among writers.

KNOWING IS BEING

Salish example: es-mi-sten
Gloss: "STATIVE-fact-transitive.1st"
Translation: 'I know it'
English source domain: seeing (Lakoff, 1992)
English example: I see what you're getting at.

MORE IS LOCATIVE

Salish example: tl'ciʔ kʷ čenčnt
Gloss: "from that you are slow"
Translation: 'You are slower'.

Salish example: tl'ciʔ kʷtunt
Gloss: "from that it is big"
Translation: 'It is bigger'.
English source domain: up (Lakoff & Johnson, 1980)
English example: His income rose.

ORGANIZING IDEAS IS A PHYSICAL STRUCTURE

Salish example: l čeň u axistn łu iqs kʼʷułm łu sckʼʷłpax̣-s
Gloss: "how DET I.IRREALIS make DET idea-his"
Translation: 'How do I put together his idea'?
English source domain: resources (Lakoff & Johnson, 1980)
English example: Let's pool our ideas.

SEEING IS FINDING

Salish example: čn x̣ʔem u wič-n
Gloss: "I search.PAST and see-TRANS.I"
Translation: 'I searched and found it'.
English source domain: touching (Lakoff, 1992)
English example: His eyes ran over the paintings.

SIMILARITY IS SMALL

Salish example: i ł-qʷ-qʷin łu šeẏ
Gloss: "indicator DIMINUTIVE-dim.REDUPLICATION-green DET that"
Translation: 'It's almost green'.
English source domain: physical closeness
English example: It touches on the same topics.

SUBVERSIVE ACTIVITY IS UNDER
Salish example: k̓ʷɬ-tqem
Gloss: "under-place.down"
Translation: 'procrastinate'

Salish example: k̓ʷɬ-x̌ʷel
Gloss: "under-abandon"
Translation: 'ruin'

Salish example: k̓ʷɬ-nq̓ʷ-mist
Gloss: "under-steal-of.the.self"
Translation: 'sneak away'

Salish example: k̓ʷɬ-ƛ̓eʔ-mist
Gloss: "under-search-of.the.self"
Translation: 'be jealous'
English source domain: under
English example: the seedy underbelly of the industry

TIME IS MOTION
Salish example: x̌ʷuy u čn k̓ʷɬči
Gloss: "go CONJUNCTION I arrived"
Translation: 'time went by and I arrived'

Salish example: put t čeṅ u kʷ iɬn
Gloss: "just(harmonious state) INDICATOR where(what state) CONJUNCTION you eat"
Translation: 'When will you eat'?
English source domain: motion (Lakoff, 1992)
English example: Time goes so slowly.

UNDERSTANDING IS HEARING
Salish example: čnes-n-sux̌ʷ-neʔ
Gloss: "1st.STATIVE-inside-recognition-ear"
Translation: 'I understand'.
English source domain: seeing (Lakoff & Johnson, 1980)
English example: I see what you're saying.

WAITING IS SITTING
Salish example: n-ʔemt-ew̓s
Gloss: "Inside-sit/dwell-between"
Translation: 'wait'
English source domain: sitting
English example: Let's just sit on this idea for a while.

Of the examples provided here, eight of the Salish source domains are the same as English (affection, control, difficulties, feelings, important, time, waiting, and subversive activity). Table 1 shows the comparison. An additional two categories are similar: extreme and more. For extreme, English has the same source domain (*at the top*), but only for one sub-category of the Salish target domain. That is, for Salish, all extremities are at the top, but for English, only the extremely good are at the top. Similarly, more is locative in both Salish and English, but in English, the locomotion is directional (i.e., upwards).

Table 1. Salish and English source domains for target domains

Target domain	Salish source domain	English source domain
Same/Similar		
affection	close proximity	close proximity
control	pressure	pressure
difficulties	burdens	burdens
extreme	at the top	at the top (*extremely good*)
feelings	substances	substances
important	big	big
more	locative	up
subversive activity	under	under
time	motion	motion
waiting	sitting	sitting
Different		
achieving	moving to a standing position	reaching a desired location
attention	fitting tightly	an object of value
categories	narrowing	containers
death	to become motionless	departure
knowing	existence	seeing
organizing ideas	a physical structure	resources
seeing	finding	touching
similarity	small	physical closeness
understanding	hearing	seeing

The remaining nine, or roughly half of the examples provided here have no comparison to English. Several of the source domains that differ (attention, knowing, seeing, death, and understanding) would appear to be very deeply rooted in sensory-motor experience, and the fact that they are different in English may appear to fly in the face of the hypothesis that fundamental metaphors embody our sensory-motor experiences. However, the differences that arise are the result of the fact that each of these experiences is complex, and can therefore give rise to a variety of different metaphors.

In fact, in two of these cases, English has phrases indicating a shared understanding of the Salish source domain, even if the English source domain differs. First, in Salish, categories are *narrowing*, while in English they are *containers*. But we also understand narrowing in the realm of categories as in the phrase, *I want to narrow down my choices before I decide.* Similarly, though death is *to become motionless* in Salish but *departure* in English, we make reference to the stillness of death in similes like, *she was as still as death.*

Another example is understanding, which is *hearing* in Salish and *seeing* in English. Both seeing and hearing have a role in our ability to learn about and eventually understand something, and a language might arbitrarily choose either to signify understanding.

One might also point to the cultural weight given to seeing or hearing as a means of understanding; in Salish culture, more importance is given to oral traditions, while in cultures that primarily speak English, more importance is often given to written traditions. However more data points would be required from other languages to make this assertion definitively. Other cultural differences are clearer. For example, in English knowing is also *seeing,* whereas in Salish it is *existence.* Indeed, the root word of the example given, *mi* (es-mi-sten >> I know it), is considered a philosophical core of Salish. It expresses the perceptive state of existence as experienced by the senses of sight, smell, touch, hearing and extrasensory perception. In Salish culture, knowledge is more than what one sees; it springs from our existence as perceptive beings.

A similar example of cultural differences embodied in linguistic metaphors is attention, which in English is *an object of value,* whereas in Salish, it is *fitting tightly.* In cultures that primarily speak English, there tends to be high value placed on competition among individuals (e.g., Steward & Bennet, 1991), whereas Salish culture tends to be highly collaborative. So for English speakers, one may view another person's attention as something one competes for, or that attention is something that one doles out (e.g., *grab his attention, give his attention to the problem*), whereas in Salish, people meet in a close collaboration (i.e., *fitting together*) in the act of attention.

Another example of how the different source domains point to differences in culture is achieving, which is *moving to a standing position (rising up)* in Salish, but is *reaching a desired location/object* in English. These source domains are fundamentally different in that achieving metaphorically arises within a person in Salish, but is something that someone goes after in English, with a focus on getting to the desired achievement, no matter where it is located. This linguistic difference is perhaps a reflection of the difference in culturally appropriate ways to attain a skill in the cultures that primarily speak the two languages. In Salish culture, it is most appropriate to quietly watch an expert, then practice a skill on one's own, not exhibiting it to others until one is fully successful – as such, the achievement comes at the end of an invisible process, appearing to rise up in one. In the mainstream culture of English speakers, on the other hand, it is appropriate to practice a skill in front of others, even failing at times, until it is finally mastered. The achievement comes at the end of a process that is fully visible to others, and so it is fitting that the metaphor is in reference to this process.

The primary implications of these findings for instruction is that heritage learners must learn to recognize that the two languages differ at a very fundamental level if their first language is English. Direct translation – even of concepts that feel "natural" in English because they are so engrained in the language – will seldom result in comprehensible Salish. On the other hand, if Salish learners become familiar with the metaphors that underlie Salish, they may have a means to unlock meanings at a very basic level without having to learn direct translations of every word and phrase. For Flathead Salish learners who are part of Salish culture, learning source domains may be a more natural process than it would be for people who are not members of the culture, because many of the domains appear to depend on the cultural interpretation of sensory-motor experiences. However, this latter point is speculation only and will have to be explored in future research. The next section delves into the notion of metaphor through task-based learning in language instruction.

4.   Task-based language learning and teaching (TBLT)

In this section we will use the acronym TBLT as shorthand for both *learning* and *teaching* through tasks. As such, tasks become the teaching vehicles through which learning transpires. A teacher's main role is planning, sequencing, and facilitating tasks, as well as demonstrating and delivering input and feedback. TBLT classrooms are learner-centered (Long, 2015; Norris, 2009).

A task is an active learning episode where language is utilized to do something. As learners engage in a task they may follow a sequence of steps that are explicitly presented to them as input, or they may have to discover the steps through trial and error. Tasks have been conceptualized as plan, structure, and frame (Breen, 1989) and more recently as "state space landscape[s]" (Larsen-Freeman & Cameron, 2008, p. 212) allowing for holistic conceptualizations of language use that in theory lead to successive restructurings of language rather than its bit-by-bit accretion which is aligned with second language learning research (Corder, 1978; McLaughlin, 1990; Larsen-Freeman, 2006).

Task input includes written or auditory language and task output is spoken or written. Learners in a TBLT class usually enact the tasks in pairs or among small groups of learners (e.g., 3–4), although there may be smaller amounts of independent work such as individual planning time. Nevertheless, if there is time for individual planning, it is often followed by planning by pairs of learners, such as when pairs are required to reach consensus on a particular topic or issue.

Meaning making in interactive tasks characterize TBLT. A task can include reading, writing, listening and speaking in the target language and usually combines these language modalities. TBLT is active, rather than passive, learning. Task-based language teaching (TBLT) focuses learners primarily on meaning, rather than formal rules for saying and understanding language, but there might be incidental foci on form, or planned input flooding of form (described below).

There are many kinds of tasks (e.g., information gap, retellings, Talmudic pair work, input flooding, and text jigsaws). We are going to present different combinations or varied sequences of retellings and Talmudic pair work for Salish Metaphor TBLT. First, we will share short sample texts that are seeded, or rich, in Salish metaphors as examples of input flooding. Then, we will define input flooding, retelling tasks and Talmudic pair work. Finally, we will discuss different task sequences as well as briefly illustrate some of those with a Salish text rich in everyday metaphors.

4.1   Sample Salish text

Two sample Flathead Salish texts were created for input flooding. Each text is followed by its translation to English. The translation is first in paragraph format that is separate and distinct from the Salish paragraph. This is followed by a word-for-word translation under each word to give the reader word-order knowledge. After this, the actual metaphors are in list format with identifications listed. The paragraphs are examples of input flooding. Input flooding is a technique in which a rich written or spoken text has been seeded with the formal structures to be utilized and internalized by the learners. In the first example, metaphors seed a short personal narrative on singing.

Salish texts: ńe u qʷo sewntm čiqs nkʷnéyi l **kʷtunt** sx̣lx̣alt še ʕʷosn łu **kʷtiłqʷelm** še čn psap u ečx̣i čnes nte čiqs **kʷłnq̇ʷmísti**, pṅ es **misten** ńe ʕʷosn łu iqs nkʷnem še čn **nʔemtéẃsm** u nq̇ʔelsmn łu **nkʷtnaqsm** qʷelm, tlʼ čeṅ u daqʷcínm kʷemt, tlʼ šeẏ **xʷuy** u **tešlš** ci qʷelm še **wičn** łu ies x̣̓ʔem, kʷemt x̣ʷa **put t čeṅ** u eł nłkʷkʷmin še nkʷen u čnes nx̣̓cini u **nx̣asq̇íni**

Translation: Whenever I'm asked to sing on special occasions I lose the important song. Then I start to get nervous and feel like sneaking away. But I know if I wait and focus on the value of the song and where it comes from, then it will come about for me to see. Right when I remember I sing it loud and clear.

Word order of translation:

ṅe   u   qʷo sewntm čiqs   nkʷnéyi l **kʷtunt** sx̣lx̣alt
when and me asked   1st.irrealis singing at big   day

še   ʕʷosn   łu   **kʷtiłqʷelm**
then I.lost.it DET important.song

še   čn psap   u   ečx̣i   čnes nte   čiqs   **k̓ʷłnq̓ʷmísti,**
then I   get.nervous and it's.like I.am want 1st.irrealis sneak.self.away

pṅ es   **misten**   ṅe   ʕʷosn   łu   iqs   nkʷnem
but STATIVE I.know.it when I.lost.it DET 1st.irrealis sing

še   čn **nʔemtew̓sm** u   nq̓ʔelsmn   **łu nkʷtnaqsm**   qʷelm,
then I   wait   and focus.attention.on.it DET valuable.thing song

tl̓   čeṅ   u   c̓łaqʷcinm
from where and voice.appeared

kʷemt tl̓   šeẏ **x̌ʷuy**   u   **tešlš**   ci   qʷelm
then from that time.goes and stand.up that song

še   **wičn**   łu   ies   ƛ̓ʔem,
then I.see.it DET 1st.stative search

kʷemt x̌ʷa   **put t čeṅ**   u   eł   nłkʷkʷmin
then   maybe just ind where and back I.remember.it

še   nkʷen   u   čnes   nx̣̓x̣cíni   u   **nx̣asqíni**
then I.sing.it and 1st.stative loud.voice and be.at.height.of.doing

Metaphor analysis:

kʷtunt sx̣lx̣alt	transliteration: *big day*
holiday	metaphorical meaning: *important is big*
skʷtił-qʷelm	transliteration: *big-song*
important-song	metaphorical meaning: *important is big*
čiqs **k̓ʷł-nq̓ʷ-místi**	transliteration: *I'm going under-steal-self*
I'm going to sneak away	metaphorical meaning: *subversive activity is under*
es **misten**	transliteration: *stative reality-1st.pronoun*
I know it	metaphorical meaning: *knowing is existence*
čn **n-ʔemt-ew̓sm**	literal translation: *I inside-sit-between*
I wait	metaphorical meaning: *waiting is sitting*
n-**kʷtn-aqsm** qʷelm	transliteration: *nominal-inside-big-narrowed song*
valued song	metaphorical meaning: *important/significant is big, categorizing is narrowing*

xʷuy u tešlš ci qʷelm   transliteration: *time goes and it rises*
it goes and come about   metaphorical meaning: *time is locative and*
                                achievements rise up

wičn   transliteration: *I see it*
I see it   metaphorical meaning: *finding is seeing*

put t čeṅ   transliteration: *harmonious state where*
right when   metaphorical meaning: *time is locative*

čnes … **n-x̣as-qin**   transliteration: *I inside-good-top*
I preform at height of ability metaphorical meaning: *extreme is at the top*

In the second example, the metaphors seed a description of a man and his dream.

Salish texts: l šeẏ u łu sqltmixʷ iše **es ntx̣ʷaqs** kʷemt łu l šeẏ u ep scc̣cox̣ʷ še es musc̣st hoy tl ci še es **q̓ʷiłčst** łu ax̣tčim še k̓ʷI̓nuis kʷemt x̣ʷa **es tuk̓ʷ** l šušewułs še iqʷem̓tmsts u **šlič** pn **ta snisaqm** u **ta sp̓l̓čus** kʷemt łu es **k̓ʷtistl̓xʷeli** łu l **aytčsmis** še x̣ʷu u sq̓si u **es nʔamtaqs** še xʷuy u aytčsmis kʷemt xʷuy u **q̓ʷm̓małqis** łu scc̣coxʷ's hoy xʷuy u iše k̓ʷI̓nuis kʷemt łu **l nk̓ʷuʔ** še šeẏ u ec̣xi łu **l snspsupps** łu es ewti ci citxʷ łu **es nṗexʷełc̣eʔ** es nʔac̣xelsi x̣ʷa stem l šeẏ hoy es čsax̣msts łu citxʷ łu **es nṗexʷełc̣eʔ** kʷemt łu es čsax̣ms hoy ec̣xi es xʷpmulexʷ u es lkʷkʷstem łu citxʷ hoy tl ci yoyoscut u čsax̣m hoy eł lkʷkʷstem kʷemt tl ci kʷtisyoyoscut še tl ci u es nṗexʷełc̣eʔ citxʷ hoy ec̣xi es kʷtntwilši łu citxʷ hoy u es kʷtisyoyoscut kʷemt axi xi ṅe u k̓ʷI̓nuis łu k̓ʷłc̣icis pn put u qs k̓ʷI̓nunms še qiłt hoy es aymti x̣ʷI̓ tas k̓ʷI̓nuis es **kʷtisnʔac̣xelsi** pn puti es **čsʔitši** hoy qmip u es miscut puti **es ntx̣ʷaqs** hoy eł itš

Translation: There was a man who lived a discerning life. When he had the gumption to do something he would do it with all the confidence in the world. He would really put his all into whatever it was and accomplish the task whatever it may be. Even when faced with great challenge in his life he would always preserver no matter how long it took. He never gave up or deviated from his goal. He would get near completion through all adversity and by his strong will complete even the most difficult task. So it was one time in a dream. He was set on sneaking up to a well-lit house in the dark. He wanted to see what or who was inside. As he drew closer it was like the distance to it would get longer and longer. It was as if the house was moving further away. He would try harder and harder. Finally through all his efforts he was almost there. As he got close, the light from the house grew brighter and brighter. After much effort and try he was almost to the house, he could almost see in, when suddenly he woke. Oh he was so angry that he didn't get to the house. He really wanted to look in. But he was still sleepy. He calmed down fully aware that he still lives a discerning life and fell back asleep.

Word order of translation:

l   šey u   łu sqltmixʷ iše   **es**   **ntx̣ʷaqs**
at that and DET man   always STATIVE straight.road

kʷemt łu l   šey u   ep   scčcoxʷ še   es   musčst
then   DET at that and have intention then STATIVE do.with.confidence

hoy   tl   ci   še   es   **q̓ʷiłčst**   łu ax̣tčim še   k̓ʷl̓nuis
INTERJ from that then STATIVE do.with.energy DET busy   then finish.it

kʷemt x̣ʷa **es**   **tuk̓ʷ**   l   šušewułs še   iqʷem̓tmsts   u   **šlič**
then   maybe STATIVE placed.down at his.road   then he.preservered.it and go.around

ta snisaqm   u   **ta sp̓lč̓us**
no turn.off.road and no turn.back

kʷemt łu   es   **kʷtistl̓x̣ʷeli**   łu l   sušweł
then   DET STATIVE really.struggling DET at road

še   x̣ʷa sq̓si   u   **es**   **n̓amtaqs** še   x̣ʷuy u   **aytčsmis**
then maybe long.time and STATIVE sit.on.road then went and exert.effort.at.it

kʷemt x̣ʷuy u   **qʷm̓małqis**   łu scčcoxʷs
then   went and nearly.accomplish.it DET his.intention

hoy   x̣ʷuy u   iše k̓ʷl̓nuis   kʷemt łu l   nk̓ʷuʔ
INTERJ went and always complete.it then   DET at one

še   šey̓ u   ec̓x̣i łu l   snspsupps
then that and it's.like DET at dream

łu es   ewti   ci   citxʷ łu es   **n̓pex̣ʷełc̓eʔ**
DET STATIVE sneak.up.on that house DET STATIVE glowing.body

es   n̓ʔac̓x̣elsix̣ʷa   stem l   šey̓
STATIVE want.to.look.inside maybe what at that

hoy   es   čsax̣msts   łu citxʷ łu es   **n̓pex̣ʷełc̓eʔ**
INTERJ STATIVE he.gets.close.to.it DET house DET STATIVE glowing.body

kʷemt łu   es   čsax̣ms
then   DET STATIVE he.gets.close.to.it

hoy   ec̓x̣i es   x̣ʷpmulexʷ u   es   lkʷkʷstem   łu citxʷ
INTERJ it's.like STATIVE land.stretches and STATIVE it.gets.moved.far.away DET house

hoy   tl   ci   yoyoscut u   čsax̣m hoy   eł   lkʷkʷstem
INTERJ from that try.hard and get.close INTERJ again it.gets.moved.far.away

kʷemt tl   ci   **kʷtisyoyoscut** še   tl̓   ci   u   es   n̓pex̣ʷełc̓eʔ citxʷ
then   from that really.try.hard then from that and STATIVE glowing.body house

hoy   ec̓x̣i es   kʷtntwilši   łu citxʷ hoy   u   es   **kʷtisyoyoscut**
INTERJ it's.like STATIVE growing.large DET house INTERJ and STATIVE really.try.hard

kʷemt aχi   χiṅe   u   k̓ʷÍnuis łu   k̓ʷłčicis
then   in.such.a.way almost and finish.it DET arrive.at.it

pn put u   qs   k̓ʷÍnunms še   qiłt
yet right and IRREALIS finish.it   then wake.up

hoy   es   aymti χʷÍ tas k̓ʷÍnuis es   **kʷtisn?ac̓χelsi**
INTERJ STATIVE angry for not finish.it STATIVE really.want.to.look.inside

pn puti es   **čs?itši**
yet still STATIVE sleepy

hoy   qmip   u   es   miscut puti **es**   **ntχʷaqs**   hoy   eł   itš
INTERJ calm.down and STATIVE aware   still stative straight.road INTERJ again sleep

Metaphor analysis:

es n-tχʷ-aqs   transliteration: *stative inside-straight-road*
he is on a straight path   metaphorical meaning: *life is a path*

q̓ʷił-čst   transliteration: *energy-hand*
do.with.energy   metaphorical meaning: *laborious activity is denoted*
                              by hands

es tuk̓ʷ l šušewułs   transliteration: *stative placed.down at his.road*
a challenge in his life   metaphorical meaning: *life is a path*

šlič   transliteration: *go.around*
overcome the obstacle   metaphorical meaning: *life is a path*

ta snisaqm   transliteration: *no turn.off.road*
he doesn't deviate   metaphorical meaning: *life is a path*

ta sp̓l̓čus   transliteration: *no turn.around/over*
he doesn't give up   metaphorical meaning: *defeat is a physical change of*
                              direction

kʷtis-tl̓xʷeli   transliteration: *big-struggle*
really struggling   metaphorical meaning: *important is big*

l sušweł   transliteration: *at/on road*
in the life   metaphorical meaning: *life is a path*

es n-?amt-aqs   transliteration: *stative inside-sit-road*
he waits (for major life event) metaphorical meaning: *waiting is sitting*

ayt-čs-mis   transliteration: *strive-hand-3rd.trans*
he exerts effort at it   metaphorical meaning: *laborious activity is denoted*
                              by hands

qʷm̓m-ałq-is he is close to completion	transliteration: *near.completion-accompany-3rd.trans* metaphorical meaning: *closely held things accompany*
l nk̓ʷuʔ one time	transliteration: *at/in one* metaphorical meaning: *recollections are locations*
l snspsupps in the dream	transliteration: *at/in dream* metaphorical meaning: *dreams are locations*
n-p̓exʷ-elčeʔ glowing inside	transliteration: *inside-glow-body.cavity* metaphorical meaning: *hollow objects are bodies*
kʷtis-yoyoscut really try hard	transliteration: *big-try.hard* metaphorical meaning: *important is big*
kʷtis-nʔačx̣elsi really want to look inside	transliteration: *big-want.to.look.inside* metaphorical meaning: *important is big*
č-sʔitši sleepy	transliteration: *go.after-sleep* metaphorical meaning: *sleep is a location*

Each Salish text above might be stripped of the translations and utilized in language classrooms. As such, successive retellings might generate opportunities for second language learners of Salish to *do* something with the language. Retelling tasks are opportunities for language learners to share information aloud in an organized way. Learners might restate information they read from a text or heard from a short talk incorporating the above texts. If either of the texts are enacted in digital film format, learners might take successive notes on repetitions of the digital clip and use their notes to support their retellings. With additional Salish texts seeded with metaphors in Salish environmental studies or Salish mathematics, digital film or audio clips might demonstrate a simple experiment or document a mathematics teacher solve a mathematical question on a whiteboard and using a think-aloud presentation to expose learners to the metaphorical language of mathematics. Each of these, then, might become grist for metaphors relevant to school subjects. However, a more interactive classroom might incorporate Talmudic Pair work too.

Talmudic pair work (Rosekrans et al., 2012; Sherris, 2009) is a hermeneutic – or interpretive – approach to the study of a short written text; in this case, a text seeded with everyday metaphors from Flathead Salish, as in the examples above. Two students alternately read aloud a line of a text, stop, and ask one another what it means. The written text can vary. It can be a simple list of words or phrases, a stanza from a poem, or a couple of paragraphs from an expository text. If we utilize the above examples, a list of everyday metaphors from the text, or the entire text, might be utilized as a pre-listening activity. It is important that the text be short and that students understand they should explore meaning together through conversation, even making predictions as to meaning. Before we continue, however, it is perhaps important to discuss the meaning of the world Talmud.

The Talmud is an important sacred Jewish text from the early middle ages that is a record of rabbinic discussions concerning history, custom, norms, laws, and ethics from centers of Jewish learning in Babylon and Jerusalem. While it is encyclopedic in length, students of the Talmud are known to partner with one another to read and question short sections of verse as in Talmudic pair work. As a result of this practice, we have chosen to call the activity Talmudic Pair Work. Figure 1 presents the instructions for Talmudic Pair Work.

Input-output interactive text hermeneutics: Talmudic Pair Work	
A reads	a sentence aloud. Stops.
B asks,	"What does it mean?"
A	Explains.
A & B	Have an option to continue to discuss and interpret the line. They might respectfully disagree with each other, request clarification, check comprehension, elaborate, share details, provide examples, make predictions about meaning, and draw inferences as they bring prior knowledge of the world and language to the interpretation(s) that emerge from the dialogic process.
B reads	a sentence aloud. Stops.
A asks,	"What does it mean?"
B	Explains.
A&B	Once again, both participants have an option to continue to discuss and interpret the line. Now they draw on past interpretations and notions and continue to develop new ones.
	The participants continue to alternately read aloud the text line by line. They engage in Talmudic Pair Work until they have reached the end of the text and exhausted the dialogic, hermeneutic approach.

Figure 1. Talmudic Pair work

Language teachers are often preoccupied with achieving an optimal balance between routine and variation, and this would be true for Salish language instruction too. Four variations on combining or sequencing retelling and Talmudic Pair Work in interactive ways are described below. Each integrates the four language modalities of listening, speaking, reading, and writing. If digital film or audio clips can be produced, different voices and speeds (e.g., high pitch, low pitch, clear and distinct phonemic enunciation, elision, fast or slow talk) and effects can be added (e.g., listening while there is background noise, music, or no distractions). Digital recordings can simulate real world situations that classroom readings sometimes cannot do.

Combination/Sequence I
1. First listening of short text (one or two paragraphs in length as in above Salish examples); students are prompted to listen for main ideas; low proficient students may circle the main idea from four to five choices; higher proficient students take notes while listening.
2. When the listening is completed, the teacher asks the students to discuss the main ideas with a partner.
    Students are debriefed in whole group on main idea.
3. Student dyads conduct Talmudic pair work (Figure 1) with transcript of text they just listened to.
4. Students independently begin guided retelling by underlining key words and phrases in the transcript.
5. Students independently make lists of key words and phrases.
6. Students use their lists to retell the text to each other without looking at the text from which they drew up their lists.
7. Students in dyads listen while their partners retell the talk.
8. Second listening of same Salish talk in order for students to add written information to their list of key words and phrases.
9. Students independently write summaries using their notes, not the full transcript.
10. They check their work by comparing their rewrites with the original.

Combination/Sequence II
1. Students engage in Talmudic pair work with a short Salish text.
2. Students individually underline words and phrases from the text.
3. Students individually list the underlined words and phrases on a separate paper.
4. Students cover the text and retell it to their partners using their lists.
5. Students listen while their partners retell the text to them using their list.

Combination/Sequence III
1. Students listen (in whole group) to a short Salish talk delivered by another student, the teacher, or an invited guest expert.
2. Students write important words and phrases in a list from the talk.
3. Students compare their lists with a partner and agree on one list that could be a combined one.
4. Students engage in Talmudic pair work with their list.
5. Students listen (in whole group) to the same short talk again.
6. Students add more information to their lists during and after the second listening.
7. Students compare their lists with their partner's and agree on one list that could be a combined one.
8. Student make a more abbreviated list from their combined notes.
9. Students use the abbreviated list to retell the talk.
10. Students listen while their partners retell the talk.

Combination/Sequence IV

1. Students watch a digital film clip of the Salish talk.
2. Students place a check mark next to each word and phrase listed that they hear in the digital film clip.
3. Students watch the digital film clip a second time and add more information to each word or phrase.
4. Students use their lists to retell what they watched to their partners.
5. Students listen while their partners retell it too.
6. Students receive a short text on the same topic, but not a transcript of the digital film clip.
7. Students engage in Talmudic pair work with the text.

4.2   Flathead Salish metaphors and language learning

The two Flathead texts are rich in metaphor. The varied combinations of retellings and Talmudic Pair Work presented above provide opportunities for negotiation of meaning and incidental focus on form among Flathead language learners. At the same time, these tasks potentially reduce calquing (i.e., word-for-word translation) among learners as the tasks potentially develop successive restructuring of metaphor in ways aligned with second language acquisition research findings. They provide ways for students to re-visit text and engage in meaning making and successive restructurings of their expanding renditions and Salish language repertoires.

5.   Conclusion

This chapter has served multiple purposes. First, it adds to the body of research documenting the Salishan languages, providing the first published description of Flathead Salish metaphors to our knowledge. Second, it has examined Flathead Salish metaphors in comparison to English metaphors, adding to our cross-linguistic understanding of how both sensory-motor experiences and culture contribute to potential source domains. In roughly half of the examples discussed in this chapter, source domains in English and Salish are shared, indicating a possible common sensory-motor origin that characterizes both languages with respect to this small corpus and might be experienced in other languages as well, at least in part. In roughly the other half of the examples, source domains differ. In some of these cases, the sensory-motor experience gives rise to different metaphors, but in other cases, cultural considerations must be taken into account. Future research in this area might explore similar considerations in other unrelated languages, building to a typology of metaphors in a variety of language families as well as sources of differences in cross-linguistic metaphor. Concordance software might be utilized to study frequencies of source domains. To our knowledge, this has yet to be conduced.

Finally, this chapter presents a method for strategically using metaphor to teach Flathead Salish through Talmudic pair work, a type of TBLT. This method potentially draws students into rich discussions of the language, building both their language skills and their metalinguistic knowledge. It draws attention to the metaphors that undergird Salish, which we believe is essential in mastery of the language. Future research might explore the effects of using this method on incidences of calquing in students' speech. Moreover, through a pretest-posttest-delayed posttest design with experimental and control classrooms, future research might measure the impact these tasks have on Salish acquisition. Indeed, beyond the policy questions of corpus planning, status planning, and acquisition planning, metaphors and other figurative language (e.g., idioms) present very real opportunities to stimulate interest in school children, youth, and adult learners. In our view, metaphor, literacy, education, and life are uniquely integrated to move the enterprise of revitalization forward. We hope others agree.

References

Breen, M. (1989). The evaluation cycle for language learning tasks. In R. K. Johnson (Ed.), *The second language curriculum*. Cambridge, UK: Cambridge University Press.

Confederated Salish and Kootenai Tribes. (2004). *People of vision*. Retrieved from http://www.cskt.org/

Corder, S. P. (1978). Language distance and the magnitude of the learning task. *Studies in Second Language Acquisition*, 2, 27–37. DOI: 10.1017/S0272263100000930

Eijk, J. P. van, & Hess, T. (1986). Noun and verb in Salish. *Lingua*, 69, 319–331. DOI: 10.1016/0024-3841(86)90061-6

Ellis, R. (2003). *Task-based language learning and teaching*. Oxford, UK: Oxford University Press.

Fishman, J. A. (Ed.). (2001). *Can threatened languages be saved? Reversing language shift, revisited: A 21st century perspective*. Clevedon, UK: Multilingual Matters Ltd.

Kinkade, M. D. (1983). Salish evidence against the universality of 'noun' and 'verb'. *Lingua*, 60, 25–40. DOI: 10.1016/0024-3841(83)90045-1

Kiyosawa, K. G., & Donna, B. (2010). *Salish applicatives*. Leiden, Netherlands: Brill Academic Publishers. DOI: 10.1163/ej.9789004183933.i-394

Kövecses, Z. (2002). *Metaphor: A practical introduction*. Oxford: Oxford University Press.

Kroeber, P. D. (1999). *The Salish language family*. Lincoln, Nebraska: University of Nebraska Press.

Lakoff, G. (1992). The contemporary theory of metaphor. In A. Ortony (Ed.), *Metaphor and thought* (pp. 202–253). Cambridge, UK: Cambridge University Press.

Lakoff, G. (1993). The contemporary theory of metaphor. In A Ortony (Ed.), *Metaphor and Thought* (pp. 202–251). Cambridge, UK: Cambridge University Press.

Lakoff, G., & Johnson, M. (1999). *Philosophy in the flesh: The embodied mind and its challenge to Western thought*. New York: Basic Books.

Lakoff, G., & Johnson, M. (1980/2003). *Metaphors we live by*. Chicago: The University of Chicago Press.

Larsen-Freeman, D. (2006). The emergence of complexity, fluency, and accuracy in the oral and written production of five Chinese learners of English. *Applied Linguistics*, 27(4), 590–619. DOI: 10.1093/applin/aml029

Larsen-Freeman, D., & Cameron, L. (2008). *Complex systems and applied linguistics*. Oxford, UK: Oxford University Press.

Long, M. (2015). *Second language acquisition and task-based language teaching*. West Sussex, UK: Wiley-Blackwell.

Lovick, O. (2012). Walking like a porcupine, talking like a raven: Figurative language in Upper Tanana Athabascan. In A. Idström & E. Piirainen (Eds.), *Endangered metaphors* (pp. 103–121). Amsterdam: John Benjamins. DOI: 10.1075/clscc.2.05lov

Matsuki, K. (1995). Metaphors of anger in Japanese. In J. R. Taylor & R. E. MacLaury (Eds.), *Language and the cognitive construal of the world* (pp. 137–151). Berlin: Mouton de Gruyter.

McLaughlin, B. (1990). Restructuring. *Applied Linguistics*, 11, 113–128. DOI: 10.1093/applin/11.2.113

Nk̓ʷusm Language Institute. (2013). *About Nk̓ʷusm*. Retrieved from http://www.salishworld.com/About.htm

Norris, J. (2009). Task-based teaching and testing. In M. H. Long & C. J. Doughty (Eds.), *The handbook of language teaching* (pp. 578–594). Malden, MA: Wiley-Blackwell. DOI: 10.1002/9781444315783.ch30

Palmer, G. B. (1998). Foraging for patterns in Interior Salish semantic domains. In E. Czaykowska-Higgins & M. Kinkade (Eds.), *Salish languages and linguistics: Theoretical and descriptive perspectives*. Berlin: Mouton de Gruyter. Accessed from http://books.google.com/books?id=VBvD52-QKcAC&printsec=frontcover&source=gbs_ge_summary_r&cad=0#v=onepage&q&f=false

Pasamonik, C. (2012). "My heart falls out": Conceptualizations of body parts and emotion expressions in Beaver Athabascan. In A. Idström & E. Piirainen (Eds.), *Endangered Metaphors* (pp. 77–101). Amsterdam: John Benjamins. DOI: 10.1075/clscc.2.04pas

Pete, T. (Ed.). (2010). *seliš nyoʔnuntn Medicine for the Salish language*. Pablo, MT: Salish Kootenai College Press.

Reddy, M. (1979). The conduit metaphor. In A. Ortony (Ed.), *Metaphor and thought* (pp. 284–324). Cambridge, UK: Cambridge University Press.

Reyhner, J., & Eder, J. (2004). *American Indian education: A history*. Norman, OK: University of Oklahoma Press.

Rice, S. (2012). "Our language is very literal": Figurative expression in Dene Sųłiné [Athapaskan]. In A. Idström & E. Piirainen (Eds.), *Endangered Metaphors* (pp. 21–76). Amsterdam: John Benjamins. DOI: 10.1075/clscc.2.03ric

Rosekrans, K., Sherris, A., & Chatry-Komarek, M. (2012). Education reform for the expansion of mother-tongue education in Ghana. *International Review of Education*, 58(5), 593–618. DOI: 10.1007/s11159-012-9312-6

Sherris, A. (2009). A hermeneutic approach to teacher education: Talmudic pair work. In A. Gallup (Chair), *Responding to the needs of language teachers: Reconceptualizing professional development*. Symposium conducted at the *International conference on Language Teacher Education*, Washington, DC.

Sherris, A., Pete, T., Thompson, L., & Haynes, E. (2013). Task-based language teaching practices that support Salish language revitalization. In M. C. Jones & S. Ogilvie (Eds.), *Keeping languages alive: Documentation, pedagogy, and revitalization* (pp. 155–166). Cambridge, UK: Cambridge University Press. DOI: 10.1017/CBO9781139245890.015

Steward, E., & Bennett, M. (1991). *American cultural patterns: A cross cultural perspective*. Boston, MA: Nicholas Brealey Publishing.

Thomason, L. (1994). Transitivity-related morphological alternations in Montana Salish. *ICSNL*, 29, 265–287.

Thomason, S. G. (2006). *Salish Languages*. In K. Brown (Ed.), *Encyclopedia of language and linguistics* (pp. 732–734). Oxford, UK: Elsevier.

Thompson, M., & Egesdal, S. (2008). *Salish myths and legends: One people's stories*.

Van den Branden, K., Bygate, M., & Norris, J. (Eds.). (2009). *Task-based language teaching: A reader*. Amsterdam: John Benjamins. DOI: 10.1075/tblt.1

CHAPTER 7

Idioms and proverbs in Bete language and culture

A metaphorical analysis of their aetiology, meaning and usage

Jean-Philippe Zouogbo

Clillac-Arp Research Group, University of Paris Diderot-Paris 7,
Paris Sorbonne Cité

Metrics on language vitality indicate that Bété is an endangered language
(UNESCO, 2014). The documentation of Bété proverbs and idioms will
potentially generate renewed interest in the richness of the language and
culture. The purpose of this chapter is to discuss Bété proverbs and idioms as
reflections of universal language structures that embody affordances of specific information germane to the environment and experience of remaining
Bété speakers. To accomplish this, the chapter explores relationships among
Bété idioms, cognition, and imagery.

Keywords: Bété, endangered language, metaphor, proverbs, idioms,
worldview, idiosyncrasy, poetic language, language functions, figurative
language

1. Theoretical framework

The Bete in the Ivory Coast have a very rich culture and great oral tradition.
They speak a West African language from the Niger-Congo family: the *Bété*.
The Bété has been classified as a moribund language because of it dwindling
intergenerational transmission and non-extent use of its writing system. The
fact remains that the population has a low level of literacy. In this culture, as
with similar African cultures, idioms and proverbs are abundantly used to serve
many socio-cultural functions in the conduct of their day-to-day living. For
example, as Martinet (1970) and later Häcki-Buhofer (2001) point out, idioms
are used to express thoughts and ideas, emotions and feelings with brevity,

DOI 10.1075/clscc.7.06zou
© 2015 John Benjamins Publishing Company

clarity, and appropriateness, capturing cultural experiences and tradition in a straightforward manner by avoiding roundabout explanations; second, according to Cauvin (1980) and Zouogbo (2008), they are used as frames of reference or cultural models for a smooth and orderly conduct of social and cultural life and ensure stability of traditions and actualize them whenever they are used; and third, they are used as means for exhibiting learning and scholarship, worldly experience, and wisdom, thereby gaining social recognition, prestige, and power in view of their (proverbs and idioms) positive social valorization in the Bete culture and tradition – he who masters the language deserves the respect of his community.

In addition to these three functions which are also mentioned by Bhuvaneswar (2013), Bete proverbs also perform the other four functions given below among the 8 important specific functions in addition to the major speech act functions (assertives, directives, commissives, expressives, and declarations) performed by proverbs:

1. categorization of social praxis by prototypicalization
2. ornamentation of discourse by aesthetic appeal to the imagery, meaning, and structure of the proverb
3. instantiation and perpetuation of cultural praxis;
4. idealization of prototypical action through cultural authorization for guidance (as advice by warning, suggestion, etc.);
5. a politeness strategy and depersonalization of directive speech acts;
6. a discourse strategy;
7. sociolinguistic prestige norm;
8. as a foregrounding device in literary and social action.

Among these eight functions listed, the first function of prototype-categorical instantiation is the basic function from which the other seven functions are derived. Since metaphors in African ecology are rich in imagery, wisdom, and aesthetic appeal, they are immensely useful to perform all these functions most effectively and so are abundantly employed. Therefore, this *l'art pour l'art*, rhetorical function leads people to use many metaphors in their discourse.

It is hoped that this paper will serve as a springboard to initiate further research in integrated approaches to provide a holistic description of metaphors and idioms with more explanatory and descriptive adequacy and experiential validity; and highlight the rich world view of the Bete society through a highly developed and well-formed language of their own.

2. The Bété: Language and culture

As argued previously, Bété is a West African language from the Niger-Congo family. In the language typology, Bété used to be classified more precisely as a language from the Kru-phylum. Bété is spoken in the Midwest of the Ivory Coast by the ethnic group eponymously called Bété. Bété speakers number approximately 1 million persons and live in the Ivorian regions between Gagnoa and Daloa, including the county towns of Issia and Soubré.

This specification is very important from the linguistic point of view because even if the language spoken in those mentioned regions is called Bété, language scholars make a great difference between the different sorts of Bété spoken. That means we have as many Bété-languages as we have Bété-regions.

They are of course mutually intelligible on purely linguistic grounds. We thus speak of different dialects. The ethnonym Bété is to be considered as a generic term for all dialects in these regions. Mentioning different Bété-languages or dialects is a better and more accurate description of the linguistic reality of this rich language (cf. Zouogbo, 2008).

Even if we now can find some scriptural forms of the Bété-dialects, it must be said that they remain undescribed. They lack in a unanimously agreed upon systematic linguistic description as far as their syntax, morphology and lexicalization are concerned. Nevertheless, indigenous language professionals and others have promoted Bété while only working with what might be called, at best, sketches of the various traits of each dialect. A relevant contribution to linguistics might be a compilation and synthesis of the extant work from which solid sources and references might be drawn for future research.

Crystal (2000, p. 20) argues that Bété is an endangered language because "it is spoken by enough people to make survival a possibility, but only in favorable circumstances and with a growth in community support". According to the classification of Wurm (1998, p. 192) Bété is, if it is not endangered yet, potentially endangered because it is "socially and economically disadvantaged, under heavy pressure from a larger language". Because of French, the dominant language in the Ivory Coast, Bété and also other local languages begin to lose child speakers. The younger good speakers are indeed (young) adults. This situation has disastrous consequences from a scientific point of view: the Bété comes to be used progressively less and less throughout the community itself, with some of the functions it originally performed either dying out or gradually being supplanted by the French. Any observer can notice how the Bété and the other indigenous languages have come to play less of a role in educational and other public situations because French prevails.

Figure 1. Ivory Coast with Bété speaking regions in the quadrilateral

3.   Bété metaphors and their aetiology

The culture is largely oral transmitted and the communication also largely remains unwritten. And the language spoken is still transmitted orally, by speakers of differing proficiency: the (most) fluent speakers are old people and of course young adults who have grown up in the direct environment of the language practice. And even not all adults born and living in the villages can be considered as fully fluent speakers. The great majority of the Bété-speakers is now unfortunately based on so-called semi-speakers and also on weak semi-speakers, those who are less fluent, with most limited speaking competence.

But it is my contention that metaphor-use is a strategy "developed" by ancestors in order to overcome the problem of transmission of the tradition. For, the most important function of the language in our oral culture remains the transmission of tradition. That means the transmission of ways of thinking and acting. Sharing the same ways of thinking and acting assures stability in the society. This quest has lead people to shape linguistic models, "fixed, mnemonic, prototypical linguistic expressions" (Bhuvaneswar, 2013, p. 9) which represent the condensation of ancestral experience. They are thus shared from generation to generation. This must not lead to blanket generalizations such as people are free to think and must always reproduce the existing linguistic schemas as this is what is considered a prototype-categorical instantiation (Bhuvaneswar, 2013, p. 9). The fact remains that people who share the same social and cultural heritage must be aware of the existing tradition and must have the same references. This tradition is often fixed in proverbs and idioms based on metaphors.

Of course, proverbs and idioms are generally accepted as a mode for embellishing speech but using proverbs and idioms while speaking is not only a proof of one's language competence, but a sign that one is also involved in the tradition. And most of the time, the social importance and image of somebody is measured by his language competence and this competence is also a measurement of the capacity to use proverbs and idioms adequately.

Proverbs and idioms are based on rich image schemas which are not only simple (pre)conceptual structures. Those images which underline the metaphors are chosen, selected among a very diverse ground of elements (animals, plants, body experience, cosmologisms) which are well-known by the Bété. The semiotic import of this imagery often has culture-specific dimensions of meaning. Moreover, the relation between the images and the culture is delivered by the tradition, the experience. It is the tradition that selects the images and metaphors. And he who uses those metaphors actualizes the tradition and contributes to the vitality of the culture. This is why idioms and proverbs are very important in oral societies. The stability is also based on the common cognitive models and references most of the time fixed as metaphors in those linguistic tools. It has also been argued that each image selected is related with a special symbolism in the culture. The only one explanation we have in order to justify the fact that panther (and not lion) is the symbol of COURAGE, MAJESTY and that cat symbolizes HYPOCRISY lies in the Bété-Cosmogony and the idiosyncrasy. Of course, there are several metaphorical references which are shared with other cultures (such us occidental cultures) but in most cases, as I am going to show through the examples, the metaphors remains impenetrable for those who do not belong to the Bété-culture and even for some Bété. Most of the time, we need some more explanation to understand the daily mental and social mannerisms and idiosyncrasies. And those explanations go back to the life experience and the tradition of the Bété.

In the following chapter, I have selected some idioms and proverbs with specific metaphorical constituents. At first, I will present the expression in Bété with its literal translation in English and the global signification. I add the equivalent in English, where this exists. The selection is based on two kinds of examples: some expressions can be understood by anyone with some minor explanations. The second group of examples is more opaque and needs cultural references, which I provide.

4. Example of Bété idioms and proverbs

4.1   Selected idioms and proverbs

The examples of Bété idioms and proverbs in our sample were arranged according to the target concepts. In each example, the lexemes in bold character bears the metaphor. Those linguistic signs can be considered as Bété symbols according to the typology of Dobrovol'skij & Piirainen (2002). Most of them are well-known language and cultural symbols. That means they have the same signification in daily culture and language expressions. The **cat,** for instance, does not represent anything other than HYPOCRISY in the Bété culture. When it occurs in a linguistic expression, it also conveys the respective cultural meaning. Therefore, it can be considered as a *symbol par excellence*. Others (**wood, old lady, grave**…) are not "lexicalized" metaphors. In a linguistic expression they have an ad hoc meaning without stable referents in the culture. This makes their conceptual grasp very difficult even for somebody who belongs to the Bété speaking community.

COURAGE – TEMERITY

(1) *Ô di **djibodjè klo** glè **nôgô***
"The one who eats **sugar cane** and whose *face* is watching the **sky**"
'The one who eats sugar cane and keeps looking up'
'Praiseworthy person (because he/has achieved an (normally impossible) action'

(2) *Ô kpô **dre** ku*
"He has a big **heart**"
'He is courageous'

(3) *Pièle **dre** ku*
"Press you **heart**!"
'be courageous! Endure the situation!'

(4) *Sa **dre** kô*
"Grab your **heart in your** *hands*."
'be courageous! Endure the situation!'

LOVE

(5) *Ô di na **dre***
"He/she eats my **heart**."
'I am madly in love with him/her.'

ANGER

(6) *Na **dre** gwé*
"My **heart** is beating."
'I am really angry'

(7) *E te ame **kwlè mne** fô*
"Don't put your **hand** in my **stomach**."
'Don't try to pick a quarrel with me!'
'Don't look for trouble! Don't provoke me!'

TO BE FRIGHTENED

(8) *Ô dii na **dre** lu mé*
"He has cut my **heart** with a rope."
'He gave me a fright.'

(9) ***Hugôhun** ba ame **wili** me*
"**Soul** left my **head**."
'I was lost.'
'I had no idea what to do'

CRUELTY

(10) *Ô ne **dre** kè.*
"He doesn't have any **heart**."
'He is (a) heartless (person).'

TO BE INTELLIGENT

(11) *Ô kè **dre***
"He has got a **heart**."
'He is not that silly as you can think.'
'He is very clever'

(12) *Ô ko **wili** me*
"He has got a **head**."
'He is very intelligent'

MISERLINESS

(13) *Ô tè **kô***
"His **hand** is tough."
'He is a real tightwad.'

(14) *Tèbè ko ô posi me*
"A **snake** is in his **pocket**."
'He is very miserly.'

A PERSON ONE CANNOT RELY ON

(15) *O ku jiri ku*
"He is a person with dead **eyes**."
'He is nonchalant, pretty clueless'

TO HAVE AN HEADACHE

(16) *Na wili jôrô me*
"My **head** is tearing."
'My head aches.'

REMEMBRANCE

(17) *Siba lôbô na dre*
"Take my **heart** and put it there (were the event happens)"
'Please let me know (about it)/refresh my memory!'

(18) *È ko ame wili me*
"It is in my **head**."
'I don't forget'

TO APOLOGIZE

(19) *E sale eji bo*
"I grasp/hold your **leg**"
'I beg you pardon/Please forgive me'

RESPECT

(20) *Ô ne zo ame gni wuli*
"He doesn't put any **hair** on my **head**."
'He has no respect for me.'

SOLIDARITY

(21) *Tromalea na sô.*
"Extend my **arm**."
'Please help me take that objet which is not within my arms reach.'

(22) *Đilikwlèso è budualô kôpèsô.*
"The **right hand** washes the **left hand**."
'People have to help each other'

HYPOCRISY

(23)   *Sepu mijinjiri*
       Tears from a **cat**'s *eyes*.
       "Cat tears"
       'Crocodile tears'

(24)   *Sepu nè:"a tome e tu lè"*
       The **cat** says: "I am weeping for you"

(25)   *Te ame **gbiziabâ** me siba*
       "Don't put me in the beauty of the **owl**."
       'Don't make me praise the beauty of the **owl**.'
       'Don't oblige me to appreciate/to do something I don't want
       to appreciate/want to do.'

ASSUMING RESPONSABILITY

(26)   *Gbèmegbôtô gbo*
       "A cleaning-the-**basket** affair."
       'This affair happened because I cleaned my basket (out).'
       'I am not directly involved in this accident/misfortune'

EXPRESSION OF DEATH

(27)   ***Digbotetiagazoa** jo kome*
       "**Digbotetiagazoa** (Bété-denomination of death) has taken him away"
       'He is dead.'

(28)   *ja **gbili**jèrè hnonhun*
       "He has slept like a **python**."
       'He is dead.'

(29)   *Ô ja **glè** mnin*
       "He has swallowed his **teeth**."
       'He is dead.'

ORIGINS

(30)   *Su ne zo **hunmeazibi***
       "**Wood** (in the river) never become a *(water)fish*."

LIFE EXPERIENCE

(31)   ***Jua** ne di wanè tia**du***
       "**Children** (alone) can't have their own *village*."

DISCRETION

(32)   *Megbôsu ne lôbô* **hunkahnon.**
"**A tree that creaks (before falling)** doesn't hurt **the old lady.**"

GREED

(33)   *E nène* **gnèso** *nu ne* **vili** *di me*
"It is good in the mouth of **the hedgehog** and *the ground squirrel* also eats it."

SOCIAL POSITION-RESPECT

(34)   **Gnriwôbèle** *diowulu ne ôguè* **likpoa** *yuku.*
"**The old male baboon** is naked but he leads **the monkey horde.**"

(35)   **Zokubihè** *ne gnanonkule*
"**The grave settled in the village** doesn't inspire fear."

4.2   The meaning and sense of use of metaphors in Bété

As mentioned previously, the use of metaphors in the Bété-society is mainly correlated with the sense of transmitting a message by leaning the content of the information against the cultural and social environment. In this way the metaphors function as direct speech acts. That means, he who speaks wants to say something special but instead of using simply words, he embeds his message in metaphorical speech tools which lay stress on the situation he wants to describe or comment. A indirect speech act would mean people want to say something but says it by using circumlocutions. Metaphors are not circumlocutions. They represent a way to say things in a powerful way so that the person(s) being addressed might potentially be touched by the message. Of course the images used are often well-known to the interlocutors. Using the metaphors gives sense to the message in a short and powerful way. The images are sometimes funny but can also be violent or obscene. Using metaphors thus avoids long discourse but involves both the speaker and his interlocutor and also, and this is the most important thing, all the community.

The following proverb (34) is about respect for elder people and social position.

(34)   **Gnriwôbèle** *diowulu ne ôguè* **likpoa** *yuku.*
"**The old male baboon** is naked but he leads **the monkey horde.**"

The naked male baboon represents a person whose social position is not enviable but the main feature of this person is his age: he may be the eldest of his family/ community, *the monkey horde*. But just because he is poor or do not have an important social (*The naked male baboon*) status the other people use to treat him with less consideration than he normally deserves despite his age. One of the several possible significations of this proverb can be: *Social position doesn't make the person.* This is a moral value very present in the Bété-culture (and other cultures of the world) where elder people are very considered and it must be so. Sometimes, people may forget this value and follow or respect people just because they are rich or they have social power. It is very interesting to notice how another Bété-proverbs represents the opposite view by encouraging this (non) value:

> *Yuakosu ke hnonmon, kwlè wa tuè.*
> "If the child's fire burns brightly, let's show our hands and warm them up."

Just to say, we have to follow and listen to a youngest person (the child) if he has (financial, social…) power (the fire that is…). Of course, the extension or application domains of the metaphors can be diverse. And the meaning must not be reduced only to the SERVILITY.

Metaphors are also used to hide the fear people have for nature or for manifestations of life. One interesting example is the representation of DEATH. In their cosmogony, death is for the Bété, something very scaring and awful. Let us simply say: Bété people fear death. And the confrontation with it is not easy. That is why it is not called "death" but respectfully **Digbotetiagazoa** which it corresponds with. The following examples are an illustration of how Bété face up with death:

(27) *Digbotetiagazoa jo kome*
   "**Digbotetiagazoa** (Bété-denomination of death) has taken him away"
   'He is dead.'

We can see how death is personified and what it means when Bété-people say somebody is dead. The use of that denomination shows the ineluctability of people towards death and their feeling of helplessness towards this phenomenon.

In the same way, somebody who is dead "has slept like a **python**":

(28) *ja **gbilijèrè** hnonhun*
   "He has slept like a **python**."
   'He is dead.'

This can of course be understood by any stranger just because this conceptual metaphor DEATH IS A LONG SLEEP is very present all around the world. But I am not sure that everybody will understand the following idiom that also is one way to say that somebody is dead:

(29) *Ô ja **glè** mnin*
   "He has swallowed his **teeth**."
   'He is dead.'

Even competent speakers I asked could not give me a convincing answer about why one swallows one's teeth. It is my contention and my own interpretation that "teeth" represents vitality, life, the alpha and the omega: somebody who is dead no more makes use of his teeth.

The (social and cultural) position towards death, the fear or great respect people have for death is also mentioned in this proverb with **Zokubihè** "the grave settled in the village" as constituent:

(35) *Zokubihè ne gnanonkule*
"The grave settled in the village doesn't inspire fear."

As we can see, the interpretation of this proverb can be misleading if it doesn't occur to one that it is a metaphor: the source domain is of course DEATH but the application domains can be numerous. The most evident for me is RESPECT and CONSIDERATION in the sense of the French/English proverb *Nul n'est prophète en son pays – Nobody is prophet in his own country.*

Why does *The grave settled in the village not inspire fear*? First of all, this metaphor provides a very important information about (Bété) cemeteries and graveyards. They never are settled in the villages. There is, in any Bété-village, a cemetery like everywhere in the world, but the cemetery always is considered as a "second" village, *ku-duku* ("the village of death-dead people/souls") with a respectable distance with the "first" village where people use to live. When somebody dies, his grave is thus settled in *ku-duku*. And there are so much mysteries and myths bounded to the cemeteries, ghosts and the power of dead persons that it would never come to someone to go alone in the cemetery. But there is an exception: we find some graves in the villages when the dead person was for instance a person with high social position or if that person was rich enough to build his grave or vault on his property before he dies. Of course, if at the beginning this grave can frighten people like the other ones in a normal cemetery, the fear disappears with time until the grave becomes like a street furniture: no one thus fears it anymore.

With that cultural background we can now try to understand the real meaning of proverb (35): The closer (*the grave in the village*) people (your relatives, friends …) are with you the less consideration (*doesn't inspire fear*) they show for you. In this way, President Obama is "merely" a wonderful father and man at home. But for the great majority of us, he is the most powerful state president of the world.

The metaphor use in Bété-culture is correlated with life experience and most of the time with people observation. It is somebody who observes a special situation and yields from it a special image in a smashing formulae. The force of the image, the repetition and the frequent use of the linguistic formulae makes it be a proverb or an idiom under the condition that the image is related with the

tradition. But he who uses the formulae must find the most expressive and corresponding applying context:

(32)   *Megbôsu ne lôbô* **hunkahnon.**
       "**A tree that creaks (before falling)** doesn't hurt **the old lady.**"

It is well-known that (very) old lady (but why not also MEN?!) have difficulties
to walk and if they sit somewhere, it takes time for them to wake up and go. But
why **do** *a tree that creaks (before falling)* not *hurt* **the old lady?** Because there is
no more surprise! The old lady has enough time to wake up and go away before
the tree falls.

   This proverb can be seen as a warning, an invitation to (talkative) people not
to give away their project before it is realized. But another possible extension of
the meaning can also be: 'a very bad new (such as the death of somebody) has less
effect when one is already prepared to the eventuality of the event'.

   The observation is a very important aspect of the aetiology of the metaphors
but most of the time this observation is not the direct result of a real-life experience. For, it is uncertain that people have really seen the *creaking tree* or the *naked
baboon*. The observation can also be as a result of mental process or also can be
drawn from tales. As we know, oral cultures make great use of tales in order to
transmit their cultures and values. And linguistic formulae are often conclusions
or lessons drawn from those folk tales. That is the reason why an expression can
be very clear at the first sight but not the meaning, which needs the background
information to be understood. Let's take the examples of:

(31)   *Jua ne di wanè tiadu*

(24)   *Sepu nè:"a tome e tu lè"*

(26)   *Gbèmegbôtô gbo*

In what follows we deal with (once well-known) narratives/stories which manifest
themselves in proverbs. In proverb (31) it might not be clear enough why Bété say
Children (alone) can't their own village. The verbal expression "children" represents "young people" and by extension "people with not enough life experience".
This is the story:

> A young man whose father was the chief of the village one day thought, because
> he had seen his father in his job settling social problems, he was mature enough.
> So he involved all young people of his generation to get rid of the eldest people of
> the village and go away to live their own life in their own village. But they would
> have learnt soon that going without the advices of the elders is not that easy:
> During a ceremony, the young chief wore a fresh cow skin as a coat as people used
> to do in those occasions. But very soon, the skin began to stick as it began to be

very hot. The young chief couldn't remove his coat after the ceremony. His mates were also not able to help him remove the cow skin. As they realized it could have been very dangerous for their chief they all resolved to go to the elders in order to ask for […] advices. When they arrived in the village, the first old man they met gave them the advice to lay their chief in cold water and wait. All the old persons jeered at the young chief: that's why we told you *"Children (alone) can't built their own **village**"*. Which means the EXPERIENCE OF ELDER PEOPLE and their advices are precious.

The *cat* (31) is with the dog the only one animal Bété-people don't eat. In their cosmogony, when somebody dies, people use to immolate domesticated animals such as chickens, goats or cows. The animals people immolate depends on the social position of the dead or if his family is rich. The poor immolate chickens, the rich, from chickens to cows, the sign that the funerals are a success. The story:

> One day, a big, rich man was about to die. So, all the domesticated animals of the village began to be very worried. Because they also were aware of the consequences of that imminent death. While the other animals were silently mourning for their fate, the cat came crying. He looked so sad and his tears were so copious that the other animals who wanted to make clear of his mourning (because they know that the cat doesn't share the same fate with them) asked him: Why are you crying?

The cat's answer became proverbial: *Sepu nè:"a tome e tu lè"*. The **cat** answered: "I am weeping for you". This proverb and the cat metaphors stand for the HYPOCRISY. That's why Bété speaks about "Cat's tears" (23) which corresponds to English *crocodile tears*.

As we can see, animal constituents in metaphors entirely stand for human being's features. So do the use of body part symbolisms. It is a kind of metonymy that have a social background and signification. And the conceptual metaphors process is also very present in the Bété-language structure: Body parts stand in most cases for EMOTIONS (LOVE, ANGER – see expressions with constituents like HEAD, HEART, etc.), HUMAN BEHAVIOUR and so on.

Bété never use to say something by looking him straight in the face. That does not mean cowardice but respect and moreover, the sense of stability in society by avoiding conflicts. Metaphors assure this function. But we know that most of the time, the metaphor is so violent, epigrammatic, shameful and so demeaning that it would have been better to tell somebody "you're very miserly" than metaphorical "you have a snake in your pocket":

(14)   *Tèbè ko ô **posi** me*
        "A **snake** is in his **pocket**."
        'He is very miserly.'

If he puts his hand in his pocket (to withdraw some money) the snake in it will bite him. In French, people say: *avoir des oursins dans la poche*, in English: *to have urchins in the pocket*. The same considerations hold for (30):

(30)   *Su ne zo **hunmeazibi***
       "Wood (in the river) never become a (**water**)fish."

The *wood* represents a person who has forgotten where he comes from and thus is a *fish*. This is specially applicable for people who have forgotten their traditions and culture because they now live far from their original community (*water*). This proverb can be an advice to someone to forget his origins or a critical attempt to reason with somebody who behaves differently because he now prefers the way of living of his new community. He must not forget that whatever he does he will never become another person.

The next illustration is very special because it is difficult to catch despite the translation provided.

(26)   *Gbèmegbôtô gbo*
       "A cleaning-the-**basket** affair."
       'This affair happened because I cleaned my basket (out).'
       'I am not directly involved in this accident/misfortune'

And even, the translation is misleading. This expression is very short but its explanation can't be so. An exhaustive explanation is needed to make the meaning clearer because this metaphor is a blended one which embodies several associated images: an old lady (once again), a basket, a cockroach, a fox and two other persons. This is also a story:

> An old lady decided to clean her old basket. As she beat the basket, a cockroach came out of it. Then a fox came out of the bush and jumped on the cockroach. The old lady scared by the fox called out for help. Two men came and one with his gut. He failed to fire at the fox and shot at his mate and injured him. Who is the responsible of this accident, people asked? The old lady? Because this affair wouldn't have occurred if the old lady had not cleaned her basket and… and…

We can see the sequence of the event and how it brings a linguistic tangle that stands for: *I am responsible but indirectly*. Are you responsible of the accident of a friend if he had a crash on the way coming to you? This INDIRECT RESPONSABILITY is what Bété use to call *Gbèmegbôtô gbo* (26). And we can see how difficult it is to translate and understand without adding the story.

What makes Bété so fond of metaphors is their iconicity: we can see through mental process the correspondence of an image with its real referent. And this transfer is sometimes very difficult to make at the beginning but leaning it to the context provides clearer understanding. In the Bété-culture, each constituent has a special symbolism. Some can be transparent but other not. In the following case, we have the metaphor of the owl, *Gbizi*. Normally, the first level of interpretation of the owl symbolism is embedded in the culture: OWL symbolizes WISDOM, CLEAR-SIGHTEDNESS in ancient times. But in the Bété example (25) it stands for UGLINESS. The ugliness of the owl (as Bété consider it is) is the source domain. And the target domain is the HYPOCRISY of people, this way people have to have an opinion and say the opposite sometimes under pressure or in order to flatter somebody else.

(25)   *Te ame **gbiziabâ** me siba*
"Don't put me in the beauty of the **owl**."
'Don't make me praise the beauty of the **owl**.'
'Don't oblige me to appreciate/to do something I don't want to appreciate/want to do.'

In this expression, the person who is speaking doesn't want to change his opinion. *The owl is ugly and it must be so!* For instance: *I don't want to support your candidate because I don't share his opinions* or even *I am not going to tell lies just because you ask me to do so in order to help you or to do you a favor.*

5.   Conclusion

We can see that apart from its ornamental and philosophical significance metaphors have social functions:

-   amplificatory: metaphors in proverbs and idiom amplify one's position in a discourse.
-   authoritative: confer authority on a point of view.
-   educative: educate, instruct and satirize for positive behavior modification or depreciation
-   rhetorical: serve as rhetorical tools in persuasion (especially as far as proverbs are concerned),
-   image making and aesthetic uses: the imbue what is said with poeticity.

Understanding Bété-metaphors means grasping certain aspects of people's *Weltanschauung*. As such, metaphors are not only ornamental speech acts. Behind this linguistic stereotypy and the semiological isomorphism (i.e., relation between body and world's object) metaphors provide specific indications of and information about, Bété-cosmogony as well as how a people's worldview and environment are structured. We now can have an idea about what will be lost if Bété-metaphors are not safeguarded or even if the language itself disappears.

References

Bhuvaneswar, C. (2013). Proverbial linguistics: Theory and practice in the ka:rmik linguistic paradigm-creation and development of proverbs. In J. M. Benayoun, N. Kübler, & J.-P. Zouogbo (Eds.), *Parémiologie* (pp. 243–297). Sainte-Gemme: PUSG.

Cauvin, J. (1980). *L'image, la langue et la pensée*. St. Augustin: Anthropos Institut – Haus Völker und Kulturen.

Crystal, D. (2000). *Language death*. Oxford: Oxford University Press.
    DOI: 10.1017/CBO9781139106856

Dobrovol'skij, D., & Piirainen, E. (2002). *Symbole in Sprache und Kultur. Studien zur Phraseologie aus kultursemiotischer Perspektive*. Bochum: Brockmeyer.

Häcki-Buhofer, A. (2001). Zu neuen Ufern. In A. Häcki-Buhofer, H. Burger, & L. Gautier (Eds.), *Phraseologiae Amor* (pp. 5–29). Baltmannsweiler: Schneider Verlag.

Martinet, A. (1970). *Eléments de linguistique générale*. Paris: Colin.

UNESCO (2014). Retrieved from http://portal.unesco.org/ci/en/ev.php-URL_ID=9910&URL_DO=DO_TOPIC&URL_SECTION=201.html

Wurm, S. (1998). Methods of language maintenance and revival, with selected cases of language endangerment in the world. In K. Matsumura (Ed.), *Studies in endangered languages (Papers from the International Symposium on Endangered Languages, Tokyo, 18–20 November 1995)* (pp. 191–211). Tokyo: Hituzi Syobo.

Zouogbo, J.-P. (2008). *Le proverbe entre langues et cultures*. Bern: Peter Lang.

CHAPTER 8

Receding idioms in West Danish (Jutlandic)

Torben Arboe

Aarhus University

The purpose of this chapter is to present and analyze dialectal idioms because they seem to be in retreat. The study employs a theory of conventional figurative units based on the conceptual theory of metaphors. The idioms are discussed in some detail inside a broad range of semantic fields. These include idioms of oppositions (e.g., RICHNESS VS. POORNESS, CLEVERNESS VS. FOOLISHNESS, SELFISHNESS VS. COOPERATION). An additional purpose is to identify the lexicographic consequences of idioms (i.e., polysemy) due to the figurative use of words, which may influence the structure of dictionary entries. The results of the entire study are summarized in an overview-chart with key concepts from each idiom. The chart indicates characteristics that constitute each idiom's distribution and figurativeness. These characteristics lead to considerations of the possible survival of dialectal idioms, including idioms also found in Standard Danish.

Keywords: dialects, figurative units, metaphors, semantic fields, polysemy, lexicographic impact

1. Introduction

In Denmark, dialects have been receding for more than a century as in so many other countries in Europe, and in the last 50–60 years perhaps even more so than in other countries. The influence from Standard Danish in a Copenhagen version, as spoken in the media, the schools and other public institutions, has been heavily making its way throughout the country, presumably most in the towns of Sealand, but also on Funen, with Odense as the largest city, and in Jutland, with Aarhus and Aalborg as the largest cities. Traditionally, Jutland is divided in 2–4 large dialect areas, depending on the criteria chosen (e.g., East, West and Southern Jutlandic), and these may further be described as 9 main dialects (e.g., North West Jutland, East Mid Jutland, West Southern Jutland), and, at a third level, 20 smaller areas, some of them with special dialect features,

DOI 10.1075/clscc.7.07arb
© 2015 John Benjamins Publishing Company

although also showing geographical names (e.g., Thy and Mors as constituting North West Jutland, Als and Angel constituting important parts of East Southern Jutland). Generally speaking, the Jutland dialect is on the retreat, giving way to Standard Danish, especially in and around the larger cities (e.g. Aarhus and Aalborg in the East Mid Jutland and North East Jutland, respectively), but a certain Jutlandic accent is still to be heard, in some degree identifiable as characteristic of a certain region (and sometimes called a *regiolect*). The resistance towards Standard Danish is probably at its greatest in Southern Jutland (earlier also called *Nordschleswig*) due to historical reasons: the region was part of Germany 1864–1920, and the Danish language, i.e. the Southern Jutland vernacular, was used as a central stronghold against the Germanization. Thus the dialect involved national feelings and thereby obtained a stronger status than other dialects also in the following years, perhaps stretching out to the present day.

As to the vocabulary, of course very many of the former daily words have grown antiquated within the last century, due in no small measure to industrialization, the mechanization of agriculture, and the development of "station towns" following the rise of railroads from the mid to late 19th century. It is the main task for the Peter Skautrup Center to edit and publish a dictionary of these now antiquated Jutlandic words as well as the vocabulary still in use.

A complicated question is to which extent the dialects are still found in the present time. A dialect's vitality has much to do with positive social attitudes about the dialect as well as a pro-active use of the dialect. Many Danes stand on the side of dialect maintenance and preservation in principle, but do not use dialect, opting, instead, to use Standard Danish. A short survey of this process of so-called "standardization" (i.e. the dialects giving in to the standard language to a still larger degree) since the 1960's is given in Arboe, 2012. However, also in Standard Danish many words, as well as idioms, have certainly grown old-fashioned during the common process of "development", sociologically and linguistically, from the first part of the 19th century until now.

At that time some authors with a Jutlandic background argued that characteristic, pithy words from the dialects could enrich Standard Danish and thus ought to be integrated there. But this had almost no impact, the linguistic trend going in the opposite direction: the interference from Standard Danish to the dialects was too strong already at that time. Contact between dialects might have slowed down the process of standardization: if dialect speakers from (many) different areas went on using words or idioms they have in common these should be more resistant, thereby forming strongholds against the general trend. An investigation of this could be an interesting task; unfortunately, my material (see below) does not give the possibility of studying this in details.

Some idioms, both dialectal and Standard Danish, are endangered because of changed societal living conditions (socially, technically, technologically, etc.): things, tools, machines and ways of doing things have gone out of use, especially as to the farming culture and rural living which had been the source domain of many idioms, and the words or terms for them have become strange, unfamiliar and perhaps obsolete, thereby making some idioms incomprehensible or at least difficult to understand. People may therefore avoid them and try to express the same content by using other, more neutral phrases.

2.   Basics for the investigation

2.1   Material

My material is basically found in the *Jysk Ordbog* (The Jutlandic Dictionary which reference includes Jutlandic Dialects). This is an archive of 3.1 million dictionary slips together with other sources, including answers to about 120 questionnaires (of 30–50 questions each) by hundreds of informants.

A helpful source in the search for idioms is a Jutlandic dialect dictionary in 4 volumes from about 1900, namely Feilberg, 1886–1914. In this work may be found many fixed expressions and idioms, which then can be further investigated by exploring the files and slips of the Dictionary of the Jutlandic Dialects. In Feilberg many expressions are mentioned as figurative, but by far not all the possible ones, and the meaning of them, or situation(s) in which they can be used, is not always explained, presumably because of the semantic similarity corresponding expressions in Standard Danish at that time. So, one has to be careful in using and sifting this evidence; word meanings and sentence meanings may have changed during the latest century.

Many of the idioms etc. are also found in the large dictionary of Standard Danish, *Ordbog over det Danske Sprog* (Dictionary of the Danish Language), 28 volumes (1918–1956), here abbreviated ODS. This dictionary holds many dialectal idioms from Jutland as well as from the Danish Isles, but of course also has a great load from literary sources, i.e. idioms etc. not found in the Danish dialects. A certain amount of Standard Danish fixed expressions has been added in the 5 volumes *Supplement* to ODS (1992–2005), abbreviated ODS-S. With a newer text basis (from the 1980–90'es) a 6 volume dictionary has been edited, *Den Danske Ordbog* (The Danish Dictionary, 2003–2005), abbreviated DDO. Here we find some idioms etc., which are also found in the Jutland dialects, being still in use, sometimes with smaller changes.

2.2   Theoretical background

Idioms and idiomaticity have been discussed for several years in linguistics, especially as phraseology research (Burger, 2007, pp. 90–93). Inside these domains also metaphors have been discussed and analyzed, and I had collected some of the examples below to elucidate the use of metaphors in idioms in the dialects. However, in the cognitive linguistics approach (referring back to especially Lakoff & Johnson, 1980, Lakoff, 1987) metaphors and other figures of speech are more often termed *(conventional) figurative units*, and the term metaphor is used to denote *conceptual metaphors* (i.e. abstract metaphors as for instance GOOD IS UP versus BAD IS DOWN, see Dobrovol'skij & Piirainen, 2005, p. 92).[1] Figurative units may be seen as semantic irregularities (op. cit. p. 41); they belong to the basic level imagery and are called *rich images* in conceptual metaphor theory (Lakoff, 1987, p. 406).

A figurative unit is an expression which has a literal reading inside a *source frame* and a figurative reading inside a *target frame*, the figurative reading thus representing a mapping from the source frame to the target frame (Dobrovol'skij & Piirainen, 2009, p. 55f.).[2] The target frame typically belongs to one semantic field, but sometimes to more than one, as an idiom may have more than one meaning: it may be used in different contexts and situations; i.e., the pragmatics of its use has to be taken into account. Thus one might call it a *semantic-pragmatic field*; this is presupposed in my use of the notion *semantic field* below.[3] The figurative units discussed below almost inevitably draw upon the culture-based knowledge of the speakers.

For example, the figurative unit (from Section 3.8) *han har stillet træskoene* has the literal reading "he has taken off his wooden shoes and placed them at the usual place when he came into the house" and the figurative reading "he has placed his wooden shoes for the last time", 'he is dead'. Sometimes the literal reading exists only in the conceptual world, not in the real world, e.g. in Standard Danish: *hun er en rose* "she is a rose" can only be meant figuratively, 'she is beautiful', because a person cannot be a flower and because a rose is often spoken of as a beautiful flower, at least in the European cultural area; here ROSE may be said to have

---

1.   Earlier, also I have used the term *metaphor* in the traditional meaning to denote some of the idioms in this chapter.

2.   The notions *source frame* and *target frame* will only be touched upon here, but the concepts are underlying (the thoughts of) the whole manuscript. They are found in Fillmore, 1985 and used in Piirainen, 2000 as well as Dobrovol'skij & Piirainen, 2009.

3.   The problems of drawing a clear borderline between semantics and pragmatics are further discussed by e.g. Stern, 2008, especially pp. 267–269.

a symbolic function, it may be classified as a cultural symbol (Dobrovol'skij & Piirainen, 2005, p. 35) and thus semiotized.

In principle I shall only consider a few other types of related idioms such as similes (comparisons, analogies), e.g. *hun er som en rose / hun er smuk som en rose* "she is as a rose / she is as beautiful as a rose", although there are far more examples of these types of idioms.[4] The distance between a figurative unit (metaphor) and a simile may be quite little, as pointed out by Croft & Cruse, 2004, p. 214; similes may be seen as implicit metaphors although they are quite disparate. This may be illustrated by the fact that the rock singers "The Rolling Stones" used a simile, *She's like a rainbow* several times in the song titled with a figurative unit, *She's a rainbow*. Some similes evoke the same mental image as corresponding figurative units would do if they existed, e.g. (from the article *1. aske* in the Dictionary of the Jutlandic Dialects), *det flyver omkring i byen som et trug aske* "it flies around in the town as a tray of ashes" (i.e. ashes from a tray), said about news or rumors spreading quickly around the town. Here a figurative unit, as in *news/rumors are flying ashes*, would be a possibility. Accordingly, also similes may be seen as a (conventional) figurative units, and a few instances of similes will be mentioned below (especially in Section 3.2).

Sometimes the figurative element is situated in just one of the words in an idiom, e.g. *fange en gedde* "catch a pike" 'get a wet foot (wet feet)', and this may have a lexicographic consequence. As a dictionary editor, you may here consider whether to place the idiom as just a figurative use of the word *gedde* ("pike"), or whether the word has in fact obtained a new meaning, i.e. 'wet foot'. If so, you have to define a new (sub-)meaning for the polysemous word. This certainly depends on how commonly the idiom is used, and to a certain degree also on how old and established it seems to be.[5]

2.3   Rendering of the idioms

Many of the verb idioms below may be presented as either an infinitive or a whole sentence. An idiom perhaps seems more vital when rendered in a sentence instead of just as an infinitive, although a formulaic start as *han/hun er ...* (= "he/she is ...") often seems almost as schematic as an infinitive. In general, I shall follow

---

4.   In Croft & Cruse, 2004, pp. 211–215, the relations between metaphor (in the traditional sense, i.e. *figurative unit*) and *simile* are seen as tighter than often presupposed, a view I find reasonable and shall adopt here. Using the terms above, one may say that a simile only has a literal reading and no figurative reading (at least in principle).

5.   Other metaphors with such "animal lexemes" are discussed in Arboe (2014).

the mode used in the Jutlandic/Danish examples (often finite sentences), but sometimes I reduce these idioms to infinitives. Also variants in other syntactic structures are used, without a verb.

Most of the examples are given in a Standard Danish version if the differences from the dialectal version are limited, but sometimes the distance is so far that one feels a loss of authenticity in such a rendering, the "sound" of the dialect seems to fade away when "translating" the expression into Standard Danish.⁶ In such cases the dialect version is rendered roughly (i.e. without phonetic transcription), especially, (1) when the pronunciation is characteristically dialectal, and (2) when grammar deviates, first and foremost when the definite article is placed in front of the noun (West and South Jutlandic) and not as a suffix as in Standard Danish.⁷ Both aspects can be shown by an idiom pronounced (or transliterated) as *a æ å·sk å i æ ild* in Jutlandic, which in Standard Danish reads, *af asken og i ilden*. Literally this means "from the ashes into the fire", figuratively it is used for 'from better to worse' (where the better may be bad enough), the corresponding idiom in English being *out of the frying-pan into the fire* (DanEng.I.63). In stead of the "phonetic" version here, some of the examples will be written in (almost) Danish orthography, but with the definite article in front of the noun, e.g. *af æ aske og i æ ild*, in order to follow the West and South Jutlandic grammar.

The Jutlandic or Danish idiom can rarely be translated directly into English, most often there is no (direct) equivalent available. However, the best thing to do certainly is to make a word by word translation just to show the lexical structure, and after that to try to find a more idiomatic expression of the idiom in English – or to paraphrase it, or at least to describe the meaning of it in English. Sometimes a special translation or explanation of a dialectal word or an outdated Standard Danish word is needed; this will be marked as LEX, meaning "lexical information of the word" (see for instance Jutlandic *skjøssel*, Standard Danish *skydsel* in Section 3.1).

---

6. But "sound" cannot be rendered precisely without using the International Phonetic Alphabet (IPA). It would be very time consuming (and beside the point in this context) to transscribe the examples to the IPA.

7. This placing of the definite article is one of the most fundamental features or demarcation lines in Danish dialects, described in e.g. Bennike & Kristensen, 1912, pp. 154–155, Skautrup, 1944, pp. 139–141. One might say that the West and South Jutlandic dialects follow a "European" norm versus the (more) "Nordic" norm followed by the other Danish dialects and Standard Danish.

3.   Semantic fields outlined (almost) as dichotomies

In the following, idioms from a range of important semantic fields are presented, some are arranged as "oppositions", whereas others are arranged as antonyms.[8] This will provide an overview and link idioms which have related meanings. It also potentially renders transparent a negatively formulated idiom thereby pointing to the opposite notion (e.g. *he is not clever* meaning 'he is stupid', cf. Section 3.2). Some of the idioms are used in two (or more) semantic fields, e.g. *på de høje nagler* ("on the high rivets") about bad economy as well as intoxication (cf. Sections 3.1 and 3.6). Many of the idioms are explained or commented, but some are commonplace and do not need explanation, it will suffice to mention the literary and the figurative meaning.

3.1   Richness vs. poorness

RICHNESS. The first example refers to farming practice, namely *hans plov går rigtigt* "his plough goes rightly", which has the figurative meaning 'he earns much money'. – *han er ved skillingen* "he is at the shilling", 'he is rich'. Here a lexical comment is needed, LEX: Although etymologically the same word as *shilling*, the Danish *skilling* only had small value, like a farthing. In spite of this, *ved skillingen* means 'rich'. – *have noget på kistebunden* "have something at the bottom of the (money)chest", 'be rich'. English equivalents: *have put money by; have a nest egg; have provided against a rainy day* (cf. DanEng.1:674). An alternative women's interpretation is, "have a lot of clothes", literally referring to a chest with clothes, wards etc. (in stead of a wardrobe earlier, or a supplement to it).

POORNESS. *Han gik baglæns af træskoene* "he went backwards off his wooden shoes", 'he went bankrupt'. – *han skred af skydselen* (from West Jutlandic *han skræj å æ skjøssel*) "he slipped off the 'baking spade'", 'he went bankrupt'; LEX: *skydsel / skjøssel* = baking plate (or 'spade') with a shaft, for pushing the bread into the oven. This idiom also has another meaning (cf. Section 3.8). – *han er på de høje nagler* "he is on the high rivets" (or "spikes", the word's reference is not clear), 'his economy is strenuous', he is probably going bankrupt (cf. also Section 4).

---

8.   Following Croft & Cruse (2004, p. 170), most of them may be said to represent *(parallel) equipollent* systems because the properties of the two scales involved are fully symmetrical (e.g., with *rich* on the one scale vs. *poor* on the other: 'more rich' corresponds to 'less poor').

3.2   Cleverness, slyness vs. stupidity, foolishness, awkwardness

CLEVERNESS, SLYNESS. Here we find some idioms taken over from notions or percep-
tions of the fox: *han er en snu ræv* "he is a sly fox", 'he is a sly, cunning person'. – *han
har en ræv bag øret* "he has a fox behind his ear", 'he is not earnest, but joking or
cheating'. – *han er foret med rævebælg* "he is furred with foxskin", 'he is a very sly
or unreliable person', you can not trust him; or at least: 'his sayings are ambiguous',
you can not be sure of what he really means or is hinting at. – *de tobenede ræve er
de værste* "the two-legged foxes are the worst", i.e. persons may be even more sly,
unreliable etc. than foxes. Here you may speak of *polysemy*, because *ræv* (FOX) in this
sentence directly means 'sly person'. This in fact has had lexicographic consequences
because some dictionaries have it as a separate meaning, cf. *I. Ræv 3* (ODS.18,
p. 131), *ræv 2* (DDO.5, p. 164), both defined as 'sly, crafty, cunning person', whereas
the dialect dictionary only operates with the meaning 'animal' (Feilberg.3, p. 112),
thereby mentioning the idiom above between a lot of other idioms and proverbs.

At this place a few *similes* may be mentioned, especially as the last of them leads
to further idioms. As a parallel to the first idiom above we have the simile *han er
snu som en ræv* "he is as sly, cunning as a fox". This is mentioned among the wide-
spread European idioms of the type "Fables, Folk Narration (etc.)" in Piirainen,
2012, p. 512. It may be said that Jutlandic hereby shares the common European
figurative lexicon and also the semiotization of the FOX (i.e. making it a linguistic
symbol), and the symbolic meanings of SLYNESS and CLEVERNESS. But it also goes
its own way, the following similes are (presumably) not known in other European
languages. – *han er så lodden som æ ræv* "he is as hairy as the fox", and here in fact
a figurative reading, especially of the adjective *lodden* "hairy", 'he is as unreliable
as the fox'. A parallel expression is *så lodden som et får* "as hairy as a sheep", also
meaning 'unreliable'. Here again we touch upon the question of *polysemy* because
you may say that the meaning 'unreliable' is a special meaning of the adjective *lodden*.[9] This word directly translates into 'shaggy, hairy' (DanEng.1: 833), but in both
the dialects and Standard Danish it also means 'unreliable, false' (Feilberg.2, p. 519)
and 'sly, cunning' (ODS.12, p. 108), which has had the lexicographic consequence
that both these dictionaries place it as separate meaning (no. 2). In Jutlandic this
figurative meaning is by far the most common; you may speak of a person as *en
lodden hund / krabat* "a hairy dog / chap", or he may be *lodden indeni* "hairy inside"
or *lodden langt ned i æ hals* "hairy deep in throat" (Feilberg loc. cit.). Presumably,
all this imagery has the fox and its appearance and behavior as a starting point,

---

9.   The Standard Danish spelling of the word was *lådden* until the 1970's respectively *laadden*
until the spelling reform in 1948. I have changed the spellings of Feilberg, ODS and DanEng. to
the now correct one, *lodden*.

supported by the (in a way) similar appearance of sheep (woolen, hairy) and then spread out to the behavior of some dogs. The figurative meaning is not mentioned in the latest Danish dictionary (DDO.3, p. 571), but is probably still used.[10]

STUPIDITY, AWKWARDNESS etc. Idioms here may refer to processes that went wrong or were not fulfilled, and the like. *han er ikke ret hugget af træet* "he is not rightly cut out of the wood", 'he is silly'. – *han er kun halvbagt* "he is only half baked" like bread taken too early out of the oven, figuratively for 'he is simple-minded, stupid'. A similar image is underlying the idiom *han kom af ovnen med kagen* "he came out of the oven together with the white bread",[11] i.e. he came out too early, figuratively for 'he is stupid'; LEX: in the large ovens white bread and coarse bread were baked together, the white bread being taken out long before the coarse bread. This idiom corresponds to an idiom in the Low German dialect Westmünsterländisch, *he mutt noch eenmaol in'n Backowwen* "he must once more into the oven", i.e. he has to be baked one more time (cf. Piirainen, 2000.1, p. 146). – The idioms may refer to orientation abilities, e.g. *han ved hverken sønder eller nør* "he knows neither south nor north", 'he does not know the most basic things, he is really silly'. – They could be (self) ironic: *der fik jeg mine heste / tørv godt solgt* "there I had my horses (or peats) well sold", 'there I was (very) much cheated', or in terms of stupidity, 'how silly I was to let someone cheat me so much'. – As to awkwardness may be mentioned the idiom *køre med* (or *sætte de høje hjul for* "drive with (or) place the high wheels in front", figuratively for 'do things in an awkward way'; LEX: a common type of carts had high rear wheels and low front wheels (as e.g. stagecoaches), which could not be exchanged with each other. The English equivalent *to put the cart before the horse* is placed between "Proverbial units of medieval times" in Piirainen, 2012, p. 423).

3.3   Slowness, idleness vs. rapidity, hard work

SLOWNESS, IDLENESS. Here we first turn to idioms going out from the use of horses, i.e. coming from the source frame HORSE. *han vil ikke gerne stivne skagle* "he does not like to stiffen trace", 'he does not like to work (hard), he tries to evade working

---

10. Further, a few corresponding similes with *ræveunge* 'fox cub', may be mentioned. *Jeg er så uskyldig som en syvårs ræveunge*, 'I am as innocent as a seven years old fox cub', which is humorous and euphemistic because of the double joke: a fox of seven years is not a cub, but a rather grown up fox, and such an old fox is presumably very cunning. The simile is found in other versions, e.g. *så from som en tiårs ræveunge* "as gentle as ten years old fox cub", i.e. not gentle at all, and *så klog som en syvårs* ræveunge "as wise/cunning as a seven years old fox cub", i.e. rather wise, not to be cheated.

11. Or rather, bread made of bolted rye/wheat flower. Danish *kage* means "cake" nowadays, but also has had the meaning "bread, loaf" earlier in both Standard Danish and the dialects.

(hard)'. LEX: *skagle* ("trace") is a drawing rope from the horse to the swingletrees in front of the cart, the plough etc.; to *stivne* ("stiffen") this rope means to stretch it out, which is necessary for dragging the cart etc. – Similarly, *han vil helst gå med linde skagler* "he prefers to go with loose traces", 'he prefers to drag only a little', i.e. he likes easy going, not working too much. – Another aspect is touched upon in, *han rider ikke den dag, han sadler* "he does not ride the (same) day he saddles", 'he is a slow starter', 'he likes to take his time' (cf. DanEng.2, p. 226, p. 263). The noun *skagle* is also used in other idioms, cf. Section 3.7. – *han springer ikke i to kilder (brønde) på én gang* "he does not jump into two wells at the same time (when digging them)", 'he does not work more than necessary, he really does not strain himself'.[12] – A resembling image is underlying the idiom *han løber ikke i syv kålgårde på én gang* "he does not run into seven kitchen gardens at one time", 'he does not work more than necessary, he is slow'. Here the number *syv* ("seven") is of course not to be understood literally, in stead it is a "significant number symbol" as in some other European languages (Piirainen, 2007, p. 214).

RAPIDITY, HARD WORK. *Sommetider kørte han på egerne* "sometimes he drove on the spokes", meaning 'he drove extremely fast';[13] LEX: he had driven so fast that the rims of the cartwheels had fallen off and only the spokes were left. – *han har et hareskind for røven* "he has the skin of a hare on his ass", i.e. 'he is running quickly', maybe just moving restless around, or quickly away, the figurative meaning then being 'he is coward'. – As to hard work we find a parallel to the above mentioned with *skagle* ("trace"), i.e. *han måtte stinde skagler* "he had to stiffen trace", 'he had to work hard'; LEX: the verb *stinde* has almost the same meaning as *stivne* above. – Also here a simile may be mentioned, e.g. *så hurtigt som kæp(per) i hjul*, which has a corresponding English idiom, *as quick as spokes in a wheel*, 'very fast, without stop'. – The same nouns are used in an idiom with the opposite meaning, *sætte/ stikke en kæp i hjulet* in Standard Danish with the dialectal variants *sæt en kjæp i hywle* in North Jutland, respectively, *stek en kjæp i æ hywl* in West Jutland. All of these correspond to the English idiom *put a spoke in the wheel*, 'disturb, stop, make hindrances' for someone or something. It may be added that this idiom has been well-known in various languages (e.g. German *den Stock ins Rad stecken*, now obsolete) since the Late Middle Ages, cf. the depiction on Bruegels's painting "The Netherlandish Proverbs" (1559).[14]

---

12. The noun *kilde* ('fountain', 'well') is nowadays substituted by *brønd* ('well') in daily speech, also dialectal, but the idiom is not found with the noun *brønd*; it certainly is disappearing together with the word *kilde* (which by the way had rather special pronunciation forms, e.g. *tsjo·l*).

13. This idiom has (had) a further figurative reading, 'carry oneself strongly', at least in North East Jutland.

14. E. Piirainen, personal communication.

3.4   Wastefulness vs. thrift, miserliness

WASTEFULNESS. From the household of old days we have *slå alt sit smør i bagetru-get* "to use all one's butter in the baking trough" (for kneading the dough), 'be wasteful', because some of it could have been better used to butter the bread, or it could have been sold to the grocer. – *dit får har nok fået to lam* "your sheep (singular) has probably brought forth two lambs"; LEX: in earlier times of scarcity and rural home production said to a person who was in stocking feet instead of walking barefoot, thereby coming in need of wool to a new pair of stockings earlier than necessary. This yields the figurative meaning 'you are an optimistic spendthrift'. – In the same situation one may also utter *du stoler nok på, at ron-nevædderen er levende endnu* "you certainly rely on that the ram is yet alive", i.e. you believe that there will be new lambs in due time for you to get wool for new stockings, again with the figurative meaning 'you are a spendthrift'.

THRIFT, MISERLINESS. *Hun giver ikke sin sødmælksost bort* "she does not give her full-cream cheese away", 'she is miserly, close-fisted'. – *holde på skillingen* "keep the farthing", 'be close-fisted, not willing to spend much money'. Here a Standard Danish proverb has been entering the dialects, e.g. *holde på skillingen og lade daleren rulle* (or, in a Midwest Jutland dialect, *hål· å æ skjelling å la æ då·ler rul*), "keep the farthing and let the shilling roll away", with an equivalent idiom in English: *be penny-wise and pound-foolish* (DanEng.2, p. 339). Seemingly, this idiom for using double standards in economic matters was also needed in the dialects, but both versions are presumably threatened now as the coins mentioned have been out of use for a long time.

3.5   Luck vs. misfortune

LUCK. No direct idioms have been found in this semantic field, but some of the idioms of richness in Section 3.1 (e.g. *hans plov går rigtigt* "his plough goes rightly") may be used as they show luck in economic matters and thereby (perhaps) in general.

UNLUCK. Here an example from Section 2.3 may be mentioned again, *af asken i ilden*, "from the ashes into the fire", 'from the better to the worse', with the English equivalent *out of the frying-pan into the fire*. The Jutlandic and Danish idiom is still in use and understood, although many people do not use open fire at all nowadays; the underlying image is rather easy to comprehend. – In this semantic field also a proverb may be interpreted as an idiom in the function of an utterance, i.e. *det er for sent at kaste kilden/brønden til, når barnet er druknet* "it is too late to fill the well with earth when the child has drowned", 'there is nothing to do after the accident, you should have acted to prevent it instead'. An English equivalent is the proverb *it is too late to lock the stable door when the horse is stolen* (DanEng.1, p. 78).

3.6   High spirits vs. discontent, anger

HIGH SPIRITS. As in Section 3.3, we find idioms with the noun *skagle* ("trace"), especially *slå til skaglerne* "hit (or kick) the traces", 'have a good time, be out on the spree' (DanEng.2, p. 327), and, with the same figurative meaning, "kick over the traces". A little variation may be found in the dialectal version *træde over æ skawl* "tread over the trace", 'do something unfortunate'. The use of horses as draught animals was long gone in the 1970'es; yet, a famous pop song of these years alluded to it in the form *slå en skagle* "hit a trace", i.e. without a preposition which else is obligatory in Danish (cf. *til, over* above). The line of the verse goes: *når han har været på kroen at slå en skagle* "when he has been at the inn to hit a trace", i.e. 'when he has been out on the spree at the local inn and is 'ill' the day after'.[15] This alludes to the theme of DRINKING, INTOXICATION, which is a prolific semantic field for idioms, as illustrated by e.g. *han har fået målt skæppen fuld* "he has got his bushel fully allotted", 'he is intoxicated, drunk'.[16] The same figurative meaning is underlying the idioms *han har fået piben tændt* "he has got his pipe lighted", *han har vadet sin støvle over* "he has waded his boot over", and, *han har en bjørn/hund i rebet* "he has (or pulls) a bear/dog in the rope". LEX: The last idiom refers back to the 19th century markets where bears were shown publicly, and the bear leaders sometimes were a bit drunk when dragging the bears from market to market. – Other idioms are *få blus på* "get a blaze on", with the variant *have blus på lampen* "have a blaze on the lamp" (referring to oil or kerosene lamps), which in colloquial English has the equivalent *be lit up* (EngDan.1, p. 763). – *være på de høje nagler* "be on the high rivets/spikes" 'be heavily drunk'; this idiom also has other meanings, e.g. 'be going bankrupt' (cf. Section 3.2).[17] As to the situation after the drinking we find the almost realistic describing idioms, *have tømmermænd* "have carpenters", *have en smed i panden* "have a blacksmith

---

15. The title of the song was *Fut i fejemøget*, an idiom meaning that things are happening really rapidly, the normal slow routine is changed or speeded up, as a house on fire; it was written by the singer John Mogensen about 1970.

16. This metaphor also has the meaning 'he got a good scolding', from the semantic field of CRITICISM, REPROOF.

17. Further meanings and usability in other situations are shown in Arboe, 2013, p. 47f.

in the forehead" 'have a hangover'. It may be noted that to the first of these idioms a parallel is found in Westmünsterländisch, e.g. *he häff de Timmerlöö in'n Dackstohl* "he has carpenters in the roof construction" (Piirainen 2000.2, p. 390, with an illustration p. 388).

DISCONTENT, ANGER. *han er kommet baglæns i trøjen i dag* "he has put his jacket on backwards today", 'he is cross, disgruntled'. Standard Danish instead uses the idiom *han har fået det forkerte ben (først) ud af sengen* "he has got the wrong leg first out of the bed", which has the English equivalent *got out of bed the wrong side* (DanEng.2, p. 301). This idiom is also registered in Piirainen (2012, p. 328), in the chapter "Various ancient sources". – Another image is found in *de maler peber* "they are grinding pepper", 'they grumble, they are angry'. – This image is also underlying the idiom *han har en kjole fuld af peber derhjemme* "he has a (woman's) dress full of pepper at home", 'he has an ill-tempered wife'.

3.7   Selfishness vs. cooperation

SELFISHNESS. *hyppe sine egne kartofler* "earth up one's own potatoes", 'take advantage for oneself when handling a situation'; as English equivalents may be mentioned: *look after number one; feather one's own nest; have an axe to grind* (DanEng.1, p. 576). – *mele sin egen kage* "sprinkle one's own cake", 'take advantage for oneself (etc.)', as in the preceding example; here the same English equivalents will do (DanEng.1, p. 865). – Likewise, the idiom *rage sammen til sin egen potte* "scrape together for one's own (earthenware) pot" expresses this thought, earthenware pots being used for many purposes in the kitchen and larder in the households of the 19th century.[18]

COOPERATION. As in 3.3, the starting point of the idiom comes from the source frame HORSE, e.g. *trække på samme* (or *lige*) *hammel* "pull by the same/equal doubletree", 'pull together, work equally'; LEX: a doubletree has a singletree for each of the horses in the team which pull it by the traces. If the horses "pull by equal doubletree" (with "stiffened traces") they pull on a par; if one horse is weak or just relaxing the other has to work harder. Although this idiom is well known also i Standard Danish it may be threatened now as the object *hammel* ('doubletree') has not been in general use for decades.

---

18. In fact pottery was almost an industry in some areas of Jutland at this time, so much that the pots were called *jydepotter* "Jutlandic pots" in Standard Danish, the dialects more often using the term *sorte potter* "black pots".

3.8   Life vs. death

NEW LIFE. *Nu strammer æ kjowl igen om æ maw* "now the gown again fits too tight at the stomach", 'now she is pregnant again'. – *hun går med en grøn ost i maven* "she has a green cheese in her stomach", 'she is pregnant'; the image perhaps alludes to both the size of a cheese and the possible expansion of it by fermenting, perhaps as an euphemistic circumlocution as found by idioms in Westmünsterländisch (Piirainen 2000.1, p. 165), but rather just a humorous idiom. – In North Jutlandic another humorous idiom is used: *Hun har brø i her ovn* "she has bread in her oven", 'she is pregnant'. This idiom probably comes from Standard Danish, *hun har brød i ovnen* (with the same meaning); it is not found in Feilberg or ODS, but the phrase, *have noget i ovnen*, 'have something in preparation', is registered in ODS-S.5, p. 570 as slang from the 1950'es. The version above was presumably introduced to the dialects by the singer Ib Grønbech in a popular song in 1993, "Kys mig, Conny, Conny, kys mig" using the melody of "Kiss me, honey, honey, kiss me".[19] – As for the final stage, the childbirth, some dialects had the idiom, *hun har slået sin potte i stykker* "she has broken her (earthenware) pot to pieces", an image rather directly alluding to the fact that the woman could not 'contain' the baby any longer.

DEATH. *Han har stillet træskoene* "he has put his wooden shoes (for the last time)", 'he is dead' (as mentioned in Section 2.2). – West Jutlandic also has the idiom *han skræj å æ skjøssel* (Standard Danish: *Han skred af skydselen*) "he slipped off the 'baking spade'", figuratively for 'he died'; LEX: *skydsel / skjøssel* = baking plate, spade, with a shaft, for pushing the bread into the oven (as described in Section 3.1). – *han har fået en (grøn) tørv over hovedet* "he has got a (green) peat over his head", 'he is dead and buried'.

4.   Results

4.1   Overview of key lexemes and key concepts of the idioms

After the above presentation and explanation of a large selection of idioms, they may be summed up by placing their basic words, which may be called 'key lexemes' or even 'key concepts', in a covering chart (see Figure 1).[20]

---

19. The use of idioms in popular songs (cf. also the example in 3.6) is a sign of the idioms' vitality at the moment, and, on the other hand, helping them to be remembered for a longer time by a broader public.

20. Probably the chart could be constructed in a better way if more space was available, but with its compromises as to column breadth etc. this one seems the best possible for one page.

Topic groups / Semantic fields	a. farm util. etc.	b. workshop	c. animals	d. kitchen util. etc.	e. inventory	f. clothes etc.	g.–h. money/ geogr.
1. richness (vs.) poorness	plough	rivets, spikes		'baking spade'	chest	wooden shoes	farthing
2. slyness (vs.) stupidity, awkwardness	peats; cart	(axe); wheel	fox, dog, sheep, fox cub; horse; horse	oven			/south; /north
3. slowness, idleness (vs.) rapidity	trace, (saddle), wells, kitchen gardens	spokes, wheel	(horse); hare				
4. wastefulness (vs.) thriftiness			sheep, lambs, ram	'baking trough'; cheese			farthing, shilling
5. luck (vs.) misfortune	(plough); well			ashes, fire			
6. high spirits (vs.) discontent	trace, bushel	rivets, spikes	bear, dog	pepper	lamp; bed	pipe, boot; jacket, dress	
7. selfishness vs. cooperation	potatoes; double-tree			cake	(earthenware) pot		
8. life (vs.) death	peat			bread, oven; 'baking spade'	(earthenware) pot	dress; wooden shoes	

Figure 1. Chart of English equivalents to the Danish/Jutlandic key lexemes / key concepts in the idioms in Section 3.1–3.8: semantic fields (1)–(8) and topic groups (a)–(h), the semantic fields representing antonyms and other oppositions.

Comments to Figure 1. In the line 'topic groups', 'farm util.etc.' means 'farm utilities, farm surroundings', and 'kitchen util.etc.' means 'kitchen utilities, things made
or used in a kitchen'. – In the column 'semantic fields', (1)–(8) correspond to the
Sections 3.1–3.8 above. The antonyms or oppositions within a semantic field are
mentioned in the same order as in the sections; the mark *vs.* between them had to
be omitted in some cases to save space. – Inside the chart each key lexeme has got
its own line in a column, e.g. in field (1b) *rivets, spikes* (separated by a comma),
and the key lexemes belonging to the second headword of the semantic field are
placed in line with this, e.g. in field (1b) *rivets, spikes* in line with *poorness* in the
column 'semantic fields'. – In parenthesis are placed words that are not directly
mentioned, but implied in the idioms, in field (2b) '(axe)' because use of an axe
(or the like) is implied in the verb of the idiom, *han er ikke ret hugget af træet*
'he is not rightly cut (out) of the wood', and in field (3a) '(saddle)' because the
idiom *han rider ikke den dag, han sadler* does not include the noun *sadel* 'a saddle', but the verb *sadle* 'to saddle', however thereby implying use of a horse, hence
'(horse)' in field (3c). Alternatively, '(plough)' in field (5a) is used to indicate that
'plough' from field (1a) may be used also here, cf. the idiom *hans plov går rigtigt*
as mentioned in Section 3.5 above. These lexemes function as concepts and might
therefore be marked as such, i.e. AXE, SADDLE, HORSE, PLOUGH. – The parenthesis
around the plural ending in 'spoke(s)' in field (3b) points to the fact that both
Danish nouns, *kæp* and *ege*, translate into English 'spoke', the one being used in
the singular, the other in the plural in idioms mentioned in Section 3.3.

The chart sums up central parts of the vocabulary, the key lexemes and key
concepts used in the idioms in the preceding section. However, it may also be
used the other way round (i.e., for finding Danish/Jutlandic idioms equivalent to
English words). For example, from field (6c) English *bear* will in Section 3.6 lead
to the literal translation "he has a bear in the rope" of the corresponding Danish
idiom *han har en bjørn i rebet*.

As to the "topic groups" in which the idioms are found the chart shows that
especially the groups including utilities are well represented: farm utilities etc. in
group (a) form a basis for idioms in 7 of the 8 semantic fields (richness, slyness etc.);
the same holds for kitchen utilities in group (d). Most of the groups are represented
in 4 semantic fields; this holds for group (b), utensils etc. from the workshop, and
for group (c), animals, and also for groups (e) and (f), inventory and clothes, both
of them have idioms in the semantic fields (1) and (6)–(8). Group (g), money, is
represented in 2 semantic fields, and group (h), geography, only in one semantic
field. It will be seen that some of the key words are found two times in the same
topic group, for example TRACE in group (a) in semantic fields (3) and (6); this corresponds to the discussion in Section 3.3. and 3.6 of idioms (*stivne skagle* "stiffen
trace", etc.) having *trace* as an equivalent to the Danish key lexeme.

4.2   Lexicographical consequences of idioms

As mentioned in the last part of Section 2.2, idioms may cause the need for establishing an extra (sub-)meaning in a lexicon entry, if the figurative meaning is
seen as an instance of polysemy and thus cannot be subsumed under the main
meaning(s) of the entry. Two examples of this are found in this investigation and
have been mentioned in Section 3.3, i.e. the noun *ræv* ('fox'), and the adjective
lodden ('hairy'). Besides the meaning 'fox (as an animal)' of the noun *ræv*, the
figurative meaning 'sly person' is established separately in the entries of some dictionaries (the ODS. and the DDO.), a practice the *Jysk Ordbog* ("Dictionary of the
Jutlandic Dialects") certainly will follow in due time although the first dictionary
of Jutland dialects (Feilberg, 1886–1914) choose to subsume the figurative meaning under the main meaning. In idioms the adjective *lodden* ('shaggy, hairy') also
has the figurative meaning 'unreliable', which has caused the establishing of separate meaning in the lexicon entries in the ODS. and Feilberg.; the *Jysk Ordbog* will
do it in the same way.

From a phraseological point of view one could wish a systematic distinction
between literal and figurative meanings in dictionaries, and this is found in some
dictionaries, e.g. the DDO., idioms here being placed after the mark *ofø* (an abbre-
viation for *overført* 'figuratively', cf. DDO.1, p. 45). But if you deal with a figurative
unit you ought to include a detailed semantic explication, and this may be difficult,
for instance because the source texts do not always directly tell if (part of) a sentence have a figurative meaning besides the literal meaning. At least this holds for
some of the source material of the *Jysk Ordbog*, e.g. Feilberg. Thus, as an editor of
a dictionary of this type you sometimes have to cite a phraseme only in its literal
reading although you – because of your linguistic and cultural intuition, empathy
or knowledge – are almost sure that it is meant figuratively.

5.   Conclusion

Above I have presented various figurative units from important semantic fields,
but many more could be found in these as well as in many other fields. They are
preserved alongside similes and other types of idioms in archives and dictionaries of the Danish dialects and Standard Danish, and perhaps the dictionaries include even more figurative units than directly pointed to because of the
uncertainty as to figurativeness mentioned just above. There is no doubt that
idioms and figurative units, with roothold in the local or regional culture, have
played a central role in the everyday communication in the communities in

question.[21] For how long they will stay in use is a difficult question because it is to some degree idiosyncratic when persons stop to use older words, be they dialectal or standard language, as touched upon in the introduction, and as mentioned about idioms with names of obsolete coins and an obsolete farming utility (Sections 3.4, 3.7). The tendency to use a rather neutral vocabulary in order to be understood easily by as many as possible will also cause a loss of older idioms, but a good deal of them will presumably be in use some decades yet, especially the ones also found in Standard Danish.

One of the aims of the "Dictionary of the Jutlandic dialects" is to preserve these unique metaphors and figurative expressions; it must be secured that they will not be lost if the dialects will not be spoken anymore. And if some idioms show polysemy of the lexemes involved (Section 4.2) we even allow for lexicographical consequences to the entries of the dictionary by establishing additional (sub-)meanings in the entries concerned.

References

Arboe, T. (2012). Dialekter og standardsprog – synspunkter og undersøgelser siden 1960 [Dialects and standard language – viewpoints and investigations since 1960]. *Ord & Sag*, 32, 18–34.

Arboe, T. (2013). En- og flertydige idiomer (metaforer) i jysk og rigsdansk [Idioms (metaphors) with one or more meanings in Jutlandic and Standard Danish]. In S. Borchmann, I. Schoonderbeek Hansen, T. T. Hougaard, O. Togeby, & P. Widell (Eds.), *Gode ord er bedre end guld. Festskrift til Henrik Jørgensen i anledning af 60-års dagen* (pp. 43–51). Aarhus: Aarhus Universitet.

Arboe, T. (2014). Phraseology – central parts of culture treated in a dictionary. In V. Jesenšek & P. Grzybek (Eds.), *Phraseologie im Wörterbuch und Korpus – Phraseology in Dictionaries and Corpora* (pp. 27–38). Maribor (etc.): Tiskarna Saje d.o.o.

Bennike, V., & Kristensen, M. (1912). *Kort over de danske folkemål* [Maps concerning the Danish vernaculars]. København: Gyldendal.

Burger, H. (2007). Semantic aspects of phrasemes. In H. Burger, D. Dobrovol'skij, P. Kühn, & N. R. Norrick (Eds.), *Phraseology. An international handbook of contemporary research* (pp. 90–109). Berlin/New York: de Gruyter.

Croft, W., & Cruse, A. D. (2004). *Cognitive linguistics*. Cambridge: Cambridge University Press. DOI: 10.1017/CBO9780511803864

---

21. It might be interesting to make a further, general study of which idioms have turned obsolete in Standard Danish, but remain in the dialects. According to an introductory study of conditions in Luxemburg, phrasemes that are disappearing in High German there seem to belong to the most commonly used in the dialect of "Lëtzebuergesch" (Filatkina, 2007, p. 150), and perhaps at least traces of a similar pattern could be found as to idioms in Danish dialects and Standard Danish.

DanEng. = Vinterberg, H., og Bodelsen, C. A. (1966). *Dansk-Engelsk Ordbog* [Danish-English Dictionary]. 1–2. København: Gyldendal.

DDO = *Den danske ordbog* [The Danish Dictionary]. (2002–2005). 1–6. København: Gyldendal.

Dobrovol'skij, D., & Piirainen, E. (2005). *Figurative language. Cross-cultural and cross-linguistic perspectives*. Amsterdam [etc.]: Elsevier.

Dobrovol'skij, D., & Piirainen, E. (2009). *Zur Theorie der Phraseologie. Kognitive und kulturelle Aspekte*. Tübingen: Stauffenburg.

Feilberg. = Feilberg, H. F. (1886–1914). *Ordbog over jyske almuesmål* [Dictionary of Jutlandic vernaculars]. 1–4. København: Thieles Bogtrykkeri.

Filatkina, N. (2007). Pragmatische Beschreibungsansätze. In H. Burger, D. Dobrovol'skij, P. Kühn & N. R. Norrick (Eds.) *Phraseology. An international handbook of contemporary research* (pp. 132–158). Berlin/New York: de Gruyter.

Fillmore, C. F. (1985). Frames and the semantics of understanding. *Quaderni di Semantica*, 85(1), 222–254. Bologna: Società editrice el Mulino.

Jysk Ordbog [Dictionary of the Jutlandic dialects]. www.jyskordbog.dk (A–I), manuscript (J–KL), card index (KN – Å/AA). Peter Skautrup Center of Jutlandic Dialect Research, Aarhus University.

Lakoff, G. (1987). *Women, fire and dangerous things*. Chicago/London: The University of Chicago Press. DOI: 10.7208/chicago/9780226471013.001.0001

Lakoff, G., & Johnson, M. (1980/2003). *Metaphors we live by*. Chicago/London: The University of Chicago Press.

ODS = *Ordbog over det danske Sprog* [Dictionary of the Danish Language]. (1918–1956). 1–28. København: Gyldendal.

ODS-S = *Ordbog over det danske Sprog. Supplement* [Dictionary of the Danish Language. Supplement]. (1992–2005). 1–5. København: Gyldendal.

Piirainen, E. (2000). *Phraseologie der westmünsterländischen Mundart. 1–2*. Baltmannsweiler: Schneider Verlag.

Piirainen, E. (2007). Phrasemes from a cultural semiotic perspective. In H. Burger, D. Dobrovol'skij, P. Kühn, & N. R. Norrick (Eds.) *Phraseology. An international handbook of contemporary research* (pp. 208–219). Berlin/New York: de Gruyter.

Piirainen, E. (2012). *Widespread idioms in Europe and beyond. Toward a Lexicon of common figurative units*. New York [etc.]: Peter Lang.

Skautrup, P. (1944). *Det danske Sprogs Historie* [History of the Danish language]. 1. København: Gyldendal.

Stern, J. (2008). Metaphor, semantics, and context. In Gibbs (Ed.), *The Cambridge handbook of metaphor and thought* (pp. 262–279). Cambridge: University Press. DOI: 10.1017/CBO9780511816802.017

CHAPTER 9

A nation without a language is a nation without heart

On vanishing Tatar idioms*

Guzel Gizatova

Kazan State Agrarian University, Kazan, Russia

The Tatar language has been exposed to significant transformations under the pressure of the Russian language. The nature of this pressure has been characterized as political, social, and cultural by different disciplinary traditions, with no small part being played by globalization. The purpose of this chapter is to explore endangered Tatar idioms along two revealing lines of enquiry. The first line of enquiry analyzes culture-specific Tatar idioms; the second line interrogates borrowed idioms from Russian sources. The paper argues that Russian idiom-adoption leads to loss of Tatar-specific knowledge as well as loss of Tatar-specific encodings of that knowledge otherwise found in traditional idioms. This indelibly transforms Tatar history and culture.

Keywords: Tatar, endangered metaphors, unique idioms, culture

1. Introduction

The purpose of this paper is to present new empirical material and new thinking, which is now subsumed in a new paradigm for considering the powerful impact of metaphors on the language and culture of the Tatar people. Russification of the Tatar language, resulting in some of the "weed-metaphors" borrowed from the Russian language is growing steadily. It is interesting to note that while using words of their mother tongue the younger generation borrows metaphors from the intruding dominate language. This chapter documents many cases of the Russian idioms being adopted by Tatar native speakers in oral and written discourse instead of keeping their own phraseology. Using

---

* Welsh proverb.

DOI 10.1075/clscc.7.08giz
© 2015 John Benjamins Publishing Company

Russian metaphors and neglecting at the same time their existing national Tatar equivalents causes severe erosion of the native language. This destructive process can be classified as language shift that cumulatively leads to language death after several generations. So the fate of any language is in the minds of its present and future native speakers.

The chapter is structured as follows: after a brief introduction to the Tatar language, I present the origin of the ethnonym *Tatar*, relevant historical and cultural background, followed by a theoretical framework. Next, I present unique and archaic idioms and arrange a typology of aspects of cultural knowledge that are found in these idioms. I conclude by analyzing metaphors exposed to transformations in conditions of bilingualism in Tatarstan.

1.1   The Tatar language and its current status

The Tatar language belongs to a Turkic branch of an Altaic family of languages. About 7 million people speak Tatar. Currently the language as a whole cannot be characterized as immediately endangered, because it has quite a number of current speakers and according to the all-Russian census conducted in 2010, the Tatars were the second largest ethnic group in the Russian Federation after the Russians (Rossijskaja Gazeta, 2011, December 16, pp. 14–15). Nevertheless, increasing numbers of Tatars are dispersing, with more than 900,000 people live in Moscow and significant numbers live in the Urals, Siberia, Middle Asia. Moreover, Tatar diasporas are growing in the USA, Australia, Finland, Canada and many other countries. Hence, due to geographic dispersal as well as political and social factors the Tatar language is yielding its prime position to the Russian language, which is considerably larger and functions as a lingua franca in many contexts. The Tatar language is being exposed to serious changes and there is mounting evidence that it will not be safely passed to new generations. During the last twenty years Tatarstan (as a federation unity) has lost many attributes constituting national identity. Early in 2000, Moscow embarked on a policy of "eliminating the cultural identity of non-Russians and abolishing the political rights of the national republics" (Devlet, 2009).

Additionally, the Tatar nation is deprived of the right to select and employ the Roman writing system, which is more suitable for the phonetic system of Tatar than the Cyrillic writing system. The Roman writing system has been characterized as constituting a threat to the safety and integrity of the Russian Federation. Moreover, during the last several years the Tatars were deprived of national universities and schools. In 2007 radio broadcasting in Tatar was reduced, and the rebroadcasting of Radio Free Europe/Radio Liberty's daily Tatar-Bashkir program by the local Yanga Gasir/Novy vek radio was forbidden. That move effectively deprived Tatars of access to free information in their native tongues. Today in Tatarstan, there is no round-the-clock radio or television broadcasting in Tatar (Devlet, 2009). Taken together, these actions by Moscow represent an unprecedented attack on Tatar, and by implication the social, cultural, and national identity of the Tatar people.

Devlet (2009) argues that Moscow is in violation of minority language rights. Indeed, Moscow contravenes both international laws on the rights of ethnic minorities, and the Constitution of the Russian Federation itself, which in Article 26/2 empowers every Russian citizen to use his native language and to choose freely the language medium of education.[1]

1.2   The origin of the ethnonym Tatar

The problem of ethnogenesis of the Volga *Tatars* is still being debated among scholars, both inside and outside Russia. A fair number of monographs and other academic works have been written by the early and contemporary scholars about Tatars, their origin, language, history and culture. But even in Russia, little is known about their rich 1000-years-old history. One of the most important features of the Tatar nation is riddled with general misunderstanding and misinterpretation. This nation, the people of Tatarstan, is actually completely unknown as the Volga *Tatars* are traditionally identified with Mongol Tatars of the 13th century. There is a habitual, but nevertheless natural, bias against Tatars, which results from the notion that Tatarstan is inhabited by descendants of Genghis Khan who had brought destruction to the greater part of the continent. This section will deal with a brief background of the term accepted by the majority of Russian and Western researches.

Without knowledge of history and culture of the language in many cases it is practically impossible to understand the meaning of a metaphor, to comprehend its semantic motivation. In order to uncover the hidden conceptual structures of metaphors we have to understand the historical, cultural, material and mental concepts of the nation because "[…] metaphor is built into conceptual system of the culture in which we live" (Lakoff & Johnson, 2003, p. 64). Rorlich (1986) puts forward a Mongol and Turkic thesis on Volga Tatars. She explains, that according to the *first thesis* the etymology of Tatar has been derived from Chinese Ta-Tan or Da-Dan, a contemptuous term applied to Mongols by the Chinese. The (*second –* G. G.) *Turkic thesis* was advanced by scholars who rely heavily on the *Diwan-i*

---

1. For earlier discussions in this field compare also Bakhtin (1981) and Anderson (1983), among others.

Lugat-it-Turk, a dictionary of the Turkic languages compiled by Mahmud al-Kashgari during the period 1072 to 1074. In this book, al-Kashgari mentions that west of the Irtysh river (in Siberia – G.G.) there existed a Tatar branch of the Turkic languages (Rorlich, 1986, p. 4).

Zakiev (1995) considers the ethnonym *Tatar* to be of authentically Turkic origin. He places emphasis upon the fact that all ethnonyms of one etymological system with the ending *-ar* (vowel harmony variations: *-ar, -ir, -oor*) are the names of Turkic tribes, and therefore it is a good reason to consider the word *Tatar* to be an ethnonym of a Turkic tribe (Zakiev, 1995, pp. 249–253). It is known from historical records that since before Christ there were tribes which lived on the neighboring territories of China and they were called Tatars. According to a Persian historian Rashid al-din, Tatars presented a very strong union before the rise of the Mongols. It is important to note that two powerful tribes – Mongols and Tatars – conducted a destructive war against each other for domination in the steppe. Genghis Khan completely destroyed the hostile Tatar tribe. Those who survived were disseminated amongst other Mongol tribes and started calling themselves Mongols.

So why were the Mongols called Tatars in Europe and in early Rus? The linguistic explanation is the following: "Ethnonym *Tatar* consists of two parts: *tat* "alien, stranger" and *ar* "people". So the meaning of the word is: "people of an alien tribe". The Mongols got this name from the Turks since the Mongol tribes were strangers, aliens to them (Zakiev 1995, pp. 249–253).

As the Golden Horde broke up many of the Mongols who had served the khan remained in Russia and Genghis Khan's descendants held a prominent position in the Moscow court and, by any estimate, a sizeable proportion of the Russian aristocracy had the great khan's blood running through their veins (Figes, 2002, p. 369). Many Russian families had Mongol origins. The saying "Scratch a Russian and you will find a Tatar" became world-famous.

Since Russia was separated from Western world it "[…] sought to redefine itself as a European empire with a presence in the West. If Russia was to be styled as a Western state, it needed to construct a clearer cultural boundary to set itself apart from this 'Asiatic other' in the Orient. Religion was the easiest of these categories. All the Tsar's non-Christian tribes were lumped together as 'Tartars', whatever their origins or faith, Muslim, shamanic or Buddhist. To reinforce this 'good and evil' split, the word *Tartar* was deliberately misspelled (with the extra 'r') to bring it into line with the Greek word for 'hell' (*tartaros*). More generally, there was a tendency to think of all Russia's newly conquered territories (Siberia, the Caucasus and Central Asia) as one undifferentiated 'east' – an 'Aziatshchina' – which became a byword for 'oriental languor' and 'backwardness'" (Figes, 2002, pp. 377–378).

Rorlich writes about the rehabilitation of the ethnonym *Tatar*:

> At the end of the nineteenth century, enlightened Tatar thinkers, such as Kayum
> Nasiri and Shihabeddin Merjani, played a major role in the rehabilitation of the
> ethnonym *Tatar*. Merjani argued the Kazanis not to be ashamed to call themselves
> Tatars. He noted that, because Russians employed the name *Tatar* as a curse, 'some
> have regarded being a Tatar a shortcoming, hated it, and insisted 'we are not
> Tatars, we are Muslims' [...] If you are not a Tatar, an Arab, Tajik, Nogay, Chinese,
> Russian, French [...] then, who are you?' challenged Merjani. (Rorlich, 1986, p. 4)

1.3   Outline of Tatar history and culture

There are several ethnic groups under the general name of *Tatars* in Russia: the
Volga Tatars (the overwhelming majority of all Tatars in the country), Siberian
Tatars, Crimean Tatars, "each of them with a different historical background, locale
and language [...] from an ethnic point of view, the legendary Tatars of Genghis
Khan bear to [...] these groups no more relation than to any other constituent
peoples of the Golden Horde, including ethnic Russians" (Bukharaev, 1999, p. 46).

Mirfatyh Zakiev states that modern Tatars didn't accept any ethnical, anthropological, linguistic and cultural characteristics from the Mongol-Tatar conquer-
ors. The ethnic roots of Tatars go up to ancient Turkic tribes, which inhabited
the above-mentioned territories in the period of their formation (Zakiev, 1995,
pp. 12–35). Their history begins as early as the 7th century AD. The earliest written
records belong to that time. In 922 AD the Volga Tatars officially accepted Islam
as their state religion.

Below I employ Bukharaev's[2] facts and concepts to structure the Tatar history and culture, which I bring into the present by adding information about the
destruction of the language. Bukharaev argues that the Volga Bulgars – the ancestors of today's Kazan Tatars – attained a high level of civilization manifesting itself
both in large and wonderful cities with civic buildings, systems of central heat-
ing, developed industries, agriculture, trade, and also developed science, art and
literature. The poem of Kol Gali "Qyissa-I-Yusuf" about Joseph and his brothers
was written in 1233. It is referred to as a classical work of Tatar literature which
had impact on all Oriental literature. The Golden Horde conquest (1236) actually
demolished this glorious civilization and annexed it to the Genghis Khan Empire
together with the Kiev Rus and Vladimir-Suzdal Rus. The Volga Bulgars "were able

---

2. R. Bukharaev (1951–2012) is an ethnic Tatar and a writer, historian and a journalist for the
BBC World Service in London who widely published and lectured on his native culture and
history in Russia, Hungary, UK, USA and other countries. For details see Bukharaev (1999,
pp. 44–63).

to very soon rebuild it from scratch, thus […] proving the nation's innate vitality and stoicism. In the 14th century, the Volga Bulgar capital city Bilyar became the largest city in Eastern Europe boasting a territory of 530 hectares (In comparison, Paris of the time covered an area of some 430 hectares)" (Bukharaev, 1999, p. 47). Upon the dissipation of the Golden Horde at the end of the 14th century the Kazan Khanate emerging on the same lands as the Volga Bulgaria acquired its language, ethnic roots, culture, religion and economy.

By 1552 the Kazan Khanate was a powerful economic, political and cultural entity with a network of schools, the graduates of which were able to develop national culture on the level of advanced civilizations of the time. The 2nd of October, 1552, the date of conquest of Kazan, marked the start of spiritual genocide of the Tatar nation in Russia.

Kazan Tatars were subjected to political persecution and severe economic and religious pressures during the two centuries following the fall of Kazan. Muslim Tatars were forcibly converted to Christianity and those, who resented forced conversion, were driven away from the city and for many years forbidden to enter it under threat of capital punishment. The Muslim architectural heritage of the city and all Tatar schools were fully destroyed. In the countryside, the most fertile agricultural lands were given to Russian Orthodox settlers. Even today, there are no ethnic Tatar villages within a thirty-miles radius of Kazan.

Kazan Tatars were allowed to have their own media only in 1905, whereas they had possessed their own literature since the 10th century. Throughout the 19th century, Tatar writers, scholars and encyclopedists tried to get permission to publish a Tatar newspaper, but had to remain content with annual calendars full of various kinds of religious and secular knowledge. In the field of book-publishing, things only brightened up with the establishment in Kazan, in 1804, of the university. In some years, the combined print run of those books reached 2 million copies, supplying not only the Kazan province with books, but also readers as far afield as Kazakhstan and Turkey. In 1913, there were eleven magazines and twelve newspapers in the Tatar language, whereas Kazan alone published twenty-four magazines and thirteen newspapers in both the Russian and Tatar languages.

Fuks (1844) writes:

> This nation, having been conquered for more than two centuries and scattered nowadays among Russians, preserved its traditions, morals and popular pride in such a surprising way, as if it had lived separately […]. Any visitor, no doubt, will be surprised to find in the Kazan Tatars a nation, generally speaking, more educated, than other nations, even those of Europe. A Tatar who does not know how to read and write is despised by his fellow countrymen and is not respected by others as citizen.
> (Fuks, 1844, pp. 18–19)

After the Revolution of 1917 and during the Soviet era a "supervising" political domination of the Tatars by Russian authorities that had characterized the tsarist period continued. In the 1980s there was a significant decline of the Tatar culture and language. Gorenburg (2005) writes that during that time "the Tatar language was being used less than during any other time in modern history [...] and the number of books and newspapers published in Tatar annually in the late 1980s was lower than the number published in 1913" (Gorenburg, 2005, p. 78). During Perestroika as a result of adopting "The Law on Languages" (1992) the revival of the Tatar language education began and some significant steps were taken in this direction.

But since the beginning of the 2000s the situation has changed dramatically. Although the Republic of Tatarstan remains an independent nation *de jure*, it is becoming *de facto* an indistinguishable cog on the Russian wheel for the deliberately intrusive and dominate Russian language and culture is replacing the native language and cultural traits at an alarming rate.

Today the preserving and development of the Tatar language is one of the most important political matters of world significance. Each language – regardless of whether it belongs to a powerful nation with a large population or a small ethnos – is a priceless treasure, created by one or another peoples. If the language is functioning, the nation using this language also exists. If the language dies, the nation also dies (Yusupov, 2013).

2.   Theoretical framework

This research is based on the principles of the Conventional Figurative Language Theory (CFLT) developed by Dobrovol'skij & Piirainen (2005). The role of cultural knowledge in idiom motivation is put forward in it. The core idea of the theory is "that, first, the concepts of the basic level of categorization (in the sense of Rosch, 1978) are more crucial for idiom motivation than the abstract concepts of the super-ordinate level, and, second, that culture-specific concepts, are, as a rule, more crucial than universal, biologically based concepts" (Dobrovol'skij, 2007, p. 795).

According to Piirainen[3] European tradition distinguishes "between two principle types of semantic motivation: the *metaphoric motivation* and the *symbol-based motivation* [...]. Idioms of standard literary language can additionally be

---

3.   See Piirainen (2012, pp. 341–345) for a more detailed description of all three types of motivation.

affected by a third, not purely semantic type of motivation, namely *intertextuality*" (Piirainen, 2012, pp. 342–343).

All three types of motivation are important for the purpose of describing Tatar idioms. The analysis of symbol-based idioms is essential in the current study because motivation of many idioms is based on symbols that differ from an occidental symbolic tradition. Intertextual motivation is of utmost importance to figurative units especially in languages with literary tradition, such as the Tatar language. The sources under analysis in this chapter are rich in idioms motivated by ancient works of literature and allusions to well-known texts. But the larger part of idioms is traditionally motivated metaphorically with Tatar idioms no exception.

According to CFLT, the description of an idiom on the basic level allows us to understand its semantics better than on the abstract super-ordinate level. Let us illustrate this with an idiom from the target domain STUPIDITY.

(1)   *тугыз төймә*
       "nine buttons"
       'stupid person'

When we describe a stupid person we usually try to avoid direct naming of this property and use euphemisms, coded language or idioms to make the situation sound a little better than it is. The motivation of the idiom is based on the knowledge about social behavior codes with mentally retarded people. There was a custom in Tatar social culture to sew exactly nine buttons – apotropes – on the clothing of mentally deficient people. They were supposed to ward off evil and protect a person from it. The source domain of the idiom is LACK OF SOMETHING expressed by the quantity of buttons, which are nine. It is not a round figure, one button is missing to ten. Nine buttons are compared with the brain of a person. As well as one button is missing to ten, so "one" is missing in one's brain, it is not full (having in mind that brain constitutes the "number ten"). So a person having insufficient cognitive ability can be compared with an insufficient quantity of buttons on his clothes. The conceptual mapping of the image of lacking buttons to a lack of cognitive ability evokes a metaphor STUPIDITY IS LACK OF SOMETHING. The images behind the idiom are closely related to Tatar culture knowledge. If the knowledge is not available in current cultural exchanges, the semantic import of the idiom is lost.

3. Typology of aspects of cultural knowledge in Tatar metaphors and symbols

There are many idioms in the Tatar language that have very similar metaphorical meanings or are based on the same cultural symbols as idioms from occidental languages. But at the same time there are also a number of unique figurative units in the Tatar language. In this section, the Tatar idioms under consideration are culture-based, and have few if any parallels in other European languages. These idioms help us to unveil a complex socio-cultural world of the Tatar nation. Indeed, these idioms as a result of their figurative lexical import have different iconic and symbolic meanings than those of other European languages.

In the framework of the Conventional Figurative Language Theory the analysis turns to the typology of the principal cultural phenomena that occur in figurative units.[4] I added one more type to the existing typology, dealing with historical knowledge underlying the images of various idioms. We consider ethnic history of the Tatar ancestors belonging to medieval civilization, the Volga Bulgaria, the Kazan Khanate to be essential for describing national figurative language. This knowledge about Tatar history belongs to the world knowledge of the Tatar language community and, as will be shown, manifests itself in the figurative lexicon.

3.1 History

Although "ethnic history" partly overlaps with "material culture" and "intertextuality" we consider this category helpful to capture the specifics of Tatar figurative units, as idiom (2) illustrates. The idiom is dated and used by the older generation in written and oral discourse.

> (2) *чабаталы морза*
> "prince in bast shoes"
> 'poor person who used to be rich and important'

For comprehension of the idiom, the constituent *morza* must be explained. *Morza* was an aristocratic title in Turkic states, such as Kazan, Astrakhan and Crimean Khanates, the highest layer of the Turkic nobility, corresponding to the Russian prince. In 1552, when Kazan was conquered by the Russian armies of Ivan IV (Ivan the Terrible) many Tatars were forcibly converted to Christianity (Bukharaev, 1999, 2000; Zakiev, 1995, 2003; Karimullin,1988; Rorlich, 1986;

---

4. See Dobrovol'skij & Piirainen, 2005, pp. 215–240 for more details.

Selbach, 2001). Most of them resented the conversion. So at the beginning of the 18th century Peter the Great issued a decree according to which Tatar princes refusing to become Christians were deprived of their titles, lands, serfs, money. Such people were called *чабаталы морза* (prince in bast shoes) by the common people because bast shoes were traditionally worn only by the poor Russian and Tatar peasants.

The image of a prince in peasant shoes serves as a metaphor of a poor person who used to be rich and important. The idiom is motivated by a conceptual metaphor POVERTY IS LACK OF ADEQUATE CLOTHING. But we cannot judge about semantics of the given metaphor only by "this abstract *superordinate level* [...] because it does not show the real semantic complexity of the idiom" (Piirainen, 2012, p. 343). Knowledge of the world that is based on everyday experiences contributes to understanding of this metaphor.

The metaphor is embedded into the conceptual system of the culture in which we live, in our physical and cultural experience. That's why the description of the idiom on the *basic level* (Piirainen, 2012, p. 343) allows us to make a deeper access into the specific cultural information known to the native speakers. The motivation for the metaphor comes from the socio-material environment of the native speakers, from our knowledge about traditional clothing of the peasants and the symbolism of bast shoes in the Tatar culture. Thus, bast shoes were worn until the 30s–40s of the 20th century by many ethnic groups, such as Russians, Ukrainians, Belorussians, Tatars, Finns, Mordva, Estonians, and some other nationalities. Bast shoes are one of the most outstanding symbols of the traditional Tatar culture reflected in different cultural codes (e.g., in language, folklore, and ritual). It is usually used as a derogatory term and associated with such features of a person as simplicity, stupidity, lack of culture, and ignorance in the Tatar culture. Bast shoes were plaited and were made of bast, a part of a tree bark. This knowledge about bast shoes explains the conceptual metaphor POVERTY IS LACK OF ADEQUATE CLOTHING. The more concrete source domain of the metaphor is PRINCE IN BAST (PEASANT) SHOES and the target domain is POOR PERSON (who used to be rich and important).

(3)   *Питрау күкесе*
      "Pitrau's cuckoo"
      'sb. who speaks out of place'

Idiom (3) is used as a nickname for a person who speaks at a wrong time, when the conversation is over. The expression is connected with conversation norms. According to the Tatar tradition *Питрау* (The Peter's Day) is celebrated on July 12th and marks the end of the summer and the beginning of the haying time in the villages. Originally it is a Christian holiday and that's why it is celebrated mainly by Christian Tatars. It became popular among Tatars at the beginning of the 20th century. Nature starts "preparing" to the fall after this day.

You can't hear the nightingale's songs any more, and they say that even the grass loses its juice and taste. The native speakers who have grown in rural environment say that cuckoo birds also stop singing by the *Пumpay*, because they lose their voice. The story goes that if a cuckoo tries to sing after the *Пumpay*, it will only demonstrate its being voiceless. Here, the image of a talkative cuckoo, as it is present in the minds of speakers, serves as source concept for a person who speaks at a wrong time and in a wrong place. The conceptual metaphor is BEHAVIOR OF A PERSON IS BEHAVIOR OF A BIRD. The idiom is now rarely used.

Let us look at another idiom in which historical factors combine with elements of material culture (4).

(4)   *кирта сикеру*
    "to jump over the barrier"
    'to betray one's faith' (earlier); 'to violate accepted norms' (currently)

This is an archaic idiom and comes from the times when people used to live in portable felt-covered houses. "To jump over the barrier" means to break loose outside the territory of your house, to go beyond the pale. It is motivated by the historical background of the Tatar people and connected with the times when people were changing their religion from one to another or refusing their religion. This could happen due to different factors: converting Muslims into Christianity by force; changing religion of their own free will, and other reasons. There was a complex of different motivational causes for changing religion in those years. But mainly they were social and material resources and privileges. The knowledge of the ethnic history of the Tatar people helps us to establish motivated links between literal and figurative meaning of the idiom. Since the old times this metaphor was applied to people who betrayed their faith for different privileges.

On the basic level, the idiom is motivated by fragments of the world knowledge about the ancient portable felt-covered houses while the conceptual metaphor can be formulated as OVERCOMING MORAL NORMS IS OVERCOMING A PHYSICAL OBSTACLE. During centuries the idiom has transformed its meaning and nowadays it is used to describe an immoral, disobedient person who has passed all the bounds, got out of hand. The target domain of the idiom now is VIOLATION OF ACCEPTED NORMS.

3.2   Social interaction

Cultural knowledge about interaction of people in society and their behavior are of vital importance for understanding culture-based idioms of a language. This section analyzes coded communication, which is only one aspect of social interaction. Metaphors of code in the Tatar language are used to transfer information between people of one group in a veiled form so that it cannot be comprehended by strangers. The message is understood only by those who know the code. Coded metaphors demonstrate the flexibility of the language and most of them are passed from generation to generation. Example (5) illustrates an idiom which used to be wide-spread, but at present is seldom employed:

> (5)   *түбәсе тишек*
>   "(one's) roof has a hole"
>   '(said as a warning) you should be careful in his presence, he understands our language'

Here, the source domain is THE ROOF WITH A HOLE and the target domain is UNDESIRED AMOUNT OF UNDERSTANDING OF SOMEONE'S CONVERSATION BY A STRANGER. The source domain at the abstract level, DAMAGED CONTAINER, only opens up the door for understanding of the idiom; it cannot explain the complex semantic relationships. Only the world knowledge, i.e. our life experience with material resources can help us to understand that if the roof of the house is damaged, it starts leaking with the rain, it is exposed to the wind and snow and other climatic misfortunes. The damaged roof is compared with the brain of a person. As well as the rain leaks in the house through a hole in the roof, so the words "leak" into one's brain through a hole in the head.

It is interesting to note that the Russian idiom *крыша протекает* "the roof is leaking" (which is motivated by the same conceptual metaphor of a DAMAGED CONTAINER as in Tatar) has an opposite meaning: 'someone is losing ability to think'. The Tatar idiom can be misinterpreted due to different fragments of world knowledge of the Tatars and other ethnic groups living side by side as neighbors for many centuries. From the point of view of a Russian speaker the idiom (5) can be interpreted by a conceptual metaphor STUPIDITY IS DAMAGED CONTAINER. But in the Tatar language DAMAGED CONTAINER directs to a different target domain – UNDESIRED AMOUNT OF UNDERSTANDING OF SOMEONE'S CONVERSATION BY A STRANGER, it has nothing to do with STUPIDITY. So the idiom can be understood only by the Tatar native speakers.

There are some other idioms with the same figurative meaning in the Tatar corpus which are worth consideration:

(6) *чабатасы тишек*
  "(his) bast-shoes have a hole"

(7) *салам баш*
  "a head covered with straw"

(8) *салам түбә*
  "a straw roof"

(9) *түбәсе(башы) карабодай саламы белән каплаган*
  "(his) roof (head) is covered with buckwheat straw"
  all roughly meaning 'one should be careful in his presence, he understands our language'

With respect to idioms (6)–(9) only (6) is used today. Others are practically unfamiliar to the younger generation. The older generation remembers something from what they have heard from the elder people. Idiom (6) contains the constituent *чабата* "bast-shoes", which is explained in (2). Since such shoes were plaited and made of bast, they didn't last long and frayed in a week or two, especially in spring or fall due to the rainy weather. In this metaphor a bast-shoe (*чабата*) is compared with a person's brain. As well as the rain leaks in the bast-shoe through a hole in it, so the words "leak" into one's brain through a hole in the head.

Idioms in (7), (8) and (9) are motivated by a conceptual metaphor UNDESIRED AMOUNT OF UNDERSTANDING OF SOMEONE'S CONVERSATION BY A STRANGER IS INADEQUATE COVER OF A CONTAINER. All of them contain a constituent meaning "straw". Knowledge about straw is based on our everyday experiences. Straw used to be the most common roof covering material in rural areas and sometimes in towns as well. But it is a common knowledge that straw absorbs moisture and the roofs used to leak, so straw and especially buckwheat straw were not the best covering material. Simply there was no choice. So in figurative language if one's "head or the roof of a house are covered with straw" it means that someone understands your native language and while using it in his presence you have to be very careful. This idiom is used to warn people from one group involved in conversation with a person outside the group to be careful in order to avoid social embarrassment.

There is an idiom with an opposite meaning in Tatar:

(10) *түбәсе калай, яңгыр үтми*
  "(his) roof is covered with iron, the rain does not leak in"
  'he does not understand our language, you can speak safely in his presence'

The next idiom (11) is used as a nickname for evil spirits. According to peoples' beliefs the evil spirits could change their image and being among people could listen to their talks. If they heard people speaking about them, they would be proud that they had been recognized. So in order to calm them down and to scare them away people would give the spirits bad names and, being insulted, they would leave people and disappear.

(11)   *иске чабата*
       "old bast shoe"
       'evil spirit'

Idiom (12) supposedly belongs to the coded language. We could not find any motivating link between the source domain and the target domain. There should be some explanation to the origin of this idiom, but it has not been established. It is possible that it could be some kind of a coded expression too. Anyway, the idiom deserves attention:

(12)   *яшелгә буяу*
       "to paint in green color"
       'to steal'

3.3   Phenomena of material culture

Some aspects of the specific Tatar material culture have already been mentioned, such as the bast shoes (2) and the traditional felt-covered houses (4). There is a variety of idioms whose constituents reflect specifics of traditional Tatar material culture. They denote objects which are typical of everyday life of the people. We will describe idioms that, on the basic level, refer to fundamental housing artifacts. For example:

(13)   *балта мае ялаган*
       "(he) has licked an axe oil"
       'he is very experienced'

The idiom is motivated by world knowledge which is based on everyday experiences of the people living in the climate of severe winter conditions. Geographically the Volga Tatars live in a part of Russia which has so-called harsh continental climate characterized by a big difference between summer and winter temperatures. It gets hot in summer and very cold in winter. So people living in high latitudes know perfectly that winter is not the time to stick one's tongue to metal. In winter when an axe is brought into a warm house from the cold, its blade is glistening because of melting frost and its drops look like oil drops. When kids are curious enough they lick the blade and immediately their tongue sticks to it. So the tongue is injured most frequently.

(14) *балтасы суга төшү*
       "(his) axe has fallen down in water"
       'to be in low spirits"

The conceptual mapping of the image of an axe falling down in water to psychological imbalance results in the metaphor DOWN IS BAD. Loosing something goes along with sadness and low mood very frequently. It is interesting to note that there is a Finnish idiom with similar image component: *heittää kirveensä järveen* "to throw one's hatchet into the lake" meaning figuratively 'to give up in despair, to stop doing something (for good) because of discouragement, not to feel like doing something any more'.[5] But semantically the two idioms differ significantly. First difference is on the level of mental images, when in the Tatar language "the axe is let drop in water quite by chance", but in the Finnish language it is "deliberately thrown in the lake". The second difference is on the level of figurative meanings of the two idioms. The Tatar idiom means 'to be in low spirits' and the Finnish 'to give up in despair'. In the first case DESPAIR is the target frame of the idiom and in the second case DESPAIR is a slot of the frame TO GIVE UP.

(15) *капчык авызын артык җәеп тоту*
       "to keep the mouth of sack too loose"
       'to ignore one's own native language, using many borrowed words
       with the purpose of showing off'

An OPEN CONTAINER is the source concept of idiom (15). A sack with an open mouth serves as a metaphor of a person who uses too many "crappy" words of a strange language when he could use his own native language. This "crap" is so much that it overflows the sack since its mouth is too loose, or open. The cultural knowledge behind the idiom gives us a clue to a better understanding of the idiom. We are aware that some Tatars, as well as other ethnic minorities of Russia, are ashamed of their native language. The problem is in assimilation and destruction policy, which has been followed by the Russian authorities to minorities of the country for centuries where ethnic identity, culture, religion and language have been oppressed.[6] No wonder when some Tatars are ashamed of their language.

---

5. For details see Dobrovol'skij & Piirainen, 2005, p. 228.

6. See Sections 1–2 of this paper for details.

3.4   Intertextual phenomena

There are quite a number of idioms in the Tatar language which can be ascribed to intertextual phenomena. In this paper we use the term *textual dependence* "to refer to the intertextual relation between conventional figurative units and texts that can be identified as their sources" (Dobrovol'skij & Piirainen, 2005, p. 230). We are considering here a textual dependence referring to a whole text or a large part of it from the Tatar literature. The metaphor is motivated by some knowledge of a text. For example:

(16)   *авызына Хозыр түкергән*
"Hozyr has spat into his mouth"
'he is a notable speaker'

Idiom (16) is connected with Sufi[7] mythology. According to a Sufi legend, Hozyr or Hozyr-Ilyas was an immortal saint who drank living water from the source of life and obtained eternity. In Sufizm "spitting in one's mouth by Hozyr" has a symbolic meaning: 'giving wisdom, learnedness, wit, eloquence' (Sibgatullina, 1998, pp. 28–29). This metaphor was born in the 12th century due to a book of fairy tales *Хәким Ата* ("Father Hakim") about a famous Turkic poet Suleiman Bakyrgani (the book was published in Kazan in 1846). As it is written in the book, Hozyr-Ilyas spat into his mouth and due to this Suleiman acquired a gift for poetry. Since Hozyr was immortal, Suleiman's poems also obtained eternity. He became a learned poet and created immortal philosophic works of poetry.

(17)   *Гали кылычы кебек*
"like Gali's sword"
'a smart and efficient person'

In (17) the source domain is A SHARP SWORD and the target domain is A SMART PERSON. A sharp sword serves as a metaphor of a smart person. The conceptual metaphor is SHARP IS SMART. Idiom (17) is motivated by the knowledge about the fantastic properties of Gali's sword described in ancient legends, literary works of the cultural heritage of the Tatar nation. It can be traced back to a popular Tatar *dastan* (heroic epos) *Кисекбаш* ("A Daredevil") where Gali's exclusive bravery is described. Caliph Gali was the closest associate of the prophet Muhammad.

---

7.   Sufism is a mystic trend which emerged in the 7th–8th centuries as a natural development of Islam. It has become a distinctive religious ideology. It is due to Sufism that Islam has been enriched by philosophical, ethical content and esthetical ideas. It is inseparable with Tatar literature as back as the first written samples up to the literary works of the beginning of the 20th century (Sibgatullina, 1998, p. 366).

Gali participated in all the wars lead by Muhammad, was wounded many times but never left the battlefield. The prophet had a fantastic sword which was inherited after his death by Gali. His magical sword never grew blunt, though several thousand enemies could be beheaded by him in a battle (Makhmutov, 1999, pp. 49–50).

Idiom (18) is motivated by a direct reference to the title of a popular fairy-tale written by the Tatar Soviet writer A. B. Alish.

(18)   *сертотмас үрдәк*
       "a duck which cannot keep secrets"
       'a loose-tongued person'

The legend is about a duck who couldn't keep secrets. For being talkative it brought misfortunes to its friends. As a result the duck was punished by its master: it could never speak again like other animals and could only quack. The fairy-tale teaches children such moral principles like commitment to one's words and being honest.

3.5   Fictive conceptual domains

Idioms "with image components traceable to concepts of unreal, fictive worlds can be subsumed under the label 'fictive conceptual domains'" (Dobrovol'skij & Piirainen, 2005, p. 236). For example:

(19)   *авызына шайтан төкергән*
       "the devil has spat into his mouth"
       'he is witty'

Devil is traditionally the personification of evil. At the same time it is a contradictory character. In some legends the devil is not frightening at all; in many cases it is funny. Some of the devils are "kind demons": they help people, they can be good servants, etc. (Gurevich, 2003, pp. 161–162). In Turkic mythology the devil also has a multi-faced character: it is talented, artful and can do boon or bane. It builds magnificent castles and cities; works marvels, giving people different miraculous properties as manifested in idiom (19).

3.6   Cultural symbols

Idioms containing animal constituents are diverse and they have rich imagery. Anthropological discoveries would seem to indicate animal imagery is among the most ancient constituents of human thought and, by implication, an important early layer of language. Watching animals, studying their habits and assuming they share human properties is found in many cultures. As a result the animals acquired different symbolic properties: the bear is a power animal and a symbol of strength; the wolf symbolizes free will, greed and destructiveness; the fox is a symbol of cunning and trickery; the hare is a symbol of cowardice, etc. The following analysis discusses the symbolic import of OWL and CROW because of their non-conventional symbolism in the Tatar language when compared to Russian and occidental languages.

3.6.1   OWL

The OWL is one of the most ancient symbols in the world culture. In Greek mythology it was a creature sacred to Pallas Athena, the goddess of wisdom and science. Due to this the OWL continues to be a symbol of WISDOM and KNOWLEDGE in occidental world. In other cultures the symbolic function of the OWL considerably differs from the Western tradition. The bird has many negative properties, it can be a symbol of bad luck (China), cold, darkness and death (Ancient Egypt), the God of Hell (Aztecs, Maya) (Chevalier, 1996, p. 730). In the Tatar language it is a demonic bird, a bad omen. It can call down curses upon places or people so that everything and everybody die, stop existing.

> (20)   *ябалак үлгэн урын*
> "a place where the owl died"
> 'a cursed place'

One of the outstanding symbolic functions of an OWL is STUPIDITY. It is dominant in Dutch, Finnish and the Low German Westmünsterland dialect (Dobrovol'skij & Piirainen, 2005, p. 349). The OWL is stupid in Hindu philosophy and in The Upper Tanana Athabaskan language spoken in Eastern interior Alaska (Lovick, 2012, p. 107). The idioms (21) and (22) show that in the Tatar language the OWL is also a symbol of STUPIDITY:

> (21)   *ябалак кебек аңгыра*
> "stupid as an owl"
> 'very stupid'

> (22)   *колаклы ябалак*
> "eagle owl"
> 'a very stupid person'

There is also a one-word metaphor (23) in the Tatar language:

> (23)   *ябалак*
> "an owl"
> 'a goggle-eyed blockhead'

It is quiet unexpected, but the OWL is also symbolically connected with DRUNKEN-NESS (Isanbet, 1990, p. 291). It is a common knowledge that alcohol is prohibited in Islam because it harms people and it is a root cause of many problems facing society. That is why there are very few idioms connected with alcohol in the Tatar language. But still, as far as we know, the OWL is maybe the only animal which is connected with such negative and highly disapproved state of a person. Idiom (24) can be found now only in the abovementioned Tatar dictionaries. It is not marked as "archaic" yet, but, probably, soon it will be. Even the older generation hardly ever uses it now.

(24)   *ябалак баш*
       "an owl head"
       'a drunkard'

Some further idioms containing the OWL constituent and denoting food or drink are symbolically connected with ALCOHOL, compare (25)–(26).

(25)   *ябалак шулпасы*
       "an owl broth"
       'an alcoholic drink'

(26)   *ак ябалак сөте*
       "milk of a white owl"
       'an alcoholic drink'

In idioms (25)–(26) food made of an owl ("broth") and an owl drink ("milk") symbolize alcohol. The idioms are motivated by knowledge that an OWL is a symbol of DRUNKENNESS. It may be an ironic hint: "If the owl is drunk, so the boiled owl broth and the owl's milk are alcoholic drinks as well".

3.6.2   CROW

In European tradition the CROW and the RAVEN have similar symbolism (Biedermann, 1994, p. 84). In the Tatar language their symbolism is different. We will analyze the concept CROW, since there are practically no idioms with the constituent RAVEN in the Tatar language in our sources. Throughout history the CROW has been associated with both positive and negative symbolic meanings. In China and Japan it is a symbol of filial gratitude and good omen. In Ancient Greece it was a solar bird sacred to Apollo (Chevalier, 1996, p. 789). The CROW is traditionally valued for its intelligence in European folklore (Roshal', 2007, p. 810). In the Tatar language the CROW symbolizes STUPIDITY and IGNORANCE. For example:

(27)   *карга мие эчкән*
       "he has drunk the brain of a crow"
       'he is stupid; he has no memory'

(28)   *карга оясы*
       "the crow's nest"
       'an empty stupid head'

(29)   *карга баласы тизәк чукыр*
       "a crow's child will peck droppings"
       '(said when) an ignorant person will do stupid things'

The idioms (27)–(29) are motivated by symbolic knowledge about stupidity of the CROW in Tatar culture.

4.   Metaphors exposed to transformations

Over the last years the Tatar language has undergone many transformations under the influence of the dominant Russian language and there is no reason to believe that this tendency is not strengthening because it is a natural phenomenon in conditions of bilingualism and languages in contact. In Tatarstan the Russian language definitely influences the Tatar language on a system level because it is a "dominant language". It is a two-sided process, which has positive and negative sides. Positive effects of bilingualism are: enrichment of the Tatar language due to intercultural communication; people have wider world perspective since it widens their horizons; cognitive benefits since bilingual children may develop more flexibility in their thinking as a result of processing information through two different languages; economic benefits; bridge building. The latter is one of the most important and it is pointed out by Colin Baker: "those who speak two (and more – G. G.) languages symbolize the essential humanity of building bridges between people of different color, creed, culture and language" (as cited in Cavaluzzi, 2013). But there are negative sides of bilingualism as well: Russification of the Tatar language, which results in an amount of "weed-words" collected from the Russian language, borrowed figurative and non-figurative expressions which are not typical of the Tatar national uniqueness. And, borrowed metaphors, of course. "Importantly, whilst continuing to use words of their traditional languages, the metaphors many young people live by are those of the languages that dominate them" (Mühlhäusler, 2012, p. 6). We can't but agree with this statement since we have documented many cases of the usage of metaphors of the dominant language by Tatar native speakers in oral and written discourse instead of using our own phraseology.

The analysis that follows explores idioms from Tatar writers embed Russian idioms in Tatar discourse.

(30) *вот*   *кайда* *собака*   *зарыта*   (T. Mingnullin, 2002.V, p. 55)[8]
     "that is   where   the dog   is buried"
     (Russian) (Tatar) (Russian) (Russian)
     'that's the heart of the matter'

The motivation of the idiom is not transparent. There are many versions of the origin of this popular Russian idiom *вот где собака зарыта*. One of them says that it is a borrowed expression from the German language, i.e. *Da liegt der Hund begraben!* The idiom is known in other European languages as well, e.g. Finnish and Hungarian (Birikh & Mokienko, 2005, pp. 649–650). It corresponds to such English idioms as: *that's where the nut is; that's where the dog is*.

As we can see in (30), three constituents of the idiom used by T. Mingnullin are in the Russian language and one constituent (*kaida* "where") is in Tatar. As a result both (Russian and Tatar) idioms are deformed and the stylistic effect is rather grotesque and comic. Why not to use **our own** national linguistic treasures? Tatar has its own idioms to convey similar meaning. For example:

(31) *имəндə (юкəдə) икəн чиклəвек*
     "it turns out that the nut is on the oak-tree (lime-tree)"
     'that's the heart of the matter'

In this idiom there is no logical connection between the figurative meaning of the idiom and the meaning of its constituents. The idiom is focused on a phenomenon which is logically impossible: nuts can grow neither on an oak-tree nor on a lime-tree.

In (32) there is a typical case of Russian loan translation into the Tatar language.

(32) *галошка утырту*[9]
     "to put someone into rubbers (rubber overshoes)"
     'to put someone in a ridiculous, awkward, foolish spot'

Galosh are low rubber overshoes put on the boots to protect them from water. The idiom is Russian proper, its motivation is not transparent. The following Tatar idioms could be used instead:

---

8.   Mingnullin, Tufan (2002): Selected works (in 10 volumes). Volume 5. Kazan: Tatknigoizdat.

9.   Examples (32)–(33) are drawn from R. Yusupov's monograph "Theory and practice of translation" (2010, pp. 177–196).

(32) a. *чабатага утырту*
          "to put sb. in a bast shoe"
          'to put sb. in a ridiculous, awkward, foolish spot'

     b. *тепсез чуманга утырту*
          "to put sb. in a big twiggen box without a bottom"
          'to put sb. in a ridiculous, awkward, foolish spot'

Let us consider one more example (a proverb):

(33) *хыйтланмыйча судан балык тоталмассың*
     "you can't catch fish without hard work"
     roughly corresponding to a proverb like *No pains, no gains*

It is an old Russian metaphor about labor and hard work. Tatar language has the following metaphors with the same figurative meaning:

(33) a. *аусыз куян тотылмый*
          "one can't catch a hare without hunting"
          'no pains, no gains'

     b. *көл булмый, гөл булмый*
          "no ash, no flower"
          'no pains, no gains'

Examples in (33) are proverbs. They differ from idioms structurally (they are sentences) and have more diverse translation potentials in comparison with idioms. But the problem is that in many cases Tatar writers and translators do not take into consideration typological difference of the Tatar and Russian languages and transfer mechanically forms of one language into another. As a result there are many cases of calquing and artificial proverbs inserted in the Tatar language.

Using Russian proverbs instead of the Tatar ones (especially in the case when national Tatar equivalents with rich images exist) causes big damage to our native language which can be classified as language shift and further on language death. According to Florian Coulmas the language death with an exception of cases of absolute genocide, is more appropriately called "language suicide", since the language dies with the complicity of its speakers (Coulmas, 1992). A very interesting and profound study has been accomplished by Campbell and Muntzel (1989) about language death. They developed a typology of language death situations: (1) sudden death, where all of a language's speakers suddenly die or are killed (e.g., Tasmanian); (2) radical death, where as a result of severe repression and genocide, remaining speakers of a minority language shift immediately to the dominant language in order to avoid a potentially life-threatening ethnic identification (e.g., some languages of El Salvador); (3) gradual death, with a gradual shift to the dominant language via extensive contact (this is the vast majority of language death situations, and is the typological category for most of the languages of Russia); and (4) bottom-to-top death, where the language remains only in ritual contexts (e.g. Mayan languages of southern Mexico that are used only in religious ceremonies). Suzanne Wertheim, examining sociolinguistic context, language ideologies, and linguistic performance of the Tatar language states:

> Although there are more than one million speakers of Tatar in Tatarstan alone, absolute number of speakers is no guarantee of a language's health, as proven in this century by the spectacularly fast reduction in the number of speakers of such languages as Breton and Navajo, to name just two [...]. Tatar can potentially be classified as a case of the third type of language death in Campbell and Muntzel's typology: gradual death with a multigenerational shift involving at least one bilingual generation. (Wertheim, 2002, p. 3)

5. Conclusion

In this article, I have analyzed data on figurative nature of Tatar idioms from a linguistic and a cultural perspective. I used the theoretical principles developed by Dobrovol'skij and Piirainen in the Theory of Conventional Figurative Language to accomplish my task. The study was built on the principles of the Theory oriented towards cultural phenomena and a cognitive analysis of linguistic phenomena. Indeed, Tatar language data confirmed once more that the problem of endangered metaphors exists even in a language with 7 million speakers and that it may be no less an acute problem than in a smaller language.

Two types of idioms were identified in the study. The first type is unique and archaic and based on culturally specific images which are not influenced by Russian. I didn't restrict myself only to synchronic analysis of the empirical material, but I described the metaphors from a diachronic perspective as well, reflecting on them in terms of historic and cultural development. I analyzed metaphors from the angle of their encoding of culturally specific cognitive systems. In this way, documentation preserves the meaning of figurative language units that otherwise would be lost as they go out of use. The second type presents the transformation of the figurative lexicon of a linguistic variety functioning under the pressure of a dominant language. I showed in this paper that such phenomena may damage a minority language which can be classified as language shift and further on – language death.

As Idström and Piirainen have argued, to save a language and its figurative units, it is necessary that "the documentation of figurative expressions should be started immediately when a language becomes potentially endangered. In such a situation metaphors and figurative nuances are the first to vanish, even if the language continues to exist" (Idström & Piirainen, 2012, p. 18).

References

Anderson, B. (1983). *Imagined communities*. New York: Verso.

Bakhtin, M. (1981). *The dialogic imagination*. Austin and London: University of Texas Press.

Biedermann, H. (1994). *Dictionary of symbolism*. New York: Meridian.

Birikh, A., & Mokienko, V. M. (2005). *Русская фразеология. Историко-этимологический словарь* (Russian Phraseology. Etymological dictionary). Moscow: Astrel.AST.Luks.

Bukharaev, R. (1999). *The model of Tatarstan*. London: Curzon Press Limited.

Bukharaev, R. (2000). *Historical anthology of Kazan Tatar Verse*. London: Curzon Press Limited.

Campbell, L., & Muntzel, M. C. (Eds.). (1989). *The structural consequences of language death [Investigating obsolescence: Studies in Language Contraction and Death]*. Cambridge: Cambridge University Press.

Cavaluzzi, M. (2013). Promoting cultural and linguistic diversity: Supporting bilingualism in the early childhood classroom. *Texas Child Care Quarterly*. Retrieved from http://www.childcarequarterly.com/spring10_story1.html

Chevalier, J., & Gheerbrant, J. (1996). *Dictionary of symbols*. London: Penguin Books.

Coulmas, F. (1992). Language careers: Economic determinants of language evolution. In F. Coulmas (Ed.), *Language and economy – Economic aspects. Sociolinguistics* (p. 153). Oxford/New York: Blackwell.

Devlet, N. (2009). Russian government policies pose threat to Tatar language. *Radio Free Europe/ Radio Liberty*. Retrieved from www.rferl.org/russian.../1775794.html

Dobrovol'skij, D., & Piirainen, E. (2005). *Figurative language: Cross-cultural and cross-linguistic perspectives*. Amsterdam: Elsevier.

Dobrovol'skij, D. (2007). Cognitive approaches to idiom analysis. In H. Burger, D. Dobrovol'skij, P. Kühn, & N. R. Norrick (Eds.), *Phraseology. An international handbook of contemporary research* (Vol. 2, pp. 789–818). Berlin/New York: de Gruyter.

Figes, O. (2002). *Natasha's dance: A cultural history of Russia*. London: Penguin Books Limited.

Fuks, K. (1844). *The Kazan Tatars in statistical and ethnographic profile*. Kazan [No Publisher].

Gorenburg, D. (2005). The failure of Tatar language revival. *PONARS Policy Memo, 379*, 77–82.

Gurevich, A. (2003). *Толковый словарь средневековой культуры* (Dictionary of medieval culture). Moscow: Rossijskaja politicheskaja entsiklopedija.

Idström, A., & Piirainen, E. (2012). Endangered metaphors. Introduction. In A. Idström & E. Piirainen (Eds.), *Endangered metaphors* (pp. 15–19). Amsterdam: John Benjamins. DOI: 10.1075/clscc.2.02ids

Isanbet, N. (1990). *Татар теленең фразеологик сүзлеге* (Dictionary of the Tatar Phraseology). Kazan: Tatknigoizdat.

Karimullin, A. (1988). *Татары. Этнос и этноним* (Tatars. Ethnos and Ethnonym). Kazan: Tatknigoizdat.

Lakoff, G., & Johnson, M. (2003). *Metaphors we live by*. Chicago/London: The University of Chicago Press. DOI: 10.7208/chicago/9780226470993.001.0001

Lovick, O. (2012). Walking like a porcupine, talking like a raven. In A. Idström & E. Piirainen (Eds.), *Endangered metaphors* (pp. 103–121). Amsterdam: John Benjamins. DOI: 10.1075/clscc.2.05lov

Makhmutov, H. (1999). *Канатлы сүз – хикмәтле сүз* (Aphoristic words are magic words). Kazan: Magarif.

Mühlhäusler, P. (2012). Prologue. In A. Idström & E. Piirainen (Eds.), *Endangered metaphors* (pp. 1–14). Amsterdam: John Benjamins. DOI: 10.1075/clscc.2.01muh

Piirainen, E. (2012). Metaphors of an endangered Low Saxon basis dialect. In A. Idström & E. Piirainen (Eds.), *Endangered metaphors* (pp. 339–357). Amsterdam: John Benjamins. DOI: 10.1075/clscc.2.16pii

Rorlich, A.-A. (1986). *The Volga Tatars. A profile in national resilience*. Stanford CA: Hoover Institution Press.

Rosch, E. (1978). Principles of categorization. In E. Rosch & B. B. Lloyd (Eds.), *Cognition and categorization* (pp. 27–48). Hillsdale NJ: Erlbaum.

Roshal', V. (2007). *Энциклопедия символов* (Encyclopedia of symbols). Moscow: AST.

Rossijskaja Gazeta. (2011). December 16, pp. 14–15. Retrieved from http://www.rg.ru/2011/12/16/stst.html.

Selbach, C. (2001). *E-book The Volga Tatars under Russian domination*. Retrieved from http://www.grin.com

Sibgatullina, A. (1998). *Суфичылык серләре* (Mysteries of Sufizm). Kazan: Zaman.

Wertheim, S. (2002). *Language "Purity" and the de-Russification of Tatar*. Berkeley, CA: University of California.

Yusupov, R. (2010). *Теория и практика перевода* (Theory and Practice of Translation). Kazan: Tatar State Humanitarian University Press.

Yusupov, R. (2013). The Tatar Republic or Province? *Zvezda Povolzhija*, 40(2).

Zakiev, M. (1995). *Татары. Проблемы истории и языка* (The Tatars. Problems of History and Language). Kazan: Institute of Language, Literature and History Press.

Zakiev, M. (2003). *Происхождение тюрков и татар* (Origin of the Turks and Tatars). Moscow: Insan.

Index of conceptual metaphors/metonymies

Subject index